This book has been sponsored by:

Apple Tree Print

HSBC
The world's local bank

West Yorkshire Windows
LIMITED

PaperCo
Rothera & Brereton

In association with

StoraEnso

No Onward Ticket

This is a limited edition book, number **0594**

Please go to www.huntersjourney.net to register your purchase.

'No Onward Ticket' has been published by Peter Hunter
as a chronicle of his round the world trip.

Peter has asserted his right to be identified as the author
of this book in accordance with the Copyright Designs
and Patents Act (1988) as amended from time to time.

ISBN 189475232-5
First published in 2003

Set in Palatino and designed by Stuart Pearcey
at Words and Spaces Ltd, Scotter, near Gainsborough, UK

Printed by Apple Tree Print, Balby, Doncaster, UK. Tel: 01302 314011

www.huntersjourney.net

There is no question about to whom this book is dedicated; it's Melody and Alastair, my mum and dad.

Where would I have been without you?

Also in memory of my nephew Matthew Richard Booth

Peter hopes his journey will inspire

NOEL MURPHY

BRITISH travel-hound Peter Hunter has run into his fair share of strife since leaving home last September.

Still, that's what the Yorkshire social worker expected when he set out with a 48-nation itinerary he hoped would inspire people to make the most of their lives.

He's escaped a high-speed train fire in Italy and another fire aboard an English Channel ferry. He wasn't so lucky in South Africa when his car went down a ditch, landing him in hospital for six days.

It's not exactly what he was expecting. After all, he set out without visas for any of the countries he wanted to visit and with no ticket home either.

The idea was to show that post-September 11 security around the world should not stop people from exploring.

"Many of the people that I work with could never imagine this kind of journey and it is therefore important to come back and show them that their life can be a challenge of success," 35-year-old Peter says.

The trip, now halfway complete, has taken him to 28 countries. He's been refused entry by Vietnam, China and Russia but otherwise, after explaining his trip, found almost invariably officials surprisingly welcoming.

Peter is filming his trip, maintaining a journal and website, and compiling details he plans to publish in book form.

To date, he's travelled 47,850 kilometres through 19 time zones and 28 countries, picking up 45 passport stamps. He's travelled on eight boats, 24 trains, 11 buses, six cars and 15 planes.

Yesterday Peter left Geelong after a whistlestop visit to Mark Ellis, brother of his boss back home.

"I've been meeting lots of people by visiting schools and different projects I do," he says.

"I feel I'm giving a little bit of inspiration to people to get out and do something.

"With the kids it might to get yourself to uni go or maybe just go home kiss Mum and say 'I love you'.

"I hope my inspiration is, if you want to do something, to help you get out and do it, to get the most out of life — that's my job in England."

OUT THERE: Peter Hunt hopes to inspire people to live life to the full.

Man of the world: this is how The Advertiser newspaper in Geelong, Australia, told Peter's story - but their headline has a global message, and the picture could have been taken anywhere too...

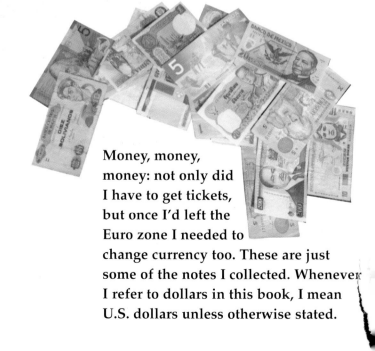

Money, money, money: not only did I have to get tickets, but once I'd left the Euro zone I needed to change currency too. These are just some of the notes I collected. Whenever I refer to dollars in this book, I mean U.S. dollars unless otherwise stated.

Acknowledgements

There are so many people in England and throughout the world without whose help, energy and enthusiasm 'Hunter's Journey' would not have been achievable. Besides those who are already mentioned in the book, I would very much like to thank Giles Hunter, Alex Dockers and Ioene Davidson who were always there for me when I needed help, guidance, advice and contacts! Their drive and determination was an inspiration (without knowing) to my keeping going.

To Graham Pickles, Stuart Grace, Andy Dewart and Julie (my hairdresser) who had some doubts that I could do it; or maybe just missed me and wanted me home!

Special thanks go to my nephew Ross Davidson who spurred me to reach Africa, and then kept me alive when we narrowly missed death, Dr Johann Lochner and the staff of B.J. Kempen Hospital who helped me to recovery, and the tabloid newspapers in the UK who named me 'Plucky Pete'!

I would also like to thank Stuart Pearcey, Dave Murray and Malcolm Poole for their infectious enthusiasm and encouragement on this book (and my test readers dad and big brother Nick).

Particular thanks must go to you, the reader, for allowing me to share my dream with so many people.

And finally thank you to Jayne and my family who were there before, during and after this most amazing adventure.

They believed in me, worried about me, and will always be there for me – how lucky am I?

Peter

Contents

Living the Dream

We all dream - but I'm not talking about when we sleep, or even our 'daydreams'! The dictionary defines dream as a distant ambition, and I think we all have one of those too! My ambition was simple - I wanted to travel the world. I sought a journey that would take me on a global adventure, non-stop and predominantly by land. I did not want to backpack nor did I want pre-booked tickets that would take me on a round the world holiday. I wanted to try and capture the whole world in one go, to get a feel for the world as one planet - knowing that there would be so many differences in people, cultures and landscapes for me to experience.

As a past pupil of a Salesian School, I had begun to recognise that I was part of a worldwide network of former pupils from schools associated with the Salesians of Don Bosco, a religious order whose rationale is to educate young people around the world to be good citizens and to provide aid and assistance to the world's poorer communities. So, I began planning a journey that would not only see me exploring the world's physical terrain, but would also see me discovering real people in communities both large and small, rich and poor, with differing cultures and colours.

I was adopted as a child into a family of twelve, and brought up as a Roman Catholic. After attending a Salesian boarding school in Cheshire I undertook a social care course at my local college in Wakefield, and finished my studies at university in Huddersfield with a degree in community education. I then spent a number of years working in the social work field, mainly in residential homes. Without seeking it, I've achieved a level of local notoriety for my work with communities in Wakefield since 1998. Part of this work had been for a Community Development Project, facilitating community initiatives. This European-funded project involved rebuilding community spirit to improve people's quality of life in a disaffected inner-city estate. The success of this regeneration programme led to a newly-built Community Centre owned and managed by the community, which has opened during the first half of 2003.

The events of September 11th 2001 shocked the world. That day I was with some friends in my local pub when one of them said: "You won't be going round the world now then Pete?" I knew that national security was going to close the door for so many travellers, but I believed terrorist activities should not stop people from exploring our world. I was now more determined than ever to see the world and defy the hurdles that would be my challenge.

I had spent over two years researching and building up a database of contacts throughout the world, and also saving up the money to fund the trip. Many of the contacts I made were through the Salesian network. A great advantage for me in wanting to meet the 'real' people was having invitations to visit schools established throughout the world through the work of Don Bosco. I was able to cut through red tape that would otherwise had obstructed any chance I might have had of visiting a school or college to meet local young people from that country. They were the people I wanted to talk with; they could tell me about where they lived, how they lived and what global issues concerned them (if any!).

Although the journey was about getting round the world, there were some places I really wanted to visit and for special reasons.

I wanted to see where my father had been fighting during the Second World War in Europe and re-trace his footsteps when he then travelled across India. I wanted to see the changes that have been made in South Africa since Apartheid, which dominated world news during my time at College. I wanted to take a journey across Canada and experience this vast country with its huge diversity in landscape.

So, with contacts and specific places I wanted to visit – I mapped out a route that I could work from. I was not sure which countries would allow me through, what kind of transport I would be using or where I would be sleeping but I was ready to go!

I had a new passport with no visas issued for any country and no pre-booked tickets at all but with determination I was going to leave England and travel east around the world. I would avoid using aircraft unless it was absolutely necessary and work out my mode of transport country by country. This was certainly a challenge – having no evidence that I would only be visiting some countries as a way of travelling to others may prevent me gaining entry as I would not have a return ticket. A web site was established to allow people to follow my journey around the world. Using it, they were able to pinpoint my whereabouts daily, and allow them to be a part of 'Hunter's Journey'. A guest book was also set up for people to leave messages from all over the world.

My rucksack contained all I would need for the differing climates, and I relied on just my HSBC credit card to use cash machines throughout the world to withdraw local currency. In addition, I carried with me a video camera to record three things: the travel from one country to another, a person to interview from each country, and my own video diary.

This is my journal, telling the story of where I went, the people I met and what happened to me. It is a story of accidents, emotions, friendships and fun. It is a story of danger, empathy, tragedy and terror. It is a story of calamity, companionship, people and poverty. I am just an ordinary person from an ordinary background who found himself in some most extraordinary situations and places with other ordinary people from ordinary backgrounds. Strangers became friends and the strangest of places became my home! Awe-inspiring views left me speechless as I travelled around the globe and provided some amazing backdrops to people's daily life. Border security was at its highest and my appearance and purpose of travelling meant a frustrating and constant battle through many countries.

Finally, my experience of the world was certainly the envy of many but it left me with one simple conclusion. The world may be a beautiful landscape but so many people around the world are also living in such horrible and dreadful surroundings. In reading this book you will encounter with me what poverty really is! From famine and lack of water in Africa, to disease and lack of sanitation in India, to tyranny and lack of education in Cambodia, join me in my journey of reality.

This was an expedition; an organised journey with a purpose. Now I can share my experiences of people and culture with so many, but it was also a challenge as I did not know where it would take me! One thing is certain; it was a chance for me to fulfil my ambition - to live my dream!

Peter Hunter
Back at home in Wakefield,
October 2003

The Salesians of Don Bosco

Who is St John Bosco?

St John Bosco is remembered as a man who dedicated his life to the service of abandoned young people. Over 150 years ago he challenged the way young people were treated in the desperate poverty that existed at that time in the city of Turin, Italy. He was driven by first-hand experience of the effects of dreadful poverty and hunger on the young people he came across, he was determined to change their condition. Others were inspired to follow him in responding to the needs of the young. John Bosco created an order in the Catholic Church, called the Salesians. They were founded in the poverty of one city and now work in countries all over the world.

A man with a dream

Everyone needs a dream, a vision to inspire them. John Bosco, when he was very young, had a dream. A Man and a Lady, both of great majesty instructed him to prepare himself for a great battle. The battle appeared to be on behalf of a multitude of poor, unruly and neglected children. He was told in this dream that he had the traits and skills to conquer the unruliness of these children, and make them his friends. He learned to become a leader for the young people he grew up with, many of whom were very badly behaved and in order to relate to them he needed to develop certain skills. He learned that by combining entertainment with teaching and praying he could achieve positive results.

Making the dream come true

Upon becoming a priest, Don (Father) Bosco realised how he needed to live out his vocation. The Industrial Revolution was spreading into Northern Italy; there was a great deal of poverty, desolation, turmoil and revolution on the streets of the city. Young people had been abandoned and lived in hopelessness. They lived their awful lives whatever the cost to themselves or others. He was shocked at the conditions they endured and the things they did to enable them to eat and to survive. This was the cost of the industrial 'improvement' that would bring us all the high standards we have enjoyed last century.

A dream shared

His followers, the Salesians, became numerous. A phenomenal growth was achieved through a combination of factors, not least Don Bosco's determination and his inspiration from his dream. The Salesians are to be found working throughout the world, in every continent; thousands of Priests and Brothers who in turn have inspired huge numbers of people.

A dream becomes a system

Don Bosco was more than just a dreamer. He knew that education was the key to helping these young people. He sought to teach them and to get fairer treatment for them. He looked to help other young people who still slept under bridges and on the streets. Don Bosco started technical schools to educate the young people in skilled jobs like printing, bookbinding and mechanics. In those days, these were the skills that would guarantee better conditions and a better future for them. He started the Salesian Missions throughout the world to provide an education that would be of help to the young people – responding to their needs, giving them the opportunities.

The Journal: It's Another World

Chapter 1:
September

Foreword

by Alex Dockers,
First Vice-President of the World
Confederation of Past Pupils of Don Bosco

It is with great honour that I agreed to write a foreword for this book by my good friend Peter Hunter.

When I heard for the first time about his ideas to make a trip around the world, I was amazed about it, but seeing how strong his belief was, I immediately supported and promoted his journey.

My biggest reason for that was that he did this journey as a real Past Pupil of Don Bosco, testifying wherever he went about his identity as a Past Pupil. Especially in his contacts with the youngsters all over in the world that he met, in his growing stories which delighted hundreds of people and which saw in him maybe the realisation of their own dream. Therefore, he was a real 'Ambassador' for our Past Pupils Movement of Don Bosco.

It was with a great pleasure that, in his journey planning, I could give him a lot of contacts in the different places and countries that he visited, so that improvisation could be limited. But this could not avoid the boat disasters, the train fires, the car accidents and other unexpected circumstances … But he had in Don Bosco, a very good guardian angel!

I hope that every reader, in the stories and histories in this book mentioned, may feel a little bit of the flame which drives a Past Pupil of Don Bosco, and that you may discover what it means to be a real Past Pupil of Don Bosco.

Day 1: Hull, England

After a final week of preparations, emotions and goodbyes I was now ready to set off on this epic journey... 'Hunter's Journey'!

I was however, becoming more apprehensive and thinking to myself that this could be a mistake. Many people had given me so much support and a lot of advice about the trip, with a final message from a friend "Don't bottle it!"

I joined my parents for a Sunday dinner and had the chance to say my farewells. I suppose it's the fact that I was saying goodbye for more than just a couple of weeks that made things a little difficult. I wouldn't be home for Christmas!

Anyway, the journey began as I left my home in Wakefield with a small entourage and arrived in Hull for the 19.00hrs crossing to Zeebrugge. With my final goodbyes to my girlfriend and other close friends it was 'All Aboard'. Tears, rucksack and camera! I was immediately invited to meet the Captain and stayed on the bridge until we were out of the docks.

After a meal I visited the bar and sat in tears thinking to myself - am I doing the right thing? After two beers I was still thinking the same, so I went to my upgraded cabin (courtesy of P&O) and got ready for bed!

Day 2: Zebrugge, Belgium

Gentleman of the Press: safe on dry land, and on the BBC.

Many of you may already know that today began with what was to be the longest day! (so far...) At 3am we were awoken by the fire alarms ringing. Staff opened each cabin door and we were told to get dressed immediately and proceed to the Assembly Point. Although I wanted to panic, I was numb, I didn't quite know what to do except put on my trousers and pick up my camera. I began filming straight away and as the cabins were evacuated we were given life jackets, head counted and ushered to a designated safety area. OK, so some people were saying: "Look at him with the camera!" and there was an air of silence broken only by the deep grinding noises of the cranes that lower the lifeboats. As each lifeboat held 140 people, they were huge against the deck windows and I took my camera over to film! Over the next seven hours I captured the whole incident, and really didn't think too much about anything else! Well, OK, I did remember the ferry disaster in Zeebrugge and I did think that we were going to be evacuated from the ship!

I continued to record the images outside as Sea King helicopters arrived and began lowering fire-fighters on board. Lifeguards were also arriving and I was filming the whole experience! It was 9.30am when we were given the all clear. The fire in the engine room had been put out, we were no longer drifting, and the two remaining engines began the slow journey to Belgium. It took nearly twenty-five hours to get to Zeebrugge and I had not slept at all. Tired and dumbstruck, I left the ship to be ambushed by television crews! My good friend Alex Dockers, who was waiting for me in the arrivals lounge, had mentioned to them that I had recorded the whole emergency incident on camera and they were wanting to interview me!

So, only 24 hours into my journey around the world, I was interviewed for BBC and VRT television and my 'amateur' footage was broadcast halfway round the world. My journey had certainly begun with an interesting experience and I looked forward to many more exciting things but no more fires! After an evening meal with Alex and his family in Waregem and the after effects of my day, I collapsed in bed at Don Bosco Zwijnaarde (DBZ) a college and Salesian community near Ghent in Belgium.

A warm welcome from bearded Alex Dockers and my first group of Salesian pupils.

No Onward Ticket

Day 3: Ghent, Belgium

Today I awoke feeling refreshed after a good sleep and was invited to visit the classes of the final year group in the college. I gave eight talks on the purpose of Hunter's Journey and of course I mentioned my previous 48 hours and why I had now shot to fame! It was a great experience to speak about what I hoped to do and also to invite these pupils to now be part of my journey. Already the guest book on the website had messages from my captive audience!

Later, I gave an interview to a Belgian national newspaper (Het Nieuwsblad) and invited some of the pupils to join me for a photograph so that they too could be famous! The day concluded with yet another talk to a group of Salesian Past Pupils and now I am prepared for many more talks and press conferences.

Day 4: Ghent, Belgium

I had a really bad sleep. Having killed three mosquitoes, there was still one left in my room and it kept flying past my ears... Bzzz! I had five bites on my face and a mozzi filled with blood!

When I went for my breakfast Alex greeted me with a half-page article in the morning newspaper, including the photograph with the pupils. So, when he then took me for a sightseeing tour of Ghent, I really did feel like a local celebrity. Anyway, enough about the shopping; the Dockers' home is magnificent and the garden outside is picturesque. A huge marble ball rotates in the middle of a pond with the force of water pumped through a rock.

After a visit to the bank to change money received from the Belgian TV station (hartelijk dank) we then set off to the Netherlands. Alex had offered to drive the three hour journey in his posh Mercedes, and who was I to refuse? Into a screen on the dashboard he typed the street where we were to go and we just followed a visual route with audio instructions. Amazing!

Fien and Trudy live in Zoetermeer and are friends of my

Mum and Dad. They always told me that if I was to go around the world, I must call in to see them! Thank you very much! Can you put me up for the night?

It was peace and tranquillity at Fien and Trudy's house because the view from my bedroom was a lake of 100 hectares. Breakfast was served with 'uitsmijter' and was delicious! It is made using slices of bread with ham and melted cheese topped with fried eggs - Mmm!

Day 5: Zoetermeer, Netherlands

After breakfast I was taken to meet Jos Spekman. He had walked from Zoetermeer to Santiago de Compostella (Spain) three years ago and it was a pilgrimage that he paced for more than 2,700kms. He wanted to meet me so we could share notes. I just listened, with my journey I would be doing little walking and had travelled only 645kms so far.

Can you believe, yet another interview with a journalist this time from the Haagsche Courant (The Hague Daily). Things were going so well! Later, since I would now not see the coastline again until I arrived in Italy, Fien and Trudy took me to Scheveningen (the North Sea beach) and then a drive past the prison used for the Yugoslavia Tribunal and where the former dictator Milosevic is held. It felt strange for me this evening.

The conflict in the Balkans was a few years ago and yet it was all very close to home now as we passed the prison. What we heard so much about on the news for so many years felt so much more real when you could see the building that was home to such a tyrant.

Press interest: the only two words of it I understood were 'Peter' and 'Hunter'.

Day 6: Zoetermeer, Netherlands

Today my journey took me first to a weigh-house in Oudewater where over the decades women were weighed to decide if they were witches. Yes, if the person weighed under or over a certain weight they were deemed to be a witch and killed! I was duly placed on a huge wooden plank and weighed, lucky for me I was found to be a good weight and given a testimony of proof!

Puiflyk, Netherlands

After an hour's drive I arrived in Puiflyk, a small town that was of particular importance to my father during the Second World War. He was in the 49th West Riding Reconnaissance Regiment and this was one of the many towns they liberated. Two of his friends were killed and are buried here, so I went to pay my respects and reflect on a piece of my Dad's history.

Utrecht, Netherlands

Arriving in Utrecht I was shown the road that Dad paraded through on 7th May 1945 and then taken to the Polar Bear Statue, a memorial to his Regiment. Here I laid flowers and spent a few moments of reflection for the many thousands of soldiers who fought and gave their lives during the War for the world we live in today and also to those that returned with memories that will never leave them but are often shared. (Thanks Dad and love you loads!)

Day 7: Berlin, Germany

I arrived in Berlin late last night by train. An old school friend from England called Paddy met me and took me straight to an Irish Bar called The Emerald Isle, where the owner Rupert and all the staff wanted to meet me, and since it was a bar, why not down a few litres of German beer!

Today was spent recovering at Paddy's apartment, and then back to The Emerald Isle where I would have access to the Internet for the duration of my stay.

Medieval weight-watching: being too heavy or too light would have meant you were a witch and for the chop as a result.

Day 8: Berlin, Germany

Off the beer today and on the sightseeing! First visit was to a Bavarian beer hall but alas! I have to say, I only had a small one, but thoroughly enjoyed the music! Oh what fun listening to such renditions as 'Oh! When the Saints' sung in a very strange language.

The new centre of Berlin is Potsdamer Platz and most of this modern area of development was the former space between the Berlin Wall and the East. It was hard to imagine what had happened in the last twelve years, but the city has changed so much since my first visit in 1990 when I hacked away at the wall to bring back pieces of history!

I also visited Gedachtniskirche known as the memorial church that was left as it was after the war as a constant reminder of what happened. It is like a half demolished building, but now stands as a sign of peace to the world. It was strange to see this partly destroyed historical building overshadowed by the modern structures of post war Germany. An early night beckoned and I had my train ticket for Warsaw.

"Auf Wiedersehen Berlin und bis bald!"

Day 9: Warsaw, Poland

I arrived in Central Station, Warsaw, at dusk and having taken advice from the Tourist Information Centre proceeded to board the No.23 bus which would take me to my hotel. Yes, this could only happen to me! I had misunderstood the man at the desk who told me five stops and I thought he said fifteen. I ended up on the outskirts of the city, some 12kms from the centre and in the middle of a huge housing estate. Now the only one left on the bus (and with a bloody rucksack) I attempted to speak to the driver. He spoke and understood English about as much as an average English bus driver speaks and understands Polish, but eventually I gathered that I should sit down behind him and return to the city. I could not guess where the five stops from the station were, and the driver did not understand a word I was saying so I went back to Central Station, Warsaw and started again!

No Onward Ticket

**Another ticket, another country:
Crossing from Germany to Poland.**

I arrived at my hotel nearly three hours after I had arrived in Warsaw (it should have been just twenty minutes) and settled in for an early night!

Day 10: Still in Warsaw, Poland

Up at 7am, can you believe, and off for some breakfast. Then I took directions to the Salesian School, which is in Kaweczynska and set off using the tram. The public transport in Warsaw is very good and everybody seems to use it. I saw the church 'Santo Stanislao Kostka' in the distance and as I approached I could see in front of the church, a statue of Don Bosco. I knew I had come to the right place and knocked on the door of the adjacent house.

The man looked at me rather strangely and simply closed the door when I asked if he spoke English! It was a poor start, but just a few minutes later I was greeted by Fr Tadeusz, who spoke good English and after telling him who I was and what I was doing, I was invited to stay.

Arrangements were made for me to talk later that day with a group of students from a nearby Salesian boarding house and so off I went sightseeing. Warsaw is a strange city with much to discover, there are memorials and statues related to the war all around but when you arrive in the 'old town', although it is rather small, it is beautiful.

Overshadowed by a monument to Zygmunt III Wazy (don't ask!) the Castle Square is tranquil. I sat at one of its café bars for over an hour gazing at the view. I began thinking about things back home, wondering what my family and friends were doing and what was happening in the news. It was becoming strange for me that I would not be going home for such a long time and although I was feeling homesick, I was enjoying the experience of being on my own exploring the world.

I met about sixty youngsters at the Salesian house and yet again was treated like a celebrity. Having shared with them my story in a very slow, broken English which most could then understand, they wanted to discuss football - now I was dumbstruck! It is not my easiest subject even in English, but I nodded and agreed with them, well almost; after all I support Leeds United!

Day 11: Warsaw, Poland

Now, to get to Moscow I needed to go through Belarus and so I thought maybe I should go to Minsk and then on to Russia (are you with me?).

First thing in the morning, Fr Tadeusz took me to the Belarus Consulate for a visa. They told me I must first get a Russian visa, as this was my next destination. So, we drove to the other side of the city to the Russian Embassy. They told me that they did not issue visas on Wednesdays. So, we went to the Tourist Information Centre for advice (thank you Margaret) and then we went to the Belarus Embassy. They did not issue visas; you had to go to the Consulate. Okay, back to the Belarus Consulate. This time I said I would like to go to Minsk and then I would come back to Poland. I was issued a form to fill in, an invoice for $90 to pay at the bank in the city and I had to get proof of my accommodation in Minsk!

It took Fr Tadeusz and I nearly four hours to complete the paperwork and book my accommodation in Minsk, but now I could go to Belarus. When I got there I would go to the Russian Embassy and ask if they would very kindly give me a visa! I was told that what I encountered today is what it has been like for many years for the Polish people who have struggled to travel out of their country. Travel

23

for Polish citizens is expensive and border documents are not easy to obtain if you want to travel to another country - for many it is just a dream to see the world!

Well, this evening I will get on the train to Minsk, which will take me eleven hours. I have a bed, a torch and a book!

"Szla dzieweczka do laseczka do zielonego.... Te wesole slowa pozostawiam dla wszystkich Polaków.

Zycze wszystkiego najlepszego i dziekuje za goscine."

Day 12: Minsk, Belarus

Arrived in Minsk at 7.30am. The journey through the night was fascinating. Two hours into the journey and the train stopped at the Polish border and the Police boarded the train to check our passports.

An hour later and we arrived at the Belarusian border and the Police boarded the train. They were very official and not so friendly. They did not speak English but my companion in the cabin, Darek, spoke Belaruse and English and so was a great help to me!

Two hours later, the train pulled into a huge depot with men waiting on either side of the track. Huge hydraulic jacks with the aid of a crane raised each carriage over a metre above the track where the wheels were rolled out and a different size of wheels were rolled underneath. The carriage was lowered back down and the process repeated with all the other carriages. In the former Soviet Union the railway lines have a completely different gauge system to the rest of Europe. Amazing! After almost eleven hours and with very little sleep, this step of my journey was over.

The former Communist building in Minsk

It is only in the last twelve years that Belarus has become independent from what was the Soviet Union, but here, right before my eyes was what I imagined a dictator state would be. There were Police everywhere - so you could say that I felt safe, but the next few days were to be my first real experience of being alone, in a very strange

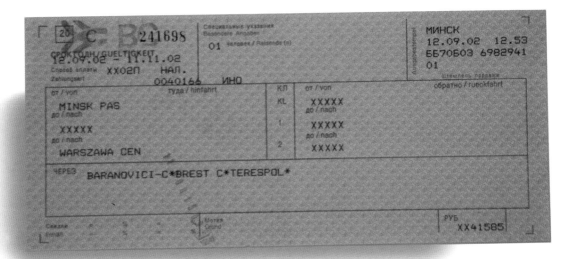

country and feeling a little scared. Nothing about Belarus made sense to me - after all, they speak a different language, have a different currency, the words on signs are incomprehensible, the roads are six lanes wide, the buildings are huge concrete block apartments where everyone seems to live and I seemed to be the only tourist! Everywhere I went people stared at me and I felt very nervous!

X marks the spot: For the independent traveller, all roads from Minsk led straight back to Warsaw...

With Darek's help today was spent trying to persuade the Russian Embassy to allow me to visit Moscow. They demanded that I should first have my ticket for the next country to which I would be travelling, but the Ukrainian Embassy would not give me a visa until the Russian Embassy had. What a debacle! At the British Embassy there was nothing they could do and as my visitor's visa for Belarus was only for 48 hours I must arrange to return to Poland.

This journey was meant to challenge how the world was open and free and this was my first example of how I would not be able to travel exactly where I wanted to go. If I had flown directly from the UK I would have had no problems in visiting Russia, but travelling with 'no onward ticket' I was experiencing barriers at the border!

I stayed at one of only five hotels in the city near Pushkinska and first thing in the morning I walked to a

No Onward Ticket

Day 13: Minsk, Belarus

local supermarket. The only thing I recognised was the bottled water and luckily for me, that was all I wanted. Most of the shops are owned by the government and are therefore controlled.

Walking past one particular clothes shop I was amused that in the window the mannequins were actually real people. Yes, male and female models were dressed in clothes that were for sale in the shop and they were posing in the window keeping very still.

It wasn't until you got closer that this bizarre window display became apparent. I began filming and the models smiled but the shop manager ran out shouting at me whilst placing his hand over the lens. It was so weird!

A young lady called Natascho who worked in one of the nearby shops approached me. She spoke English and explained that people don't like being filmed. Over a coffee I explained about my journey and she shared her experiences of living in this strange country.

Belarus has a population of 10 million of which over two million live in Minsk. The average salary is $20 a week, but unemployment is not high. Communism may be a banned word here but it was a word I used repeatedly! The Police often stopped me when filming and people would just turn away. In a land of dictator rule and the KGB, I just wanted to get out!

Day 14: Minsk, Belarus

I met Natascho again so she could show me around Minsk. Today was a celebration day for the people of Minsk and I could not believe my eyes. In Victory Square and along the 2km road to the National Square there were thousands of people. In fact, the local news reported over a million celebrating in what I can only describe as a huge carnival. Many were dressed in traditional costume and there was music being played along the sidewalk. The whole atmosphere softened my attitude towards Minsk. The people are so friendly and helpful and among this mass of people, I really enjoyed myself. Special thanks must go to Janusz, the manager of the casino in the hotel. Now, before you begin thinking, I did not spend a penny - in fact Janusz gave me some chips to play with and I lost and won them all back!

Janusz is from Krakow, but has worked for many years in Minsk. He spent much time talking with me and sharing his experience of this very strange country. I am indebted to his hospitality and knowledge of the country and its people.

At 9pm, I boarded the train which would take me back to Warsaw and then on to Krakow, as I was now travelling south. Farewell Belarus!

"Cnacisa za npizuauiemie nocetiyu ienapycb za nasazemme."

The overnight journey was yet another experience. I spent most of the night drinking Russian vodka sharing my sleeping compartment with three Belarusians - Valery and Leonid (two crazy guys travelling to Germany for work) and Lyuba (she was a student on her way to Lodz in Poland). The language was no barrier when it came to drinking and as we went through the same border checks and the changing of the wheels, the evening turned into morning and we were in Warsaw.

Feeling quite tired, I changed trains and headed south to Krakow. I shared my journey with a student called Katherina who was returning from Crete where she had been working during the summer. We had a very interesting conversation about how young people feel living in Poland and she happily allowed me to film the 'interview'. Late afternoon and I was settled in my hotel for a rest.

I thought I would venture out this evening and treat myself to a meal. Having walked for about ten minutes I found myself gazing into a huge square, it was a lovely sight, lit up with a few people walking through. After eating my pizza, I walked back through the square, just as

Student Katherina was on her way home from Crete to Krakow; I was still heading away from home.

Day 15: Krakow, Poland

it was approaching midnight. As the bells rang out from the church overlooking the square, high above in a window you could just see a man peering out playing a bugle - then suddenly the sound stopped. A few seconds later and from another window high above the church, the bugle began to play again - and then abruptly stopped! Now, it was quite cold and there was no one else in the square. Was somebody playing a practical joke? Anyhow, it was at least my birthday now and so; well, I just wished myself a happy birthday and returned to my hotel.

Day 16: Krakow, Poland my birthday

Remember the manager of the casino in Minsk? Well, his family is from Krakow and he arranged for his daughter Joanna to meet with and show me the sights of this 'City of Culture'. My first visit was to the Market Square (the largest medieval square in Europe) and a familiar sight from the previous night! I discovered that the bugle call, which I now knew was called a hejnal, is played from the higher tower in order to commemorate the destruction of the city during the 13th century Tartar raids. The reason it stops abruptly is because the bugle player was shot with an arrow while he was warning the townsfolk of an attack!

Krakow is certainly a beautiful city and thanks to Joanna for taking me around and listening to me moan about how homesick I was on my birthday. I would have so liked to have been at home. Just to be with my friends and see my family and then return to my journey – this was not going to happen and so I just had to be strong and shake myself. Early evening and I was on my way to Oswiecim (Auschwitz) on a local train. This was a real experience for me; it stopped at 24 stations en route and took over two hours. I had a real opportunity to see how people live in the countryside and small villages from my carriage window. Most of the houses were set in small farm surrounds and I can imagine the people were pretty self-sufficient. The train had only local people getting on and off between the isolated stations that were merely

Krakow: very Eastern European - but there's a McDonald's on this street.

Auschwitz, Poland

small platforms with the name of the place inscribed on signs fixed to small huts. I felt uneasy on this train ride, maybe because there seemed to be nobody else travelling the full journey with me, just lots of people using it to travel short distances. I guessed that most could not speak any English and so I just kept my eyes focused on the world outside.

Oswiecim had its name changed by the Third Reich in 1939 to Auschwitz and for five long years its name aroused fear among the populations of the Nazi-occupied territories. It was here that the concentration camp was established, and it has been estimated that as many as 1.5 million prisoners were killed. Just a mile away is the Salesian school, a huge building for more than 600 students, many of whom live and study on the site. During the Nazi occupation most of the building was used as a hospital for German soldiers, but a small part of the school was kept open for propaganda reasons! Many students were taken to the concentration camp and did not return.

Birthday cake: probably the loneliest birthday I've ever spent.

The Director of the school welcomed me with open arms and I would spend the next few days talking to the students about my journey.

I lay in bed this evening feeling exhausted, my birthday had been and gone and I felt quite lonely.

The school bell rang at 7am at 'Zespol Szkol Towarzystwa Salezjanskiego' not for breakfast but for morning prayers. The meal followed and the school day began at 8.00am. By lunchtime I had visited half the school and given a talk on Hunter's Journey. The Director, Tadeusz, was a great host and the school regime was very similar to my boarding school experiences at a Salesian School in England. The only difference (and a big one I might add!) is that during the day, girls share the school with the boys as day pupils!

After lunch in the priest's refectory, I was assigned three girls - Monica, Anna and Patricia - who were to accompany me to the Auschwitz Museum and generally

Day 17: Oscwiecm, Poland

Inhumanity in history: the torment of Auschwitz must always reduce us to tears.

look after me for the afternoon.

Auschwitz is only 2kms from the school and when we arrived I began to film the gate entrance. On visiting the first block in the camp I turned my camera off because I was feeling sick. It is very hard to describe what you see here. Most of the Jews condemned to extinction in Auschwitz arrived convinced that they had been deported for 'resettlement' in Eastern Europe. For this reason the deportees always brought their most valuable possessions with them. What you see in the different halls are thousands of empty suitcases with names on, shoes and spectacles in huge piles and haircloth made of human hair. Evidence throughout the camp shows how many of the prisoners perished from hunger, executions, hard labour, punishments or as a result of the poor sanitary conditions.

It is difficult to imagine the tragic scenes that took place in the camp and the anguish and despair felt by those who came here - but what did happen has been respectfully kept here in Auschwitz as a reminder of a part of history that should never happen again and, moreover, as an international monument to the victims of Auschwitz.

Day 18: Kosice, Slovakia

Another early rise and eventually I was on my way back to Krakow and then on the train to Slovakia. Now, this **was** a journey. The train was fairly 'prehistoric' and primitive. After an hour it stopped at a station and we were all asked to leave and ushered on to buses. An hour later we arrived at another station and boarded another train and we were on our way once more. Again the train stopped and the Police boarded to check our passports at the border with Slovakia.

I was now one of the only passengers left on the train - I guess Slovakia is not a popular destination. After seven hours on a very slow train we arrived in Kosice (pronounced Kooshitsa) and I was met by Dominika (married to Chris – another old school friend) and driven the last leg of today's journey to Presov.

I was shattered. I met her family and 'Mum' fed me - then it was time for a good sleep!

Day 19: Presov, Slovakia

Time to get some washing done and a long soak in the bath and then a long shower before breakfast. Later we went to the railway station to sort out my ticket to Bratislava for the following day, taking me west towards Italy.

In the afternoon I had the guided tour of Presov with Dominika, her Mum, Auntie and baby Joseph. Yes, with all these women it was shops that we visited.

The town is very well kept, with only public transport allowed into the centre. I ate cakes and drank Krusovice (the King's beer!) in 'Vino Veritas' and enjoyed a day of just relaxing.

Day 20: Bratislava, Slovakia

Although today I was up and on the train by 6am, the journey was pleasant enough. I slept nearly all the way - I did notice the huge mountain range, the third highest in Europe, called Vysoke Tatry; they were a great sight to see.

Once in Bratislava I was ravenous and sought out the nearest restaurant. I didn't understand the menu at all, but thanks to Stanislav who was sitting near to me, I was able to order some food. Afterwards, he invited me to his office to access the Internet and arranged to meet me in the evening to take me round the town.

Bratislava is the capital of the Slovak Republic and one of the youngest capital cities in Europe. Sitting on the banks of the 'Dunaj' (Danube) it became the focal point for the movement of the national uprising of the Slovaks in the 19th Century and the peaceful division of the joint state of Czechs and Slovaks in 1993, although many people did flee to nearby Austria and Switzerland.

I had a whistle-stop tour of the city, by night and in the rain, as Stan showed me some of the sights. I was most fascinated by a small wooden hut at the side of the river

31

that recorded the water level - the data recorded that during its peak in August 2002, it had reached the highest levels ever recorded. The city was on high alert with the threat of severe flooding as the river level reached its most critical point.

I was grateful to Stan for giving up his time to show me around. I had met a complete stranger who wanted to help me. This was just one example, only three weeks into my journey, of how so many people whom I did not know were prepared to share their time and knowledge in showing me around where they lived. These were not tourist guides but ordinary people who wanted to be a part of my journey!

Day 21: Nitra, Slovakia

My hotel, The Arcus, was just a short distance from the centre of town - and was the best hotel I had stayed in so far. Today I travelled about an hour out of town to a place called Nitra. I came here to meet Lubica (a friend of Jos Spekman - the guy I met in Zoetermeer) who works on a community project with housing estates in the town.

The mission of the project is to improve the quality of life and motivate the citizens of Nitra and be involved in solving public issues. All of this reflected on similar work that I had been doing back in my home town of Wakefield. Many of the projects developed here are about improving local resources for young people, in particular with public green spaces.

Slovakia was to hold its general elections the following day, and many hoped the results would enable them to join the European Union. The EU financially supported so much of my work in England, but here in Slovakia communities have to find other ways to raise funds.

Stan: My new friend in Bratislava.

When King Svatopluk of Moravia felt his death was near, he asked his three sons to visit. He placed branches on the ground and ordered his sons to pick one up and break it. Surprised, they did as they were told! They were successful and so he asked them to pick two branches and break them. Again they were successful. When he offered them three branches to break, no son was able to do it. After that King Svatopluk said: "My dear sons, if you keep together, nobody will be able to defeat your kingdom." The sons promised him they would, but after his death they broke their promises and began to quarrel. Soon after, the kingdom of Moravia was destroyed by enemies.

The reason for this story is that the three branches became a symbol of unity in the Slovak nation and the people of Nitra designed a coin that they would sell to raise funds for their projects. One of my first souvenirs of the journey – and not too heavy!

The Nitra coin: made of clay, it was my first souvenir.

Day 22: Bratislava, Slovakia

I woke this morning with a cold and feeling pretty ill. I stayed in my hotel most of the day - it was cold and raining outside. It is certainly times like this that it would be so nice to be at home!

In the evening I went to Limbach to visit Marek and his family. Marek is the President of the Salesian Past Pupils in Slovakia and was one of the first pupils to attend a Salesian School in Slovakia after the communist regime had been overthrown. His English was a little poor but it was better than my Slovakian and with the aid of two of his sisters we were able to exchange ideas and talk. His family had a vineyard and most of our talk was done whilst sampling their home-made wine. Needless to say the talk flowed just as much as the wine!

As with many young people in Slovakia, learning English is very important. One youngster told me that for each language you know you are another person! Slovakia has come a long way in the last 12 years, it is (in my opinion) a very poor country but the people are genuine and full of hope. The next few years of change will be so important to the future of this country and I

No Onward Ticket

hope that they are successful, with the full support and recognition of the European Union.

Day 23: Vienna, Austria

It was only a two hour bus journey to Wien (Vienna) but the border control was a very slow process – no doubt due to previous problems of illegal immigration. Firstly, the Slovak Police boarded the bus and took away our passports. After checks were made and the passports returned, we travelled a short distance to the Austrian border where we had to disembark and go through Passport Control.

Vienna was cold and raining and I just wanted to get warm. Having found a hotel near to the railway station, I unpacked and got into bed. I was cold and tired and hoped that a good sleep would help. I awoke late in the evening and decided just to stay where I was until the morning.

Day 24: Vienna, Austria

Still feeling pretty miserable, I went to the restaurant for an eagerly-awaited breakfast. To my horror I was informed that my room was booked for tonight and with no other vacancies I would have to find alternative accommodation. What a nightmare!

Vienna was not very kind to me. It was raining and I was not sure where to go. After two hours I found another hotel, left my rucksack and wandered into the town centre.

There are many landmarks here that are hundreds of years old and preserved in their historical substance as outstanding buildings, including St Stephan's Cathedral, the Imperial Palace (Hofburg) and the State Opera (Staatsoper). I spent only a few hours looking round and decided to make my way to the railway station to plan my escape!

At the station's Information Centre I was informed of the timetable for trains to Switzerland. I then had to go to the Reservation Office to 'reserve' my seat. I then had to go the Ticket Desk to purchase my ticket! I still had not finished - I then had to go to the International Ticket Desk for a stamp and finally I had my ticket for the early morning departure the following day from Wien to Lausanne.

With the cold weather, and the fact that I did not feel so good, maybe I had not given Vienna much credit. I had met no one, people did not seem very approachable, and I was looking forward to leaving.

"In Wien find'st nur die kultur, im reslichen osterreich herrscht nature pur!"

Day 25: Lausanne, Switzerland

I left Vienna very early this morning and having reserved my seat, this guy who did not speak English, would not move from his seat that was my reserved seat! Anyhow, it gave me my first chance to complain to somebody after such a miserable few days. The train conductor was so cool, he just upgraded me to first class and I sat in comfort, with leather seats and waiter service as I ate my breakfast. Vienna was smiling on me at last.

After almost seven hours the train arrived at St Anton am Arlberg. This is the station before the long tunnel through the Alps that takes you into Switzerland. It was flooded due to the unseasonal heavy rains and so off the train we got and onto buses for the most amazing hour-long ride over the mountains. My first glimpse of snow and there was plenty of it!

When we arrived at Bludenz to board another train, the conductor ushered me back into first class and the carriage had a glass roof! Now this was a real treat and the views I got through Switzerland were breathtaking, simply breathtaking! The Alps are a spectacle that shapes the national character of this country. I was in awe at such a view from my seat in the glass-roofed carriage as we travelled across the border.

Finally, after nearly 14 hours I arrived in Lausanne and James was there to meet me. James is an old friend from back home and a few years earlier I was invited to

Zimbabwe where he and his fiancé Lynne had chosen to get married. This was one of the first times I recall getting that urge to do more travelling in the future! We drove a further twenty minutes up through Grandvaux to a beautiful house nestling into the mountains. I was shattered and it was time to sleep!

Day 26 and 27: Lausanne, Switzerland

Sorry, Day 26 was given over to sleeping and relaxing. This was my first rest day since leaving England, and I was in dire need of the chance to recharge my batteries.

On Day 27 I was able to appreciate the scenery much more. The mountains are what many will think of when you hear the name Switzerland. Until I reached Lausanne, I had no idea of the view I would now get from where my friends James and Lynn live. The panoramic view of Lake Geneva (Lac Lemen or Genfersee - depending on where you actually live around the lake and therefore whether you speak French or German) and the famous peak of Evian were just part of what your eyes captured from the house set in the mountain hillside. I was spoilt!

Switzerland's views take your breath away.

Lausanne is in the most gorgeous of settings and other than the steep hills I could find nothing to complain about. The gradients between the harbour, town and house are incredible - added to the view of the mountain peaks with clouds above are all just amazing! Everything about this country was fantastic but it was time to move on.

"Alles hat eine ende, nur die wurst hat zwei!"

Day 28:
Padua, Italy

This was to be another day of travelling, but again I was spoilt with the most splendid views you can imagine! Having left Switzerland we travelled through a tunnel over 17kms long as we reached the border of Italy. The Police boarded the train to check passports and specially trained dogs were checking for other things I guess!

I was so pleased to reach Italy; I have been many times before and I do love this country! At last, as I arrived in Milan I could feel some warmth!

Maria Acazi, a past pupil from a Salesian school who I first met last year whilst attending a conference in Turin, met me in Padova. She took me to her family home out in the country and I joined her family for a taste of real Italian home cooking. We then joined some of her friends for a taste of Italian beer - well, not exactly - we were at a bar called the 'English Cockney Pub' and it was like being back in bloody England. It was a replica of an English pub, with English beer and… well, what more can I say? I really wanted to be in an Italian café bar!

Day 29:
Still in Padua

Today was Sunday and in a country where most of the people are Catholic, it was off to Church! Afterwards, I watched a Scout Ceremony, as Maria is a Scouter.

It was all too complicated for me to follow, but it was a glorious day sitting outside with the sun shining and it gave me my first opportunity to improve my suntan!

Unfortunately, I was feeling pretty lousy and so my afternoon siesta took me through to early evening, when I was taken out for a traditional Italian pizza. No complaining though, it was scrumptious!

In the morning I visited Instituto Don Bosco - a school in Padova. I gave another exciting talk on Hunter's Journey to some very interested Italian students and met some of the teachers, most of whom are Salesian Sisters.

No Onward Ticket

Day 30: First Padova, then on to Venice, Italy

Venice is only an hour's drive from Padova, and Maria, together with her friend Fili, were great hosts as they took me to see this most spectacular of Italian cities. Most of the evidence from recent floods had gone, but there is still plenty of water! The first half hour of wandering through the narrow pathways and over the bridges was enough to leave me really enjoying the experience. The network of waterways that link the town together are quite something, but after reaching St Mark's Square, things changed!

Firstly, the price of a coffee! I know it is Italy, and a traditional drink but at nearly nine euros a cup AND you had to pay a further five for the string quartet playing nearby - well, no way!

Secondly, after leaving the square it was shop after shop after shop! Jewellery, watches and high street fashion had

What trip around the world would be complete without Venice and a gondola?

all come to the streets of Venice and I was not very happy! It may be a lovely city with its history, culture and narrow waterways with gondoliers, but it was also tourist heaven and I was happy to leave!

Chapter 2:
October

Foreword

by Fr Pascual Chavez V
Rector Major – Salesians of Don Bosco

"Our life is just exactly what you are doing, a pilgrimage on the world. Indeed our country is not here but in heaven. May God lead your life and God bless you."

Foreword

by Fr Francis Preston SDB
Provincial – Great Britain

The late Cardinal Basil Hume, when reflecting on the life and achievements of St Benedict, the founder of the Benedictine Order to which he himself belonged, had this interesting comment to make. "When a man dreams a dream it remains a dream. But when that man can share his dream with others, then it can become a reality." The greatness of Benedict and John Bosco lay in their ability to get others to share their dream and thereby make our world a better place.

Peter Hunter had a dream – to travel the world in an original and exciting way and thereby make contact with many young people in very different circumstances to those he had known in and around Wakefield, UK. I am delighted that in the weeks before his departure Peter chose to share something of his dream with me. I found his enthusiasm infectious. I didn't doubt for a moment that Peter would succeed in his venture. And of course I wasn't disappointed!

I am sure that you will find Peter's account of how he realised his dream as enthralling and inspiring as I have.

Day 31: Rome, Italy

Throw a coin backwards into the Trevi Fountain and it's said you'll return...

I woke up this morning and I think I must have slept awkwardly - because my back was really painful. I wasn't sure why, but I was in agony. So, get rid of the cold and let's have something else! Early departure again and I was on the train to Rome and to the Salesian Headquarters at Via della Pisana.

I love Rome, and took a bus from the Termini - Central Train Station - to Via dei Capasso. It was so strange, standing on the bus gazing as we passed the Coliseum and the great big Spanish Steps! We know Rome wasn't built in a day; nor was there a chance that I would get to see it all in two. Captivated by the scenery, I missed my bus stop and had to walk with rucksack on back for ten minutes to the gates of my destination - a huge complex set in acres of land just outside Rome.

Here, in the home of the Salesian 'Cabinet', I got lost just walking from my room to the dining hall. It is like a big hotel with offices on one side and conference facilities on the other.

I had now been travelling for a month and had completed 6,240kms and done 112 hours journey time, visiting nine countries - but I was still in Europe!

Day 32: Still in Rome

Had a good sleep today and when I went for lunch I met Salesian Priests from all over the world. As this is their Headquarters, there were representatives from most of the countries in which Don Bosco's work is based and it was a great way to make some contacts.

Fr Bernard represents the Salesian Province of Great Britain and was so helpful to me with introductions and of course, translation.

The rest of the day I spent time on the computer, firstly to read e-mails and then to update my journey log. It is sometimes difficult to access a computer, so I wanted to make the most of the opportunity!

When in Rome, by all means do as the Romans do - but spend some time as a tourist too. Therefore, armed with my camera, I went to downtown Rome. I visited Piazza Navona, Piazza Venezia, Colosseo, Pantheon and Citta' del Vaticano, my 10th and smallest country. I went into San Pietro's Basilica and saw the marble statue of St John Bosco high above the statue of St Peter and a portrait of Pope Pius IX. In a dream back in 1858, Don Bosco found himself looking down from a niche high on the right hand side of the central nave, directly above the bronze statue of the prince of the apostles St Peter and the mosaic medallion of Pius IX. Don Bosco couldn't imagine how he got there and found the situation to be quite disturbing. In 1936 the statue was inaugurated in one of only 39 niches here in Rome. It is amazing to think that Don Bosco, an inspiration to me, had fulfilled his final dream. He began his work after a number of remarkable dreams about what his vocation in life was to be and his monument is in such a fitting place for him to be remembered.

Day 33:
Still in Rome, but The Vatican too...

The time, the place: Peter Hunter, News at Ten, The Vatican.

Later this evening I had the opportunity to meet with the Salesian Rector Major - Don Pascual Chavez - the 9th successor of Don Bosco, who was thrilled with my plans to travel the world and gave me some great words of support. I have been fascinated by the way people have wanted to help me, so thanks to you all!

Day 34: Naples, Italy

On my way to Naples (a stopover to Sicily) I made a short detour to Cassino, 150kms southeast of Rome.

On September 3rd, 1943, the Allies invaded the Italian mainland just as Italy re-entered the war on the Allied side. The German position known as the Gustav Line stretched across the middle of Italy as a defence but in January 1944 Allied troops landed behind this line and by May 18th the main city of Cassino was taken. 4,266 men lost their lives and are buried in the Commonwealth War Cemetery here in Cassino.

Reflection: remembering a major sacrifice.

I came here to find the grave of Stanley Thomas Powell, the grandfather of a friend back home and pay my respects. The cemetery is a mile's walk from the station and when I arrived I was overwhelmed at its size. I was unable to find the grave and went to ask for assistance. What happened next was bizarre! As I walked down towards the entrance I met a man called Carlo who has worked at the cemetery for six years - now what was amazing was that he came from Yorkshire! (my home county). In fact, his grandfather Joe was in the Royal Engineers and had been assigned to the British Number 5 War Graves Registration Unit. With the help of the Italians, they buried the British soldiers here in Cassino.

Joe married an Italian, came back to live in Yorkshire and later Carlo's mother also married an Italian and she came back to live in Italy. With help I was able to find Stanley's grave and I planted a small flower there before paying respects on behalf of my friend and all his family.

Late in the evening I arrived in Naples and found a hotel near the railway station. After eating pizza I went for a walk around the city centre. It was late and maybe I was not in the safest part of town, so I actually felt uncomfortable and even a little scared and returned to my hotel and went to bed.

Day 35: Palermo, Italy

After a sleepless night in Naples I was on the express train to Palermo in Sicily. The journey takes over nine hours and although Sicily is an island, it is separated by only three kilometres of water. A boat carries the train across! After only an hour on the train there were problems. With the smell of burning, I was to experience another fire, but this time on a train! The train did not stop immediately and all the passengers from one of the carriages were evacuated to other parts of the train. They all looked rather shaken and worried - but I was also very concerned and all sorts of things were going through my head – memories of the first night's fire on the ferry were still very fresh! We arrived at a station where fire fighters were waiting to examine the train. We were all evacuated from our carriages and waited anxiously. Apparently, the undercarriage of one section of the train was overheating and this had caused the problems. After all sorts of confusion, in the good old Italian way, we boarded the train to continue our journey - three hours late.

Five hours later we arrived in Villa S. Giovanni. The train was divided into four sections and shunted on board a boat. This was an amazing experience - I was now on the train and on a boat too! Sailing across the Straits of Messina passengers were allowed to get off the train and walk about the ship but had to return to the same carriage, because once in Sicily some of the carriages were going no further. Luckily, I was OK and after twelve hours arrived safely in Palermo. So yet again, my journey in a boat proved to be quite exciting - but today the train was too!

Day 36: Palermo, Sicily

I had found it very difficult to find a hotel last night and then also to get food. I had walked from the station along the main road with all the shops, restaurants and hotels and it was pouring down with rain. Every hotel was full and no-one seemed to have any ideas where to go. Even when it was suggested about trying a particular hotel, I walked for ages with my rucksack on my back, getting soaking wet and the place would be full! I was becoming very upset. I was cold, wet, hungry and absolutely shattered and after almost three hours I was back at the station and in tears.

It was now early morning and there seemed to be nobody about. Eventually, I began walking again and as I made my way in the opposite direction I saw a small hotel and was saved.

After such a late night I was slow to get up and felt exhausted. I had lunch at the Salesian House in Via Liberta and then had a walk around the city. On Sundays all the main roads in the centre are closed to reduce pollution - for such a small island, there are cars everywhere!

It is hard to explain my discomfort with Sicily. No-one seemed to speak English and this was very frustrating because I could get no information to help me with my journey. The thought of the Mafia may be a myth for so many, but you could certainly feel something strange in the air! Nobody seemed to want to know you at all.

I talked with my girlfriend Jayne back in England, to share my frustration (I was just so bloody annoyed) and to see how she was, of course, and I made the decision that the following day I would go immediately to the station and begin my journey to Malta.

Day 37: The journey from Sicily to Malta

Today beats every day so far! At the station in Palermo the lady at the information desk was so unhelpful! She just did not care about what I wanted to do or where I wanted to go and she would not speak English except to say: 'go to Agrigento'. Having purchased my ticket and waited for an hour, I then travelled three hours by train to Agrigento. When I arrived, I was told that there were no boats to Malta from here and I must go to Catania. This was a further four hours by train and there was no guarantee that it was the best thing to do! I could not find anywhere to go to ask for further information in Agrigento - not even an Internet café. I was left with no choice and so I was back on the train.

When I reached Catania it was getting dark and I needed to act quickly! I went to the information desk where the clerk told me that there were no boats to Malta until tomorrow and then he changed his mind and said that it would be the day after! I began to laugh; no-one seemed to know anything, or if they did - they were not going to tell me!

After looking at the cost of hotels for two nights and a boat later in the week, the clerk suggested I fly direct from Catania to Valletta in Malta. The cost was less than the cost to stay in Sicily and I really wanted to leave this part of Italy! Just to remind you, unless there was a good reason (i.e. safety or cost) then my journey was to be done by land and sea only! There were plenty of reasons to leave Sicily and by 9pm I was on the thirty-minute flight to Malta. A Sicilian man I had spoken to on the plane said **"La gente Siciliana ha il coure grande!"** I wasn't so sure!

I landed in Valletta to be greeted by Noel Camilleri, the Treasurer of the World Salesian Past Pupil Federation, together with his wife Connie. But today had not yet finished with me! MY LUGGAGE HAD NOT ARRIVED AND WAS LOST!

Day 38: Sliema, Malta

This was a calamity! My worst nightmare had happened and unless I could get my rucksack back I was surely going to have to consider the future of my journey. Packed into that rucksack were maps, power adaptors, medical supplies and countless other essential items that I would need en route.

I was staying at the Provincial House on St John Bosco Street where Fr Victor was so helpful. We spent most of the morning telephoning the baggage handlers and Air Malta to try and establish where my bag could possibly be. By late evening it became apparent that my luggage was still in Catania, Sicily. I was in despair! I never wanted to go back to Sicily!

I telephoned my brother Giles in England, who was my contact back home for any problems etc. He reassured me and urged me to be patient before beginning to think about returning home.

I felt very uneasy all day and could not relax. I needed my luggage back!

Day 39: Sliema, Malta

The work of Don Bosco began in Malta almost 100 years ago and I was astounded at how much goes on here. In the morning I visited Savio college - a school where through education, religion and loving kindness, pupils could become good Christians and honest citizens. I enjoyed a tour of the school and a chance to talk with the students about my journey!

I also visited the theatre in Sliema that has been fully restored and managed by Salesian Past Pupils. Across the road is St Patrick's Home, which caters for young boys who need residential care. There was a real sense of good, positive work going on here and with so many friendly people what else could Malta offer!

Even so I remained uneasy – there was still no news of my luggage; although I had really enjoyed today – I was not relaxed and the day had been spoilt!

Day 40: Still in Sliema

The good news was I had my luggage back! It arrived late the previous night on a flight from Catania. I was so relieved; now I could continue my journey.

Today I went to explore Malta. It was extremely hot, but the tourist season had finished. The government will not allow building work during that time of year so now... well, there was work going on all over. New high-rise apartment blocks were going up everywhere and the tourist invasion of such a beautiful island had begun.

This was my first country since leaving England where they drive on the left and all the road signs and shop signs were in English. It was a very comforting feeling not to have things translated, after nearly six weeks of no English – the only language I can speak. Malta has a great history, and was part of the British Empire until 1964, many of the old buildings are what you would expect to see in the UK but they are here and all have a story to tell!

Later today I went to visit a number of travel agents to explore the next stage of my journey to Athens and then on to Israel. You will not believe it - I had to go by boat to Catania and then by train to Brindisi on the east coast of Italy where hopefully I could get the two-day ferry to Athens! I really did not want to go back to Sicily, but I had no choice!

I went to find a hairdresser today who would bleach my hair. The first place I saw, I went in and asked if they could help me! Chris (the owner) assured me he would do a wonderful job and so I sat down. He did a great job and I was blond again! Whilst talking with him, I discovered that he was in a band and had three times been in the Eurovision Song Contest representing Malta. It was so good just to meet like this and I had to get the camera out!

Day 41: Still in Sliema

Malta is a beautiful island of friendly, English speaking people and I would be sorry to go but **"Ix-xemx shuna ta' Malta tirrifletti fil-qlub generuzi tal-Maltin"**.

Top: lightening my mood, not to mention my hair. Hairdresser Chris has represented Malta in the Eurovision Song Contest.

Left: Malta memories through the post.

Day 42: Brindisi, Italy

Last night I experienced Malta by night - visiting the tourist part of the island. After only four hours sleep at 5am today I was on the high-speed ferry to Catania in Sicily. Remember, I did not want to return to Sicily but I needed to get a boat to Greece and this meant going back! Due to high winds and a very rough sea, we were diverted to Pozzallo where we had to get a bus to Catania. Sicily was causing me problems yet again and the journey to Catania had now taken a further two hours. I missed the express train to Brindisi and had to travel on regional trains with four connections taking eleven hours! Even now, I cannot bring myself to go into the frustrating details of today's journey!

My only consolation was that I got to see Sicily's most enchanting and fascinating place - Mount Etna, the highest active volcano in Europe.

Etna is called the Garden of Sicily because of its rich and varied vegetation. The last eruption 400 years ago may have destroyed many towns and villages, but it made the land fertile and rich in minerals. The landscape around is awesome - but I still needed to reach mainland Italy.

Almost 19 hours travelling brought me to the port of Brindisi. It was almost midnight there was nowhere open for food, so I found the nearest hotel and got some sleep.

Day 43: Igoumenitsa, Greece

Another early morning and I was on the eight-hour crossing to Greece. I met a number of backpackers travelling to Corfu where the boat stopped on its way to the mainland. It was good fun chatting away to so many English speaking folk, many of whom were from Canada. I hope Steve (from Toronto) had a great week before heading back home. He had visited much of Europe over the last two months and travelled on his own AND survived, so I wasn't doing bad!

I was glad to arrive in Greece because this was my final country in Europe and I now felt that I had completed the first stage of this epic journey! First impressions of Greece were good; the people seemed to want to help, although many did not speak English. I enjoyed a pleasant evening meal at a restaurant but as I don't like Greek food, I had pizza!

Day 44: Athens, Greece

The only way to get to Athens from Igoumenitsa is by bus, and it took eight hours. It was difficult travelling as I didn't really know what was happening. When the bus stopped at the services, the driver didn't tell us how long we would stay - I just had to keep an eye out for him or I would have been left behind! A short crossing by ferry after five hours on the bus, and then a few more hours and we were in Athens.

We arrived at a huge bus station and there were hundreds of people getting on and off buses! It was total mayhem! I had no idea where to go or what to do, and so I just followed the majority who were getting on bus 51 - luckily this bus took us into the centre of Athens and I found a hotel, showered and went exploring!

After finding somewhere to eat I set off back to my hotel. It was after midnight, it was raining and I got lost! I only saw a few people whom I asked for directions and none had heard of my hotel! After almost two hours of walking I finally made it back to my hotel, wet and completely shattered. I was in tears!

Day 45: Athens, Greece

My hotel was not good - there was no bath, the shower was terrible and I had no television. I'd heard about the terrorist bomb blast in Bali and wanted to get the news. So I went in search of a better hotel and found one much cheaper, on a main road, with a bath, good shower and a television. I settled in and switched on the TV to catch up with the news and was horrified at the footage showing the nightclub attack in Bali. Events like this obviously caused me concern and made me wonder more about the route ahead - but I was determined it would not stop my

Stolen view? These are the pictures the security man didn't want me to shoot. But the Greeks have an unusual attitude to cameras; remember the arrested plane spotters?

Day 46: Still in Athens

journey. I spent the afternoon in travel agents trying to find the best and cheapest way to get to Israel. There were no flights for two more days and so I would stay in Athens until Friday.

In the evening I met Gina (a friend of Olga's in Berlin – remember Paddy? - she's his girlfriend) and she took me around the city and pointed out places I should visit over the next two days. After some persuasion we went to eat traditional Greek food at a nearby restaurant and it was very enjoyable. The dish was based on olive oil, onion, garlic, basil, spinach, tomatoes, feta cheese and plenty of vegetables - all my favourite foods...not!!!

The Greeks look very similar to Italians and Gina told me of a common phrase that they use in Greece 'una fazza una razza' which means 'one face one race'. It is used to remark on the Greeks having certain characteristics the same as Italians, like a tendency to be late and their attitude towards the law! I found this quite amusing. They may look similar but…let's not go there!

Athens is very popular with tourists who come to see the Acropolis casting its shadow over the city. I took advantage of the midday sun and set off to visit this most amazing and historical site! After almost one hour walking and suffering a little heat exhaustion, I arrived at the top of the Acropolis and there stood a piece of history, the ultimate example of Ancient Greek architecture dating back 6,000 years - the Parthenon. You have to pay 14 euros to get onto the site and having got so near I parted with my money and proceeded along a guided walkway.

I found a suitable place to film and set my camera up - but within minutes a security man approached me and made it quite clear that filming was prohibited! So, feeling hot and frustrated, I left the main entrance and headed back down into the city.

I next visited the New Parliament Buildings, the Syntagma (Constitution) Square and the Tomb of the

Unknown Soldier guarded by the famous Evzones with 'mini skirts' and shoes with pom-poms!

One thing had struck me whilst walking around this beautiful city - how would they cope with the 2004 Olympic Games? The traffic through the city is constant and many of the roads are narrow, the pavements are already packed with Athenian shoppers and public transport is very limited. I spoke with a number of people about the Olympics and I got the impression that they were not too happy with what was to come! The centre of Athens is a building site, with huge renovation projects to many of its hotels, and even to some of the historical landmarks! A number of the roads are even being dug up to retrieve old tramlines and many of the road junctions are being turned into roundabouts! I just hope that they can complete all this work in time for the Games.

Day 47: Still in Athens

Having missed breakfast, I decided to rest until lunchtime and walked into the Omonoia (main square) for a coffee. This was time for me to relax, but the heat was getting to me again - I ventured into a shopping centre and passed away three hours exploring the shops, something I have not really done since I left England.

The square attracts many beggars, and the Police are always moving them on, using physical force when they have to and I was quite shocked by one incident and left feeling rather upset. An old lady sitting at the entrance to the Subway had a small bowl that people could throw money into. A smart-looking businessman was coming out of the entrance and deliberately kicked the bowl over. As the lady tried to pick up the coins the man proceeded to stand on her hands until she screamed and he just walked away! This was upsetting for me and inhumane. I went into a nearby bakery and bought a sandwich to give to the lady. The incident had left me feeling upset; I do not want to encourage beggars, but what else could I do?

I returned to my hotel and decided to unpack and then

No Onward Ticket

repack my rucksack ready for my journey to Israel. Since I was flying and wary of losing my luggage, I also packed a second bag with essentials that I would carry separately.

Day 48: Leaving Athens

The airport in Athens is state-of-the-art and was opened only two years ago in preparation for the Olympic Games. The road network to and from it is superb, because it includes a special road directly to the Olympic Village for athletes and the media!

At the airport I went to the El Al check-in, and within two minutes I was surrounded by a number of Police and Security Officers and escorted to a private room – in security speak this was known as a 'Code 5'! Now, I have to say they were very polite and once they knew of my journey around the world - well, they found it all quite amazing! However, they wanted to search not only the entire contents of my luggage but also me! My rucksack, camera bag and additional hand luggage I had prepared were all taken away, and I was searched from top to toe!

By the time I was allowed into the other room to collect my luggage, I had been with security for two hours and the flight was due to leave in just 35 minutes. Every single item that I possessed was laid out on tables, and I had to pack immediately or miss my flight! It was absolutely heartbreaking - everything I had for a year long trip around the world had been examined! All the medical supplies I might need in Africa, India etc and all my toiletries, clothes and maps, books, camera and other electricals were all opened! I have never seen anything so soul-destroying and all I could do was throw everything into the bags! My camera and luggage were then taken from me and I would not see them again until I arrived in Tel Aviv!

I was then ushered through security and passport control and escorted onto the plane! The officer who had been with me all the way through this experience told me that I was flying with the safest airline in the world! I asked him if I looked suspicious, and he told me that the colour of my skin, a British passport and the fact I was travelling on my own were all contributing factors for me to be a 'Code 5'!

Tel Aviv, Israel

On landing at the airport in Tel Aviv I followed instructions that had been sent to me (from Fr Gianni, a Salesian priest working in Bethlehem) and did not tell the full story of my reasons for coming to Israel. This made it easier for me to be issued with an entry visa and avoid unnecessary problems.

At last I was in Israel and took the sherut (service taxi) to Jerusalem. I could not believe I was actually here in Israel and with a degree of apprehension I was actually quite excited about the next few days!

Fr Gianni met me at the Notre Dame Centre as night fell and we set off to make the journey to Bethlehem. Now, I had been instructed not to mention this at the airport. I had told them I was going directly to Nazareth.

It is very hard to both comprehend and explain the situation over here, but to get to Bethlehem we had to go through an Israeli checkpoint. It was a war zone and I was quite terrified as we were stopped. All car lights are turned off except spotlights coming from the tower, and soldiers using torches. After more than an hour, we were invited to drive the car to a concrete barricade where soldiers checked our passports. At last, we were instructed to proceed and weaved our way through a kind of no-man's-land and into Bethlehem.

Bethlehem, Palestine

It was mostly dark as the streetlights and even the traffic lights had been knocked down by tanks over the last year and the place was very quiet.

On three more occasions we were stopped - this time by Palestinian militia carrying guns. They just wanted to check who we were and allowed us to carry on. I was now in Palestine and not Israel and we finally arrived safely at the Salesian International College in Cremisan.

Day 49: Still in Bethlehem

Bethlehem is known throughout the world, and for centuries has been one of the most-visited places, attracting pilgrims and tourists from all over. Today I experienced something quite amazing. Fr Gianni took me into the town and we first visited the Salesian bakery. Here the United Nations now provides flour so that bread can be freely distributed to over 400 families. In just two years, Bethlehem has become a very poor place. It has relied on visitors for so many year and now there are none. As we walked around the streets, I was the only tourist to be seen. Every hotel was closed; there were no restaurants and only a handful of souvenir shops had stayed open in the hope that someone might visit.

I visited the Church of the Nativity, built like a citadel over the cave where it's believed that Jesus was born. It was erected in 339AD and whichever way you look at it, this is a piece of history! The sad fact is that I was its only visitor; normally hundreds of people would pass through this shrine every day and during Easter and Christmas time it would be thousands!

There was just nobody around. I was in the Holy Land, the birthplace of Christianity, but because of the Israeli and Palestinian conflict, there were no visitors. This is the reality of the situation and I found the whole thing disturbing!

In the afternoon I returned to the town on my own. I just wanted to experience this place. Everywhere I went, I was greeted by 'Marhaba' meaning welcome! People were so friendly and I was certainly an attraction to the locals but I was constantly on my guard as eyes were following my every move!

Day 50: Still in Bethlehem

Since the most recent 'intifadah' or uprising over the last two years the conflict has had a real impact on so many people in Bethlehem. Whilst a suicide bomber will enter Jerusalem killing innocent people, the Israeli army will then enter Bethlehem and carry out 'tit-for-tat' destruction of homes and killing of equally innocent people. It makes no sense to me when all these people have such strong religious beliefs that they appear to think that killing people will resolve anything.

I spent the morning in Bethlehem and the afternoon in Jerusalem. With less than 10kms separating these two places it's hard to believe the differences in the way of life - tanks and checkpoints keep the people apart from each other.

Jerusalem

Travelling from the college to Bethlehem is only a short distance but over the months the Israeli Army has blasted huge holes in all the roads around the town in an attempt to isolate it. Most have been filled in with rocks and sand, but the journey is slow and uncomfortable at times. The Salesian college in Cremisan is used as a thoroughfare for many vehicles that cannot access any other road. They drive right through the college - it's amazing!

As I walked around the town of Bethlehem I noticed many posters on walls and shop fronts. These were of Palestinians who have died in this 'intifadah' and they are regarded as martyrs here. I had the camera with me and did some filming and I kept being asked if I was the Press! It seemed that people wanted Bethlehem to be filmed so that the world could see what was actually happening! A man who wanted to show me something kept pestering me to come into his home. I followed him along the narrow streets and the adrenalin began pumping. As I entered his living quarters I could see that it was filled wall to wall with pictures of 'martyrs'. He was some kind of local Sheriff who was keeping a record and he allowed me to interview him! I was a little scared as other people arrived and before long the entrance and my only means of escape was blocked! Many of the pictures were of young men and teenagers holding guns. This was all getting too much for me and I decided to stop filming and leave!

It was difficult to get out of the room and I had never been so terrified. They had guns. I had put myself into a very dangerous situation and I was on my own. As I made my way quickly along the narrow street back to the main thoroughfare, I knew what I had done had been risky, but it was also absolute reality. I felt dreadful about the whole thing; Bethlehem is a war-zone!

After lunch I joined Louis (a student from Nazareth) on a trip to Jerusalem. At the checkpoint, soldiers boarded the bus checking passports and asking a number of questions. I wasn't travelling with a coach party of tourists, I was on the local bus from Bethlehem to Jerusalem and it was a frightening experience! I was sitting at the back and as the soldiers made their way towards me, I felt as though I was in some Hollywood movie. I knew they could take me away for questioning and again my life was in danger! After a detailed examination of my passport the bus was weaving through the concrete blocks and through the checkpoint.

There is a strong military presence at the Wailing Wall; sadly the young people nearby seem accustomed to it.

I knew that visiting Jerusalem would be dangerous but having come so far, this was to be a pilgrimage. It is the city where David united the tribes of Israel, Solomon built a temple, Mohammed ascended to heaven and where Jesus died on the cross. It is also the capital of the reborn State of Israel and continues to dominate our news with innocent people being killed.

The Wailing Wall was my first visit and after going through more security checks I was standing in front of the wall. It was all rather strange; people were pressing their heads against the wall and now and again would kiss it! They were rocking backwards and forwards and bobbing their heads in prayer. It was captivating for me and I stood there in awe!

There were only about a hundred people here and again I saw no tourists. I spoke with some soldiers who told me that normally there would be many hundreds of people here. They also told me that they preferred to be on a night shift when they could enter Gaza or Bethlehem to find Palestinian activists and arrest them! I realised that I was now experiencing people from the other side of this conflict and when I had been asked where I was staying,

Louis spoke on my behalf and explained I was staying only in Nazareth! These soldiers had no idea that in actual fact, I was staying in Bethlehem and had seen the damage that their tanks made every night when they entered the town. On the site of the hill where Jesus was crucified, there is a massive church - the Church of the Holy Sepulchre. With just a handful of visitors, I was able to walk around this central shrine of Christianity and it is breathtaking. History again encapsulates your mind as you walk around gazing at the rock that was once the hill on the outskirts of the City and which the building has now encompassed!

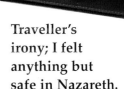

Traveller's irony; I felt anything but safe in Nazareth.

The modern-day centre of Jerusalem is like many city centres with its shops and cafés - but there is one major difference! Soldiers and Security Police are everywhere, visible by flashing red and blue lights from Army and Police vehicles. Private security staff are also on the buses and standing in shop doorways!

This is not a pleasant way to spend your time shopping but the reality is that these people must live in this environment. I felt very apprehensive and on edge all the time, probably expecting something to happen. Thankfully it didn't and we travelled back safely to Bethlehem.

This morning I had chance to read my e-mails and catch up with my journey log! Later I travelled back into Bethlehem and visited other sites including the Milk Grotto where, according to Christian tradition, the Holy Family took shelter on their journey to Egypt. It is said that a drop of the Virgin's milk fell to the floor of the cave, giving rise to a chalky stone.

Day 51: Still in Bethlehem

I spoke to a tourist guide about how quiet it was and he explained that the situation is getting very bad as no-one has any work, no-one can go anywhere and no-one visits any more!

I found an Internet café and whilst I was reading my guest book messages (love 'em!) I was to witness another amazing experience. It seems that any major news stories are broadcast immediately to the Internet through 'breaking news' flashing onto the screens. It is, however, in Arabic and I could only watch as a number of the locals in the café were shaking hands and rejoicing! The news was coming through of a suicide bombing just 35 miles north of Bethlehem in a part of Israel. This is the reality of the situation. I was stunned as we learnt that fourteen people had been killed and that the people in the café were actually pleased that a successful revenge attack had occurred! It was hard to believe that people could derive so much pleasure from this and I was beginning to feel very afraid.

It wasn't long after that all the computers went off line. I was told that this was typical after such attacks due to the Israeli Government trying to make communication difficult for the Palestinians. I was very nervous and although I had switched on my camera to film what was happening, I decided it was time to leave!

It felt very strange now as I walked back toward the bus station. It was getting dark and I have to admit I was beginning to feel afraid. The Israeli Army would normally respond to a suicide bombing by entering the Palestinian Territories and retaliating. I needed to get back to the Salesian College where I would be safe and so I took a shared taxi back to Cremisan.

Talking with the students in the evening it is very difficult to see where there can be a solution to the situation over here. Religion certainly seems to play a part in people being very stubborn but politics seems to play a part in people's human rights! Only last Monday the British Ambassador to Israel, Sherard Cowper-Coles, described the West Bank and Gaza Strip as "the biggest detention camp in the world." I have to agree!

Day 52: Nazareth, Israel

Today I was going to travel by bus to Nazareth but Fr Gianni needed to travel north and so it was decided that he would take me by car. I had made a conscious decision to try not to travel by bus in Israel, so this was great news!

We left at 8.00am and after ten kilometres we had gone through three checkpoints. Since yesterday's events the Israeli Army was certainly on a higher state of alert and traffic was beginning to build up all over. Once we were on the highway there was no traffic and we were on our way.

When we reached Jericho, Fr Gianni wanted to take me through the old town. We approached the checkpoint and, after a long wait, we were told it would be difficult to pass as the Israeli soldiers were letting nobody in or out, and so we turned back onto the highway.

When I arrived in Nazareth, looking over the whole town is the Salesian School and the Basilica of Jesus the Adolescent. This is where I would stay for a few days before heading into Africa.

The school was built as an orphanage in 1902 and is now a school for over 500 pupils, all of whom are Arab Israeli citizens. Although more than half are Christian, the remainder are Muslim. It is important to recognise that the work of the Salesians is about responding to the needs of the community in which it works, no matter what religion, culture or colour.

The view from my room was absolutely fantastic. I could see the whole of Nazareth including the Basilica of the Annunciation, one of the Christian world's most holy shrines. Nazareth was the home of Mary and Joseph and the infant Jesus and is a focal point of the Holy Land. Ironically, most of the literature on Nazareth talks about the hordes of pilgrims and visitors struggling through the narrow and congested streets!

Late afternoon and I was walking completely on my own through the streets of Nazareth. I visited the site where the

Angel Gabriel appeared to Mary inside the Basilica of the Annunciation - I was the only person there except the Franciscan Priest watching over the shrine (and he was falling asleep!). It is very depressing for me to see that no people are coming to these historical sites, but of course, we all know why!

Day 53: Still in Nazareth

Nazareth is so different from the place I had just left, people mixed with each other more although there are still isolated problems that build up. For instance, a piece of land in front of the Basilica of the Annunciation is home to a makeshift place of worship for a group of Muslims who want to build a huge Mosque directly next to a centrepiece of the Christian world and most Christians are not very happy! It seems that nothing will ever change - only last year the Burger King in the town was burnt down in a protest to the American support over the Israeli - Palestinian conflict! You cannot call this a war, but it is. The problem for me is that a war is usually fought between soldiers, but here it is between suicide activists and soldiers with innocent civilians caught up in it.

People I spoke to here just want to leave and it is so sad that you cannot be happy and feel safe in your own home! The government spends more money on its 'security' than any of its other budgets - this goes for health and education! Added to a lack of tourists (which they rely on) you have a real problem of unemployment and lack of hope!

Stunning: the view from my room in Nazareth.

Anyway, I was ready to leave Israel. Yes, it's safe on the whole, but you do feel uncomfortable. There is a real sense of nervousness and although it has been good to come and see, to experience everything about Israel and Palestine, I was glad to be leaving, to escape the apprehension and uneasiness that there is.

I went back to the town today to arrange my best route out of here. A bus? Well, it was possible but it would be dangerous for many reasons and would also be very difficult for me at the border control. There was a flight tomorrow with El Al (Israel's Airline) and since they only fly once a week to Egypt I booked a seat. This was not planned on my itinerary but since I needed to go to Ethiopia next, this was my best route.

As I walked up the steep hill to the Salesian house, puffing and panting (you should see the climb!). I would ask people if I was going the right way and would get a nod as they pointed up the hill! The name of the Salesians means something very special to many people here in Nazareth - Christians educating Muslims.

One man (Kalil) invited me into his house for water and a rest as I was near to the top of the hill! He spoke of the good work the Salesians are doing for the community and his own children. His wife then brought a tray with glasses of hot Arabic coffee and insisted that I must drink with them. The whole family then arrived and eight of us sat in the house enjoying a very strong and sweet coffee!

People really are friendly towards me! I think that as I move into warmer climates I am getting darker, I must be blending in with the local people more!

Day 54: Tel Aviv to Cairo

Fr Mario drove me to Tel Aviv to get the flight to Cairo. Just over two hours in the blistering heat and we arrived at the security checkpoint at Ben Gurion Airport. This would allow us entry into the airport grounds and after a little explanation we had made our way to the departure terminal and I said my goodbyes!

The procedure for flying with El Al is incredible. Here I was again being questioned about why I was in Israel, for example:

Where did you come from?

Where did you stay last night?

Where did you go from the moment you arrived?

Did you visit Palestine?

Did you pass through any checkpoints?

Do you have any weapons?

I know it's procedure, but after another three hours of searching and yet another escort to the aircraft... well... was it the colour of my skin or was it my blond hair?!!

The flight was just over an hour and there were about 30 passengers but we were treated to a new Boeing 747 jumbo jet! How cool it was just to pick any one of nearly 500 seats!

When I landed in Cairo I had to purchase a visa stamp before going to passport control. I followed all the instructions I had been given, but at the desk an arrogant Police Officer took my passport away with no explanation and I was just left standing! There were so many staff in different uniforms walking about, everybody looked official but nobody would explain to me what was happening! In fact, nobody would say a word to me at all! I felt as if I had been sent to Coventry! (Sorry, Coventry!)

Almost half an hour later another supercilious Police Officer came to speak to me. He told me that I would not be allowed to enter, as I had no return ticket. I explained that I was trying to get round the world by planning each stage of the journey in the country before. He said I was crazy and then just got up and left! Confused? I certainly was!

Then two guys in uniform approached me and asked if I had my luggage. I explained it was in the baggage collect area and they told me they would go and get it for me. I was worried that I may lose it and was happy at the offer! When they arrived back with my rucksack they told me it would cost US$10 and I had no choice but to pay! Almost two hours went by before the supercilious Police Officer came out of his office and called me over and gave me my passport stamped with my entry visa and I was on my way!

Well, there was still one more thing - my camera had to be registered with customs and this was to cost me a further US$20. I had to ask myself if there was any other scam they were going to come up with to get money out of me!

I left the airport to be greeted by a very patient Fr Santi who would drive me the twenty kilometres to Shubra where they had a Salesian School and I was to stay for a few days.

Day 55: Cairo, Egypt

Pyramids are the first thing that comes to mind when I think of Egypt. Most of the country is sand and 95 per cent of its population live within just a few miles of the River Nile. Over ten million people live in Cairo and as I walked from the school to the Metro station I was greeted by heat, noise and dirt. It was quite oppressive.

Shubra is a suburban district which would show me some of the reality of this vast overcrowded city. The traffic is just overwhelming and with a very basic road infrastructure, cars seem to go where they want and when they want! The pollution is so bad that when I awoke this morning and looked out of my window to see fog, I was surprised - until I was told that it is actually smog that settles over the city every morning!

Litter, dust and sand cover the pavements and you have no choice but to walk on the road; you are then battling with the cars and I just couldn't believe it! It reminded me of when we get snow in England and everyone walks on the roads; I prefer that to heat, noise and dirt!

The city itself is pretty much the same but on a larger scale. To cross a road is out of the question! I found my way to the main square overlooked by the Hilton Hotel and then wandered along the riverbank and gazed in amazement at the Nile. It had always been something I had wanted to see and I savoured the moment!

Stereotype or not, this is the image of Egypt we have in the West.

Many times during the day people would approach me offering their help. I just wanted to look around but if you stopped to look at anything somebody would come and talk with you. Every time all they wanted to do was sell you something, show you their shop, or, on one occasion, one guy did actually try to rob me of my money belt! I really did not feel safe here and yet the crazy thing is that on nearly every street corner there is a Police Officer! Even as I made my way back on the Metro, two guys talking only in Arabic made me very apprehensive. I decided to leave at the next station and took the taxi.

I knew that my arrival in Africa would be an experience …..any brochure on Egypt shows the country's amazing breadth of attractions and beautiful resorts like Luxor, but the streets of Cairo are something else!

Day 56: Still in Cairo

The Salesian school in Cairo was founded in 1926 to cater for children from Italian families living here; by 1960 the school was taking in local youngsters and now all its pupils are Egyptian. With over 500 pupils nearly half of them are Muslim; they are all very friendly and were very happy to meet and talk with me! The school building is huge with the tarmac play area the centrepiece - so typical of Salesian schools that I have already visited. The school is known locally as the 'Vatican'!

Africa was going to be far more difficult to travel through after Europe and I needed to spend a great deal more time researching and talking to people about the physical journey - how I would actually get to my destinations and what was the best route! To travel south from Egypt through Sudan is very dangerous, so I would have to take another route. In fact, the British Foreign Office advises strongly against non-essential travel through Sudan and therefore I would need to fly!

After visiting four travel agents, I had four prices to fly to Ethiopia. It became apparent that it would be cheaper if I also bought my onward flight to Uganda and it would also help with any visa problems. I visited Ethiopian

Airlines with whom I wanted to fly, but they were very unhelpful! I was told that there were no flights until Friday, as the Tuesday flight was full. I had a local guide book that recommended DeCastro Tours downtown and so after nearly three hours, there I was in their office with tickets booked for Tuesday to Addis Ababa and the onward flight to Kampala - and all at the cheapest price!

The day had been a nightmare and it wasn't over as I was now lost in the underground! It was nice when a lady called Marianne from Cairo who worked as a translator saw me looking lost and offered to show me where I should be going. I was too late for my evening meal at the Salesian School, so Marianne suggested I try some 'Koshary', a local Egyptian dish. It was made from pasta, rice, lentils, chick beans and fried onions with a tomato/garlic sauce - it had an unusual taste but I liked it and ate the lot!

I had now started taking my malaria tablets, one each day for the next twenty-one weeks. I was really worried about how they would affect my stomach and with a change in diet every four or five days - only time would tell!

Day 57: Cairo, Egypt

I had now been travelling for two months and had begun to feel the strain of the journey! This morning I received a telephone call from the Ethiopian Airlines to explain that without a visa I would not be able to fly. The caller was definitely the same woman who yesterday had told me that no flights were available. I can only guess that she had taken umbrage at the fact that I had actually got a discounted flight from a travel agent. Perhaps she just didn't like me!

I telephoned the Salesian school in Addis Ababa to confirm that I would visit them, as this would support my purpose for wanting to go to Ethiopia. I then telephoned the Ethiopian Embassy who confirmed that I could get a tourist visa on entry - this is exactly what I already knew, so I could not understand what the problem was. It's times like this when you just feel like

giving up! Not knowing what you are doing next, having nobody to assist you and battling with different languages!

After lunch I spoke with the Airline Manager and told him about the situation. He asked if I was a reporter and I said no; he asked if I was a Salesian priest and I said that I was a Salesian past pupil. Just a few minutes later he confirmed my booking and said there would be no problems!

By now it was late afternoon and I was on my way to see the Pyramids. Three pupils from the school (Karim, Morad and Ahmed) had agreed to take me to see the Pyramids in the Cairo suburb called Giza. It's hard to believe that two of the boys had never been to see the Pyramids before. The journey by bus was only forty-five minutes and as we approached I was amazed at what we saw. They are massive - over two million blocks of stone were used in the construction of the Great Pyramid and since it is over 5,000 years old I was just speechless!

Our excitement turned very quickly to disappointment because we arrived at the road leading to the Pyramids only to be told that they were closed! In wintertime they close at 4pm and we were just five minutes too late! After much heated discussion at the gate it was still no good and so I suggested that we should just walk around the wall to another side and at least get a look. We had been hassled by so many hawkers (so aggressive too!) offering to take us by horse to the other side and so I thought we could just walk round!

Oh my God! This was a big mistake - we had been walking for about twenty minutes through some really dirty narrow streets and then we were stopped by three guys on horses! They told us we could go no further and we must turn back. I was a little scared but after a long discussion in Arabic (not me of course!) it was agreed that for a small fee we could go round to the other side by horse and cart! We did and got some fantastic views of the three Pyramids and this very strange monument that is half-lion, half-man called the Sphinx. It was such good fun but I was so cautious because it was beginning to get dark and I suggested we head off back!

Karim invited me to visit his family before returning to the school. In a densely populated suburb of rundown dirty buildings, we climbed the steps five floors up to the apartment. I met his Mum, Dad and three other brothers. It was lovely to visit his home and talk with his family. This generosity certainly outweighed the small number of people who wanted to make things difficult for the tourist! We shared coffee together and I was given a toast, **"Bel hanawel shefa!"**

Day 58: Still in Cairo

I was looking forward to leaving Cairo and heading into the 'real' Africa; Egypt is very much an Arab country and I'd had enough! I did no filming today, and spent most of the time talking with pupils in the school and writing up my journey log.

In the evening I took a final walk around the area where I was staying and was still fascinated by the number of people out and about shopping and just walking around! What were people doing? Anyhow, I returned to the house to begin packing my things ready for my flight and once more planning for the unthinkable - losing my luggage!

I really struggled to sleep, it was hot and I just did not feel tired – it was 3am before I nodded off and I slept until 4.30am when the nearby Mosque began its early morning prayer rituals using loudspeakers from across the road to broadcast to the entire neighbourhood! Most mornings I had coped with it, but today… Aarghh!

"Maael Salama!"

Day 59: The flight to Addis Ababa, Ethiopia

After breakfast I was on my way to the airport! It was becoming more and more difficult to say goodbye to people now; just as I began to settle in one place, I was on the move again! I really did find it difficult saying my goodbyes this time - think I'm becoming emotional and also in the same context, very homesick!

You cannot believe that I went through all the security checks and ended up at my gate for departure with no problems whatsoever! It meant I was three hours early and had to occupy my time watching the world go by! In all my travels this was the first time I had really had to wait to go somewhere!

The flight before mine was to Jeddah, Saudi Arabia and the airport was filling up with men dressed in white towels! It was so strange and eventually I realised that they were on their way to Mecca for the Haj. I visited the toilet in the airport and it just so happens that the doorway to the toilet is in the right direction for these pilgrims to take off their shoes, roll out the carpet, and kneel down to pray!

I was really excited as we boarded the plane; I have so wanted to go to Ethiopia and I was now on my way! The aircraft was old and I just laughed to myself so many times during the flight - it was just as if I was on a plane twenty years ago! The view from my window was fantastic - mainly desert but an amazing sight! We stopped in Khartoum after four hours and the passenger in front of me had got off here - those going to Addis Ababa had to stay on the plane!

Well, as I stood up to stretch my legs I noticed a purse on the seat and realised that the lady in front had left it! I quickly picked it up and made my way to the exit door. The passengers who had just disembarked were now on the bus and the cabin crew staff asked me to go to the bus to find the lady. I jumped down the stairs and saw her sitting on the bus. She was so happy when I handed her the purse, as she had not realised that she had lost it yet! I was really happy for her and now I could say I had been to Khartoum and physically set foot on Sudanese soil!

We arrived in Addis Ababa very late and I was worried about entering with no visa! I was sent to the Immigration Desk where I explained myself, paid US$30 and smiled whilst my passport was stamped. This time there were no problems. What a contrast – and a very pleasant one too! As it was late, I took a taxi to a nearby hotel and crashed out!

No worries: my Ethiopian passport stamp.

Day 60: Addis Ababa, Ethiopia

As I left my hotel this morning I could hardly open my eyes - this was due to the sun, it was so bright. It was also very, very hot but not humid and sticky. Addis Ababa lies 2,500 feet above sea level, so there was actually a pleasant, refreshing breeze but the sun was still very strong! The city was absolutely crazy - tourists were very few and spotted quickly by the many locals wanting to escort you or sell you something! It was also quite frightening, as their way of approaching you could often seem very threatening - but these were the people and in actual fact they were very friendly and helpful!

Ethiopia has a past that goes back to the beginning of time - in the very birthplace of mankind! Fossils of the very earliest evidence of Man have been found in this country that for most of us today is only known as a country of famine! According to the U.N. it is the third poorest country in the world and the next few days were to be most incredible for me!

I went to visit Fr Dino (a Salesian Missionary priest) who is building a centre to help the street children of Addis. The project is huge and will give safe hospitality for the children during the day where they can be fed, cleaned and educated. He suggested that in the evening we should drive through the city centre and he would show me why this was to be an important project.

Very late in the evening we drove in a secure vehicle around Addis and I saw hundreds of children wrapped in cardboard, plastic or cloth materials sleeping in doorways, against walls and in the gutters! I was disgusted and horrified as Fr Dino showed me makeshift homes of blankets draped from walls with people asleep underneath! The city is very cold in the evening and I honestly could not believe my eyes when I saw children literally sleeping in the gutter at the side of the road, where they would lift the grid up to climb in! I was numb and very upset.

Day 61: Still in Addis

Today I went to Mekanisa to visit the Salesian school. This was great, I loved talking with the children, they were all so friendly with lovely happy smiling faces and followed you around trying to hold onto your hand! It was, however, to turn into one of the saddest days of my life!

After lunch we drove again in a secure vehicle just 200 metres from the school into a world of absolute poverty. People living in tents and wooden huts crammed next to each other with neither running water nor sanitation, just hundreds of people living in such terrible conditions it's hard to even imagine. I felt absolutely sick! Many of the people have walked for days to come here to the city from the drought-stricken areas in the north (which we see on TV) and they have nothing; absolutely nothing!

Adjacent to this shanty town is a small convent home run by the Salesian Sisters. Here, they look after some of the poorest individuals who are so sick and with physical abnormalities that they would have no chance of survival. I had tears in my eyes; I have never seen or imagined anything like what I was witnessing

Ethiopian currency

right in front of me. I was absolutely shocked and did not know what to do or say! Words, and I really mean this, cannot describe what has happened for some of these children and what life lies ahead for them. There were also children with leprosy and Aids and since the hospital was struggling to find beds for them they were rescued and brought here. The three buildings were made from converted shipping containers insulated with wooden panels and turned into living accommodation for the sick.

I met a boy who had been brought to them wrapped in a blanket - he had been wrapped in this blanket so long that his whole body was covered in pus. Every day for a year they had bathed him and his wounds were now healing well! He had asked the Sisters why he needed to wash with water everyday and he was twelve years old! The Sisters told me that even after they help some of the people there is nowhere for them to go and as they had to leave the Sisters they turned to begging or prostitution.

I was in complete shock and I'm sorry that you have to read this but I just wanted to come home! Even as I write this I have tears in my eyes - what kind of life did these people have with so little food, no work, no education and a home where the floor is the bare ground of dirt, dust and disease?

I kept asking myself what hope there could be? But I would say this - every child I saw would smile - and that smile was their hope!

Chapter 3:

November

Foreword

by Dr Johann Lochner
BJ Kempen Hospital, Victoria West

People cross your path in millions of ways and it was our luck to meet Pete and his nephew Ross, on a cold spring day in November 2002. They had an accident near Victoria West and Pete had a nasty laceration on his right arm. He was hospitalized at BJ Kempen Hospital in Victoria West, South Africa. Pete was quite lucky to survive the accident. They were stranded in the dead of night on a highway with no help at hand. A car eventually stopped, but the driver just searched their luggage, took what he needed and left. After hours, a good Samaritan stopped and phoned the police and ambulance, which took them to hospital. Pete was badly shaken by his ordeal, but proved to be a model patient.

His wound was checked on a daily basis and as he became stronger he was able to explore our little town and he and Ross became local celebrities! It was a privilege to get to know Ross, a police officer in Canada. Their views on policing were an insight, where a policeman is a helper and not someone to be feared.

We, as citizens of Victoria West, were privileged to have met a man who could follow and realize his dream and live to tell the tale, especially as it could have ended in a disaster.

Day 62: Langano, Ethiopia

Today I left Addis to travel by bus 200kms south to Lake Langano. I wanted to see more of Ethiopia and this was the nearest place I could get to by land and return the next day. The journey by bus was incredible, it cost me US$3 and I got the front seat with a great view and I wouldn't be squashed by the other passengers as they made use of every bit of space on Ethiopian public transport!

Out of the city and we were heading into a savannah; it was a great sight and every so often we would pass a small village of wooden huts and some cattle! Much of the area was inaccessible, an inhospitable desert that dips to the lowest point on the earth's surface.

This was real Africa and it was a spectacular sight! The road followed the Great Rift Valley, which stretches from the Red Sea to Kenya and hosts a series of small lakes with surrounding woodland.

Now, the bus journey! The road is just about straight and villages have grown up along the side, but at any moment on the journey cattle would just cross! It was amazing the way the driver steered from side to side to avoid the animals. If the vehicle in front was going too slow, the driver would do the same thing - honking his horn and nearly forcing the other vehicle off the road! I won't talk about what happened with the horse and cart, or even just PEOPLE!

After nearly three hours we arrived in the town of Ziway and this was the 'service station'. This was my first experience of public toilets and they were bad, but I needed a wee!

I was advised not to eat from the small café crowded with people (other buses had already stopped here!) and I looked round for some tourists to talk with! I was on my own and being hassled by hawkers! I went into the café and asked for a coffee with milk; the waiter did not understand and so I made the gestures for me to go behind the bar and make my own! The crowds of people laughed as I made my coffee and returned to sit down. At least I knew it was safe to drink and duly paid the equivalent of about eight pence!

Bekele Mola Hotel was a three-kilometre walk from the main road. The driver stopped along this vast highway to let me off and I was all on my own. I began to walk down the dirt-track road and suddenly young children appeared from nowhere! Through the bushes I could just make out a number of wooden huts with roofs made of dried out grass! This is where they had come from and they began to follow me - I could not believe that I was actually scared! Eventually I stopped and they stopped! It was bizarre, they were as scared as I was! I handed out my chewing gum and mumbled a few words and they left!

Lake Langano has been developed for tourists, but I was the only one there because this was not high season! It would be dark soon, so I went to look around. There are actually three lakes - Langano, Abiata and Shala, one brown, one silver and one blue, respectively. It was certainly an awesome sight but as dusk fell the mosquitoes were out - so I went in!

Day 63: Back in Addis

I'm really not cut out for wilderness adventures. Bekele Mola Hotel may sound great, but your room is actually a little isolated hut in the grounds with a small primitive bathroom attached! I heard strange animal noises in the room and I was walking back to the main road fairly promptly! This was not for me!

There is no designated bus stop so I just stood and waited - I was told just to wave at any bus that passed and if it stopped then it would be surely going to Addis, and if it stopped the driver wanted your fare! I was lucky and after just a few minutes a minibus stopped and offered me a lift. I was back in the city in four hours!

Addis Ababa is a very compact city with a population of over three million. The people are so friendly and are always saying '**Tenaistilign**' which translated from their Amharic language is a form of greeting! The problem with the city is the number of people taking refuge from the

No Onward Ticket

drought-affected areas in the north. The local newspaper reported today that the drought situation in the State had worsened and the life it was claiming, both human and livestock, was likely to increase beyond anticipation. This is a vast country, larger than France but with no real infrastructure. We see the images on our television screens and do we think that our contributions make a difference? I spoke with a number of people who told me that work is focusing on rural development activities. Soil and water conservation, sustainable food programmes, irrigation schemes, construction of educational and health buildings and new access roads were all major projects for the non-governmental organisations (NGO's) - but where does that leave the government?

I have a little secret to tell! I was tired and felt very dirty having not had a shower for three days. I stopped a taxi and asked the driver to take me to the Sheraton Hotel. I checked in to a top floor room overlooking the swimming pool and beyond. I ordered room service, sent my clothes to the hotel laundry, had a bath, then a shower – drank beer and watched a movie whilst relaxing on my large master bed! In the morning, after a swim, I went for breakfast and ate so much. On returning to my room to pack, I looked out on my balcony and could see over the wall to the hotel grounds something that really shocked me! Children dressed in shabby and dirty clothes were sleeping along the streets littered with garbage. I began filming as I wanted to record this amazing contrast of rich and poor so close together. This had been my purpose – to capture such awful poverty against the wealth and luxury of western accommodation. Why?

There's a different mentality about driving in Africa.

Day 64: Entebbe, Uganda

It was sad to leave Ethiopia; it had been a dream to visit this country but I was tired and very shocked by what I had seen. So, '**Egziabiher Yistilign**' and maybe I will come back one day!

Fr Mario, who worked at the school, drove me to the

airport and I thanked him for the hospitality his community had given me! These are dedicated people and I admire their vigour and commitment to keep going! Last year when he was driving in the city he had stopped at traffic lights, a young beggar stole his spectacles injuring his eye at the same time - and just a few months ago the school was stoned by a group of disappointed teenagers who had wanted the priests to sponsor their newly-formed football team!

Border control was simple because I had the ticket and I was on my way. The flight took us to Kilimanjaro first and on the approach I had a fantastic view of this near-extinct volcano rising out from the plain. It is almost 6,000 metres high and was breathtaking from the air and

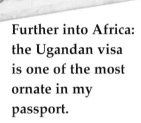

Further into Africa: the Ugandan visa is one of the most ornate in my passport.

quite staggering to imagine when we touched down at the tiny airport. At last my mobile phone had a signal again and more than 20 text messages poured in! It had been difficult for me without them. As a lone traveller I found text messages to be a great way of communicating. After an hour, we were on our way to my 18th country, Uganda.

I met a passenger called Richard who worked for The World Bank. I was unaware of their programme of Aids prevention in which they have given millions of dollars to help tackle a disease that is killing millions of people here in Africa. The work includes care, support and treatment whilst focusing on capacity building and knowledge sharing. (Thanks for your travel tips, Richard!)

I arrived at the airport very late and stayed at the Fly Motel close by. The airport is 35kms from Kampala and I preferred not to travel at night.

Day 65: Bombo, Uganda

Fr John (a Polish Salesian Missionary) met me in Kampala today and after doing a few errands we drove about an hour out of the city to a remote village called Bombo. Now, we are talking remote! The road to the village is a dirt track, water comes from small-bore holes and in the early evening, a generator provides a small amount of electricity but by nightfall it is pitch black!

Kampala was a busy place, quite attractive and modern, but now I was in the 'jungle'. I was shown to my room and I was quite shocked at the conditions in which the four priests lived. A mosquito net was essential, the floor was bare concrete and it was hot, humid and very sticky, and with no air conditioning - how could I survive?

After our evening meal, during which I discovered one of the priests was suffering from malaria and the others had all had it – there was little else to do but turn in for the night. I went to my room and there on the wall was a great big lizard! I ran out to get help and the priests just laughed! "It will not harm you", they said "and don't worry about the rats that run along the rooftop during the night!" It was a living nightmare for me! I climbed into my bed (fully clothed) and listened to the mosquitoes coming for me but unable to get through the net! I was petrified and with the rats, lizards and dogs howling, I got very little sleep!

Day 66: Still in Bombo

The missionary project had established a church, school and small hospital for the people here and I was amazed at what they provided. Since 1998 the work of providing an education for young people has been on going and it was great to see what was here, including a technical school training both boys and girls in such skills as carpentry, bricklaying and sewing - all of which is important to the empowerment and development of the local community.

The children (over 1,500) all come from poor families; many are orphans and so stay in boarding accommodation at the school. It costs only US$150 per year to fund the education of a youngster and Fr John works tirelessly getting funds to pay for their education. This amount also pays for books, clothes and shoes for each child. I spoke in the class with some of the older pupils and it was very hard for me to stand there with these people who have so little. Not one of the 60 pupils had a television and when I asked about a fridge they just laughed at me. This is the reality that so often we in the UK just hear about.

In the afternoon I went to see where many of the children live. I have never seen living conditions like it! Most lived in small huts with no electricity and no running water. Sanitation was basic and as it was now the rainy season, the dirt tracks and areas around the houses were just muddy rivers. I was helpless as I witnessed many very young children just standing around, nowhere to go and nothing to play with. It was another depressing sight for me; malaria was common and health was not even a word that people would talk about!

Harsh reality: life for Ugandan children is one of grinding poverty.

As the sun went down it became very dark and the rain had started. Our four-wheel drive vehicle was sliding all over and I was more frightened than on any ride at the theme parks! If we got stuck we would be in serious trouble as there was no rescue service! It was also very dangerous during the night and I just wanted to get back!

The whole way of life is different to the West. I was fortunate to witness again the real life of a community here in Uganda - a tourist would not see this, but thanks to my association with the Salesians I was able to do so! In fact, Uganda has a rich tourism history - its abundant forests, lakes, rivers, savannah and mountains; its variety of wildlife, game, fish and butterflies make it a popular destination throughout the world. But, internal strife in the 1970's left the people desperate and in my opinion just a small few have made it through. The rest suffer a poverty that you cannot imagine and this has led to unimaginable theft and robbery for those that even make it a little way.

No Onward Ticket

It seems that Uganda is a clear example whereby the rich get richer and the poor, poorer! The work done by the Salesian Missions brings some hope and healing to the innocent and abandoned, but...

Day 67: Still in Bombo, Uganda

Help! I cannot cope with my living conditions! Last night I was kept awake by the singing and dancing from a nearby village; it sounded just like an African tribal dance and I kept thinking they were coming to get me! The mozzies certainly did and I have three bites on my ear! How had they got through my net?

I knew it was time to leave and went into the city to get my bus ticket for Kenya. I had a wonderful day looking around Kampala, visiting an Internet café and basically enjoying life in a far more sophisticated way! What we take for granted the people outside the city do not have and I have been shocked and stunned by this!

Ethiopia had been very difficult to cope with and now I had to experience further poverty - a quality of life that is unimaginable and because I had been given an opportunity to talk with these people it made it even more difficult.

All I could say in an attempt to put my thoughts into words was 'it's another world!'

Day 68: The journey to Nairobi, Kenya

My journey began at 5.45am with the drive by jeep from the village to the city. At 7am I was on a coach to Kenya. The coach was very spacious with twelve rows of three seats, two on one side of the aisle and one on the other. (Oh, and only 11 passengers!) Things were going very well as we arrived at the border in Busia. The coach driver really pushed the vehicle to its limits though, travelling at 100kph on roads that were very old and worn - it was becoming a very bumpy ride.

After almost six hours we arrived in Kisumu for a

service stop. I was starting to feel a little unwell so I decided not to eat anything. The toilets were disgusting! Bricked cubicles but when you went inside it was just a hole in the ground - no flushing facilities and human faeces just filling the hole! I felt sick, absolutely sick! Back on board and just an hour later we had broken down! This could only happen to me.

We were in the middle of nowhere and the sun was beating down as we sat at the side of the road to wait for assistance! Another hour and two mechanics arrived; in the meantime people from a nearby village had come to watch also!

After almost two hours we were on our way again, but then the unthinkable happened - smoke was coming from the airvents and I thought the bus was on fire! The driver just ignored it and even though the smell was really bad, he just motored on! I began to think that this was my next 'fire in transit' and became quite scared that he showed not the slightest sign of stopping!

The smoke did disappear and the smell went away but the journey had now become another nightmare experience for me!

Passing through numerous Police checks, witnessing amazing views of tea plantations and stunning views of the final stretch of the African Rift Valley, we arrived very late but safe in Nairobi!

The journey had taken fifteen hours covering over 700kms and after almost ten weeks travelling, I was in my 19th country!

Day 69: Utume, Kenya

I woke up today feeling unwell; I had flu-like symptoms and was exhausted. I had stayed overnight at a hotel in the city and even though I had slept well, I felt really ill! I arranged to stay at the Salesian Theological College in Utume, on the outskirts of the city, where I spent the rest of the day in bed.

Day 70: Still in Utume, Kenya

When you consider the work of the Salesians around the world, the recruitment of Priests is very important and the college in Utume is home to over fifty theologians from all over Africa. I was given a great welcome and spoke to the residents in the evening about my journey!

Unfortunately I was still very ill and had spent most of the day just resting and making use of the Internet to read my mail. Another early night!

Day 71: Uhuru, Kenya

Still not feeling too good today, but I was invited to attend a Sunday Mass in nearby Uhuru and it was the most amazing experience. The service lasted for three hours with all Africana singing and dancing and shouts of Alleluia! In a small church packed with locals - the atmosphere was uplifting! I had tears in my eyes of sheer joy at this most mind-blowing experience of African worship. Towards the end of the service I was invited to speak and made my way through the packed audience to the front of the altar. Wow! Everything I said was greeted with shouts of praise to God! Constant clapping and people mumbling "Yeah" made my speech the best I've ever done! They loved me and I loved them!

In the evening I attended a production of the musical 'The Witness' staged at the college with over two hundred local children. It was a fantastic show and was done to raise funds to pay for the youngsters' education!

These last few days had been very hard for me; I was weak and still felt ill. Tomorrow I would visit the local hospital for some blood tests to make certain that I had nothing too serious! Travelling on your own is very difficult; I wanted to go home for a few days and sleep in my own bed but I couldn't! I could do no more than rest, drink plenty of water and get better!

Day 72: Still in Utume, Kenya

After another difficult night sleeping I was now on my way to Mater Infirmary to see the doctor. After filling in relevant forms I then had to go to the 'cashier' and pay a small amount to actually see the doctor! It was apparent that I needed a number of blood tests and after returning to the 'cashier' and making a further payment - the blood was drained from my arm and I went to lie down! It only took thirty minutes for the results to come through and thankfully malaria was ruled out! My blood count was low and it seemed that I had picked up some 'amoebic bug' whilst in Uganda! I was a little nervous but relieved that it was not malaria!!!

I returned to the college and rested for the rest of the day.

Day 73: Still in Utume, Kenya

Today I visited the work of 'Bosco Boys' - it is a project for street children in Nairobi and provides accommodation, food and education. It is also about empowering these youngsters to help themselves and encouraging them to give up bad habits like glue sniffing and taking drugs, most of which is a way for them to survive!

Later Fr Henri, who runs the 'Bosco Boys', took me to where many of the street children come from. The shanty town of Nairobi occupies a piece of land to the side of the city; here 1.5 million people live in an area known as the 'slum'. I was absolutely disgusted at what I saw and felt physically sick. The stench of rotting garbage, the dust, the heat, the people! It was an awful sight; each 'house' was made from pieces of metal which made up just one room for the many people who live, cook, eat and sleep there! I was appalled; a narrow path ran through the slum area that was also used for disposing of waste water and sewage!

What kind of life do these people have? The sight was

'hell' and yet just over the wall was 'heaven'! This was where the rich people lived in high-walled homes with security on their gates! I spoke with some of the people living in the slum, a young mother of five children who was pregnant again. To feed her children she had to go out to work - and this meant selling her body! I spoke with a 17-year-old boy who spent his time selling drugs to pay for food to share with his friends! There were no welfare benefits, they lived a life that they had not chosen and I was very upset.

On returning to the college I was keen to shower and change my clothes. I had spent my day walking through a most depressing place and yet I had wanted to experience the reality of people who lived in one of the biggest slum areas of Africa. This was another sad day for me.

Day 74: Still in Utume, Kenya

I spent the day resting and catching up with e-mails and my guest book messages from the website. In the evening I spoke with the Theologian residents about my journey and thanked them for such great hospitality!

Day 75: The journey to Dar es Salaam, Tanzania

At 6.00am I was on my way to the bus station. The only way to get to Tanzania is by bus and so I was making the 12-hour journey; I was feeling much better and glad that I was able to continue on my way. Looking out of my window you would often see Maasai tribe people; they are nomadic and spend their life on the move finding grazing land for their animals. They dress in just two pieces of attractive, decorated cloth and live a very simple life. The road just went on for miles, straight and very long.

After almost four hours we arrived at the border. I have been so lucky travelling through Africa - I get asked a few questions, pay for my visa and I'm allowed to enter!

The landscape of Tanzania was different; it seemed much greener and with a good main road infrastructure. We arrived in Dar es Salaam safely in the late evening but it was very hot - I mean really hot and humid and I found it very hard to sleep - even with the fan in my room full on. This was the hottest country I had visited so far!

Day 76: Tanzania to Zambia

Early rise because I wanted to see something of this city called Dar es Salaam. It was a very tidy place and not as dirty, dusty and congested with cars as previous cities. The sad thing was the number of Maasai people coming into the city hoping for work and somewhere to live! Over the last few years much of their livestock has perished through disease and so with little food they are left with no alternative.

What strikes me is that many world corporate companies have come here and taken so much of the land to extract things like copper and zinc. Although they may employ local people, when they leave, they leave nothing! The villages are cut off by road and with no electricity, water or telephones it makes life very difficult for these people and nobody seems to take any responsibility. The big companies could do something; they could build a school, a dispensary or - something! But instead it seems to me that they just rape the country, taking what they want and leaving behind nothing but wreckage in which the people have to try and survive.

At 3pm I was on the 'Tazara Railway' to Zambia. This was going to be an amazing experience – non-stop for 51 hours through some of the remotest parts of central Africa. I went to find my 1st class compartment on the train. These were the most expensive carriages and yet were not particularly clean or luxurious; I walked through 2nd class and was just glad that I wasn't sleeping there! I was sharing with Mayembe from Zambia and Qussay from Zanzibar - I was very apprehensive (as I did not know them at all!) and worried about my safety, the food, the toilet facilities and… well, was I doing the right thing?

After a few hours on the move, the train began to slow down and for the next hour we were travelling through the northern part of the Selous Game Reserve. I just stared out of my window hoping to catch a glimpse of African wildlife. Then I saw the most amazing sight; I encountered three huge jigsaw-patterned giraffes! As they seemed to glide past so close to the train, they looked quite massive and I was overwhelmed! It was fantastic and just as I sat back I saw a herd of elephants in the distance! This was real Africa for me. This is a fabulous, unconquered landscape of unspoilt beauty and empty windswept floodplains. This is 'Jurassic Park' - where nature is still the master, an unforgettable adventure!

Day 77: Tanzania to Zambia

This was nothing like the sleeping compartments on the European trains, very basic and pretty uncomfortable. However, I had spent a few hours in the lounge carriage having a few 'Mozi' beers chatting to Emily and Anita from England and Marco from Italy - and I had a good sleep!

I awoke to this awesome sight of Africa out of the window! Nothing had changed, it was so incredible to see this fantastic landscape - I could not get bored of this!

As people walked past the compartment we began to get to know folk and this was such fun! I would tell them of my epic journey and they seemed very interested in my experiences! It also gave me an opportunity to learn from them.

Every few hours we would stop at a station, mainly for water but a number of people would get on or off the train. The station would be packed with locals who had nothing else to do but wait for this train only twice a week - hoping to sell some of their local produce! Many children would be begging; none of them had anything on their feet and they looked so unhappy! It was very depressing seeing up to a hundred children standing along the railway line begging for anything!

I handed one boy some bread and an empty water bottle, his eyes lit up as he thanked me and ran off along the embankment to his home; you would have thought all his Christmases had come at once!

This was becoming a very long journey but the greatest experience was of making friends and watching the world go by in Africa. It was very late in the evening when we arrived at the last station in Tanzania. Immigration Officers boarded the train and my passport was stamped (after a small fee!). **"Kwaheri Tanzania nakutakia mema!"**

Day 78: Lusaka, Zambia

Today was a long day. By mid-morning I was all packed and ready to get off the train but we still had six hours to go. We arrived in Kapiri Moshi after 51 hours and 16 minutes! This was the end of the line. The Tazara Railway line was built by the Chinese in the 1970's to transport copper from Zambia to the port in Tanzania and was never extended to the capital Lusaka. I had to take the bus from the station for a further three hours into Lusaka, I was exhausted and the journey was very uncomfortable. The bus was completely packed with passengers and luggage and each bus leaving the station would only leave when it was physically impossible to get anymore people on board! At random Police checkpoints a number of passengers would have to hide behind seats so that the driver would not be fined for overcrowding! What a nightmare, I did not think we would ever make it, but we did! **"Mulishani mwena Zambia, natemwa bana ukwisa muzambia!"**

Day 79: Lusaka

I had experienced the natural beauty of Zambia, the completely unspoilt wildlife areas and tiny villages scattered on the plains, but I was now in the capital city Lusaka with a significant absence of holidaymaking crowds! This was a beautiful but simple city with neither tall buildings, nor large crowds of people at all! I stayed at the Lusaka Hotel in the centre of the main road running through the city. It was the first hotel built here and I was its only tourist.

Lusaka is not the safest of places; most tourists stay in large holiday hotels on the outskirts set in large walled off gardens. Tourists don't come into the city - they may be coming to 'The Real Africa' as it is known but they visit Victoria Falls and travel through the game reserves unfamiliar with the life of the Zambian city dweller!

As dusk falls this city becomes a very dangerous place; everywhere closes and it becomes a ghost town! There is a high level of unemployment and during the night the Police will arrest anyone walking about as suspected burglars.

Even during the day every shop, bank, café, hotel and Internet café has a security guard protecting the place. People would follow me as I walked the street and one guy even tried to grab the chain from around my neck.

This was not a good place to be on your own but in a strange way; having spent such a long time on the train enclosed, I wanted time to myself!

The hotel was cheap, the food simple and the coffee delicious. I had a television with CNN news and **'no'** mosquitoes!

Day 80: Lusaka, Zambia

Zambia was very hot; my head felt like it was burning as I made my way to the Internet café. Unfortunately my mobile did not work here, but I had received some great news from my nephew in Canada who was flying out to meet me in South Africa and would join me across India! My girlfriend Jayne had also managed to get a flight for Bangkok and would meet me there for Christmas - if I made it that far!

At the Internet café, I loaded my disk into the computer and it would not work! It seemed that the intense heat outside whilst carrying the disk may have damaged it and I was absolutely sick! I had spent so much time the previous day working on my journal and had lost everything which would now have to be re-done!

Since my nephew was meeting me in just four days time

and with the situation in Zimbabwe - I decided it would be better to fly direct to Cape Town and spent most of the day trying to get a cheap one-way flight! Having succeeded, I spent the evening chatting with a number of Zambians in the hotel bar before settling in my room to watch a movie! I was feeling very lonely today and watching a 'weepy' film had me crying and asking myself "What am I doing?"

I have been travelling for almost three months and was 100% fit again but beginning to really miss home! Earlier I had visited the supermarket and when I walked in, Christmas music was being played; it was so strange, I could not feel 'Christmassy' at all and just laughed to myself! I did not think it strange that it was by then the middle of November and I was basking in the African heat! Nevertheless, whilst I enjoyed the experience of exploring culture and meeting people it had started to become a little strenuous!

Day 81: Cape Town, South Africa

After breakfast and a very long time trying to get cash from a bank, until I found the HSBC, I was on my way to the airport. It was very quiet and the plane was only half full. It didn't take long before I arrived in Johannesburg for my connecting flight and was boarding the airport bus to the plane. It suddenly dawned on me that everyone was white! Wow! I had hardly seen a white person since Athens and I was amazed! I was in South Africa and I was so bemused! Once on board the plane it seemed I might have been travelling in Europe – I could not get over the novelty of having white faces and English-speaking voices around me! I was sitting next to two business people called Mark and Caroline. We had a great chat about my journey and they told me how great Cape Town was. I was so excited about being in South Africa; I had made it to the tip of this great continent and to my 22nd country!

Mark gave me a lift from the airport to the town and dropped me off outside the City Lodge. Unfortunately

No Onward Ticket

there were no vacancies, but the staff were so helpful and found me some nearby accommodation for the night. The mobile phone was working again and I had a great deal of work to do here, planning the next stage of my journey around the world!

Day 82: Cape Town, South Africa

So, here I was in the 'Mother City' or 'Namkelekwe entshona Koloni' and spent most of the morning exploring! The view of Table Mountain provided an awesome welcoming beacon to this city and could be seen wherever I walked - it just looked amazing. The city was modern and very cosmopolitan and having spent the last four weeks working my way down through drought stricken, barren floodplains of central Africa, this was paradise!

Early evening and I met with Sylvia (a relative of a Salesian past pupil in England) who emigrated to South Africa twenty years ago. She first took me for a drive along this fascinating Cape Peninsula and its coastline, along the mountain chain and then we arrived at 'Hout Bay'. Here we enjoyed a most splendid meal; I had never eaten so much! It was just great to have some good food and I cleaned my plate of fresh local prawns and Kingklip! (a locally caught fish – very tasty!) We talked all night about my journey and it was so strange to be talking with someone from England, I could talk fast and just talk and talk and talk without having to work hard at speaking clearly enough to make myself understood!

Day 83: Still in Cape Town, South Africa

I moved to a small guesthouse today called Altona Lodge and made arrangements for the arrival of my nephew from Canada. Most of the day was spent trying to arrange flights from Jo'burg to Bombay, which I would need to take next week. It was proving very difficult but I knew that I had to get to India and across to Calcutta by December 5th as my nephew had his return flight to Canada booked from there.

Later I was invited for an interview with the Cape Argus newspaper that wanted to cover my journey. They were pleased at my success in reaching the tip of Africa and another completed continent. I arranged for a hire car to drive to Jo'burg, although it would take over 15 hours (over 1,400kms) – it was cheaper than a bus or train!

Finally, I had confirmation of the flights needed for next week and headed back for some food and a good night's sleep. I was beginning to get really excited about meeting my nephew and any feelings of loneliness would soon be forgotten.

Day 84: Cape Town, South Africa

Meeting Ross at the airport was great and with our brand new hire car we drove straight down to the Cape of Good Hope and Cape Point. We stood at the most southern point of Africa, situated at the junction of two of earth's most contrasting water masses – the Atlantic and the Indian Oceans. Towering more than 200 metres above the sea, I peered over the viewing platform and just enjoyed the view, the experience and the thought of how far I had now got! It is difficult to recognise the two oceans meeting at this point and your eyes begin to play tricks as you try to identify the different waters. It did not matter – I was there and it was brilliant!

We drove more than 100 kilometres along this spectacular coastline through the rich and varied flora and fauna, seeing baboons that would even jump up onto the car and watching a colony of African Penguins sheltering along the beach. At times the road was almost at the edge of the cliff and although the view below was fantastic it was pretty scary!

This had been such a great day and we drove back towards Table Mountain just in time to see the most famous sight of all here in South Africa – the sunset! It was incredible; the colours in the sky were amazing as the black sky pushed down on the sun until it disappeared.

We arrived back into the city to eat and reflect on an amazing day of sightseeing. Cape Town is an

unforgettable city in a location at the southern tip of Africa – dominated by the sheer cliffs of a mountain!

Day 85: Cape Town to Johannesburg, South Africa

History has a great deal to say about South Africa and in my lifetime it will be about the 'freedom of black people' and, in particular, the determination of one man's struggle for what he believed in.

We were on our way to Robben Island where Nelson Mandela spent twenty years of incarceration.

For nearly 400 years colonial and apartheid rulers banished those they regarded as political troublemakers to this small island and the prison that had now become a World Heritage Site. It also symbolised the triumph of human spirit over enormous hardship and adversity.

The tour of the prison was given by a former political prisoner who gave some harrowing details of life in this 'hell-hole', the way they were treated by the guards and what happened to those that came to visit inmates!

I was shocked and disturbed by what we heard and saw. I had an opportunity to interview the guide later and he told me that even near to death from the beatings, he believed that one day it would all be worth it!

The new South Africa has a long way to go in my opinion. Black and white people were different here, they lived in different areas of the town and hardly ever did I see a social mix! There may be a majority black population, but they were still a minority people!

For almost three decades, this was Nelson Mandela's front door.

At 5.00pm Ross and I set off in the hire car to Johannesburg from Cape Town. We had been on the road for seven hours and having had two stops for fuel we had completed about 600kms of our journey. We were making good time, I was feeling good, and we would be in Johannesburg by morning.

Day 86: Highway N1, East of Three Sisters

Shortly after midnight our journey came to a terrible end! I was driving at about 120kph when the car began to wobble and then swerve all over the road. Seconds later we were off the road and after hitting the ditch, the car overturned and slid along upside down for what seemed like ages, before coming to a very abrupt end, landing on its side!

We were in the middle of nowhere, the headlamps still shining and they were the only source of light as I began to climb out of the window! The car was completely crushed on all sides and it was terrifying! I was covered in blood, dust and glass! It was awful. As Ross climbed out after me he asked how I was - I was petrified and in shock!

Aftermath: the largest disaster of the journey was the car accident in South Africa.

We were both alive and that was honestly amazing to believe! The car was completely wrecked but we had both climbed out alive. Both of us had our glasses knocked off our faces, and I couldn't see! My right arm was dripping blood as it had gone straight through the window and... well, what can I say? At the time I thought I was dead, I thought I was walking around watching myself! It was a living nightmare! I began to feel very cold, I was shivering and Ross and I just hugged each other!

I climbed back up to the road for help. We were completely isolated, no lights, no cars and nowhere to go! Our entire luggage had been thrown out of the boot on impact and Ross began to salvage what he could.

The dust was still in the air and I was crying! It was over ten minutes before I saw the headlights of a vehicle ahead. The first couple of wagons just went right by. I remember trying to wave and get the attention of the drivers! Ross pulled me off the road - this was a very long stretch and traffic moved very fast! A small pick-up did stop. Four black men got out and made their way down to our overturned car. They were looking all over but not really paying much attention to us. Eventually they said they would call the Police, and they returned to their vehicle and drove away! Ross realised that we must secure our belongings quickly - we were not safe and needed help!

It was a further twenty minutes before another vehicle passed. This car stopped and the driver immediately telephoned both the Police and Ambulance for assistance. They stayed with us and offered me a jacket as I was shivering violently and eventually they put me in their car to await the arrival of the ambulance (thanks Ogi Mabimba and family, you may have saved our lives!)

It was nearly a full hour after the crash before a Police car rolled up with one uniformed and one plain-clothed officer. The plain-clothed officer used his torch and shone it around on our car for a bit while the other stayed with the Police car. He wrote down our names on a scrap of paper from his pocket. They asked us what tow company we wanted - how the hell were we supposed to know? Finally, nearly a full two hours later, I was freezing cold and covered in blood, glass, and dust, and an ambulance rolled up - but it was full!

Ambulances are used to transport patients from one hospital to the other during the night! Thankfully a rescue truck pulled up shortly after and we squeezed into the cab to begin a 75 kilometre journey to the 'local' hospital in Victoria West.

I awoke in the morning having had three injections in my bum and 16 stitches in my right arm! I was in a private room at the B. J. Kempen Hospital.

Dr Johann Lochner examined both Ross and I and, due to the extensive cuts and bruises we had all over our bodies, he said we were lucky to be alive!

He also added that after accidents on that stretch of road, many people are subsequently robbed and left for dead or not even found until morning (and found dead!).

Flying Doctor Johann Lochner: was I pleased to see HIM! His horror stories of Highway N1 confirmed our fears.

Staying at the hospital was quite an experience!

Although I was getting flashbacks from the accident, Ross and I were beginning to talk about it and think about our luck in not having sustained any other injuries! My right arm was a mess, it was beginning to show the bruising and I was pretty frustrated by the whole thing!

The hospital staff treated us like celebrities and with only three other patients (in the female ward) we were certainly getting first class treatment! It's not every day they get visitors from outside and they spoilt us so much. It is disturbing however, that this hospital - vital in supporting the community of Victoria West - is so antiquated. Its medical supplies are very limited and there is no hi-tech equipment. My X-rays were even developed by hand by the radiologist whilst I waited! The food was good, but I needed everything cutting up!

We had both been shaken about in the car when it overturned and we were both beginning to feel the aches and pains all over, bruising and whiplash to the neck also. Thankfully we were both wearing seatbelts and this almost certainly saved us from any other injuries!

The car hire firm was brilliant; our car was a complete write-off, but by late afternoon another car from Cape Town arrived for us to use when we were ready! No paperwork, no hassle! We had both had our glasses smashed in the accident, and our clothes were bloodied and torn! Sorry to keep saying it, but I could only thank God for my life now and pray that I could keep going. My thoughts at the moment were about coming home because my arm was so bad but I agreed to wait until Ross returned to Canada before making a final decision!

Early evening came, and Dr Johann arrived to do the 'rounds'! He was a 'flying doctor' and agreed that we both needed some fresh air. He took us by car to the other side of the town and then invited us to fly with him in his plane! It was unbelievable. What a fantastic experience flying over the town and into the wilderness of South Africa – the view was exhilarating and the feeling in the

Day 87: Victoria West, South Africa

cockpit of this 2nd World War American plane was just awesome! The doctor was so kind to us and then he showed us an old 1950's U.S. Air Force training plane, which was open-topped - the pilot sat in the rear cockpit and flew the plane using dual controls. Well, we just had to experience this and so off into the sunset we went. He was the nicest man you could ever meet and afterwards we joined him with his family for an evening meal. We arrived back at the hospital just before midnight and I don't think the Matron was too pleased, but I took my tablets and I was soon fast asleep!

Day 88: Still in Victoria West, South Africa

I felt very sore all over today, but I attempted a left-handed shave and one-armed bath! Ross went back to visit the site of our near-fatal experience. He wanted to examine the area and look for any of our lost possessions.

The following is a summary of the car accident in South Africa that Ross made after returning to the site two days later. He's a serving Police Officer with the Ontario Provincial Police, and this is his report:

Date: Mon 25 Nov 02;

Time: 0030 hrs

Location: Hwy N1, East of Three Sisters, Western Cape, S. Africa

This paved highway runs east/west with one lane for each direction of travel. There is no restraining barrier. It is a long flat stretch of road in a desert/scrub type area. There are no settlements for what seems to be at least a 50km radius.

Two black skid marks 10 metres (m) long begin to leave the eastbound lane and enter the ditch from the start point (SP). These skids were made by the front right and rear left tires. There is a third set of marks, 4 distinct gouges in the pavement parallel to the skids. I believe these gouges were made by the steel rim of the rear right wheel.

The car entered the ditch; right side (drivers) first, 3m from the edge of the road. At this point the car had been skidding side-

ways for 12m from the SP. It flipped into the air and was airborne for 7m.

At 19m from the SP an impact of glass and debris was scattered across the ground.

At 33m from the SP a side view mirror broke off and was driven into the ground, we were sliding on our side.

At 46m from the SP the car came to rest on its left side (passengers). We were 8m away from the roads edge, suspended in air by our seatbelts.

The furthest item I found was a hubcap 53m from the SP and 13m from the road edge.

I have photos and I plan to make a scale diagram when I return to Canada to be added to the web site if possible.

Provincial Constable Ross DAVIDSON #9363

Ontario Provincial Police

I could have died there, in the dark on a lonely road at the other side of the world. I still shudder at the thought.

Later, he went for a walk around the town whilst I continued to rest. When he came back he told me how he had visited the local Police station looking to trade some Police badges. At first they just laughed at him, then a smartly dressed white man came into the front office and started handing out sweets. A gun and bullets were just sitting out on a desk.

The white fellow started talking about the station and invited Ross to look around and tour the cells. Then he began removing his belt and shoelaces, explaining that such things were not allowed in the cell area. Ross walked with the man and an officer along the corridor. He spoke about a local case before the Supreme Court, the 'Bonnie & Clyde' attempted murder case and Ross assumed he must be a lead investigator.

The officer opened the cell area and they both stepped in. At this point Ross said he realized the man was 'Clyde' on trial for attempted murder! Ross was allowed to just walk right in, no checks or anything. 'Clyde' spoke frankly

No Onward Ticket

Nephew Ross: I was so glad he was with me for this part of the journey

about hi-jacking a car, together with his girlfriend 'Bonnie'. When they got out he shot the driver in the back of the head, execution style and left him for dead. The man survived and 'Bonnie & Clyde' later turned themselves in to the authorities. Ross couldn't believe what he had just been allowed to do. They chatted in his cell for a bit about prisons and the Police before Ross left.

South Africa is a very dangerous place at the moment, crime is huge and particularly muggings and robberies! We were both aware that the most dangerous place is in Johannesburg and we would have to be very vigilant when we eventually got there!

Our flights to India had now been changed allowing us extra time to recover and we had made a decision that we would continue our journey the following day! The doctor was concerned, however, about infections to my arm and I needed to consider this very seriously! I was beginning to feel more comfortable, but we had gone through a terrible ordeal and Ross and I both kept reminding ourselves of how lucky we were.

In the evening the doctor invited us to join him at the local golf club. I noticed immediately that all the members were white! Black and white people divide this town; no matter what people say about South Africa, it will take years to mix people together in harmony! I'm not even saying that this should happen, I'm merely wanting to share with you that you could sense a divide everywhere you went.

Apartheid is wrong and nobody seemed to disagree with this fact. However, the colour of a person's skin does seem to separate people socially, politically and more apparently – in employment! We met some great people in the golf club and enjoyed a few 'Windhock' beers (strictly under doctor's orders of course!).

Day 89:
Victoria West to Johannesburg, South Africa

With my arm in a sling, a new hire car, and a full tank of fuel – we were leaving Victoria West to continue the final 11 hour drive to Johannesburg!

People had been fantastic to us both; when you are so far away from home and need help after such a terrible experience you just want to be at home but the people of Victoria West and in particular the doctor and nurses in the hospital gave us both superb hospitality and we thank you from the bottom of our hearts!

Ross now had to get us to Johannesburg safely and it was a long drive. We said farewell and we were back on the road. We took a different route taking us through a number of small towns on the way – the road was slower but probably much safer! My arm was very uncomfortable but we managed to devise a way of strapping it to the handle above the passenger window to keep it raised and avoid it swelling!

It was very late in the evening when we arrived in Jo'burg, and as we drove through the city there was a sense of danger! We had so many preconceived impressions of this place. We were in the heart of the city and the heart of South Africa where change, both good and bad, is happening very fast. By nightfall most of the shops were closed for fear of robberies (it was the customers who were worried rather than the shopkeepers) and most of the city was a ghost town. We had ended up in a black dominated part of the city with a good number of people standing on the street corners; we were very apprehensive and keenly aware that we needed to keep moving! As we approached traffic lights (called robots!) we would slow down, look both ways and then just keep going! We were told not to stop at junctions whilst driving for fear of being ambushed! What a scary thought and I was glad when we found the 'Holiday Inn', hoping it would be safe to stay here for the night!

Unfortunately they were full and absolutely useless in helping us! A security guard offered to travel with us to another hotel some fifteen minutes drive away but we

declined the offer! You really didn't know whom to trust, and I'm sorry to say this but I felt a sense of apprehension about these people who for some reason (that I cannot explain) made you feel scared! They were black South Africans and it should make no difference about the colour of anyone's skin but throughout my time so far here in South Africa, I had not felt very comfortable at all with these people!

Day 90: Johannesburg, South Africa

We had made our way to the airport to stay in a 'City Lodge' hotel, which was expensive, but we were tired and needed to rest!

In the morning, after Ross had re-done my bandages, we headed back into the city to find the Indian Embassy! My whole journey was to explore the barriers around the world; I had no visas in advance and this was one country where you could not apply on entry! The clerk told me that it would take a week to apply because they required confirmation of my status from my home country!

After much persuasion due to urgency (we had tickets to fly on Sunday and it was Friday) they agreed to fax the Indian Embassy in London and after two hours I telephoned the Embassy to ask if they would respond immediately! They agreed, and then we sat and waited for the clerk to read the fax and stamp my passport! This all took eight hours and we were both exhausted; the heat, frustration and well... just everything can get you down and I had had enough today!

We had found a hotel in a 'safe' part of the city that was cheap and booked in for two nights. It was my Dad's birthday today and it was great to phone home and talk to him and my Mum. I miss my family and Jayne so much and there was only so much sympathy I could get from Ross about my aches, pains and injured arm!

We took a drive out to get some food. It was only 10pm but everywhere was closed, for a city so big, trying to get anything when it gets dark is very difficult! We resorted to McDonald's but at least we had eaten!

Today a missionary priest of Don Bosco who works in the townships surrounding the city met us. Fr Chris McMahon, a native from Lancashire recognized my accent immediately! He took us to Ennerdale, a 'coloured' township near to Jo'burg – it was one of the growth points in this new South Africa, with many squatter camps on its borders.

Day 91: Still in Johannesburg, South Africa

Some of you may have heard of the tragic death of a missionary priest from Ireland only a week earlier. When we arrived at the church (unknown to us), flowers marked the spot where Fr Declan was found dead. We were told that he had been struck over the head with a brick and stabbed twice in the chest. A brick and kitchen knife, believed to be the murder weapons, were later found in the house. A local parishioner devastated by what had happened told me that a 'bloody struggle' had taken place in the lounge with a still unknown person who robbed him of his wallet!

We were both stunned by what we were being told and I wanted to share this tragic event with you because it is the reality of what is happening in Jo'burg. It is a sad thought that communities here need help in taking ownership of their 'new' country and becoming interactive with their neighbours - and yet robbery and murder have become an everyday occurrence here and anyone can be a victim!

Still numb from our experiences, we were then taken around this community and we saw for ourselves the shanty town life of thousands of people. Compared with Nairobi this was a more structured and organized layout, but it still shocked me that people have to live in such conditions. No electricity, no running water and primitive toilet facilities.

We still had things to sort before flying on to India and so we left Ennerdale and made our way back to the city. I

needed to have my arm cleaned and dressed – trying to find the hospital was a nightmare! We drove around the city asking people for directions, but we just could not find the place.

One of the difficulties we experienced was around communication. Whilst the 'blacks' do speak English, it's not easy to understand. Likewise they probably find it difficult to understand us! This makes any simple task like asking for directions very difficult!

It was definitely time to leave Jo'burg and yet, South Africa had been an amazing experience both in differing contrasts of cities and a day when I nearly came home!

No fake photograph: it doesn't look as if I was there, but trust me, I was.

This is as far south as South Africa goes: the next stop is Antarctica. Ross and I were glad to have made it!

No Onward Ticket

Chapter 4:

Foreword

by Ross Davidson,
nephew and procrastinator

I can't remember when exactly it was that the idea of me joining up with Peter on his world trip first came up. I seem to remember that Peter was visiting my family in Canada about 2 years ago and he was in the early stages of formulating his world voyage plan. I suspect he was only half serious when he suggested I should join him if I could, but a thought was planted in my head that I never shook after that.

In the fall of 2002 things really started coming together. Peter's trip was well under way and he was moving fast. It just so happened that I could get time off when Peter would be travelling through South Africa and India. What an opportunity! I had only travelled to conventional destinations before so this was a chance of a lifetime. My knowledge of these countries was minimal and that provided a real sense of adventure for me. I wanted to have my eyes opened to the way the world really is. Nothing could have prepared me for what I would experience.

I will have the memories of South Africa and India with me forever, from South Africa's huge, natural expanses to India's dirty, crowded streets. Both countries, while very unique, are places where the ordinary would become extraordinary and where acts of kindness from the least likely of people would have everlasting effects. But South Africa will always have a special emotional attachment for me. It is where we made it through the most frightening experiences of my life, where death was very close.

I am grateful that Peter had the determination to make it around the world in the way that he did. It meant that I too was able to share in a bit of the excitement. It took a person with tremendous vision and courage to accomplish a journey such as this. If ever there was anybody capable of making it around the world, I knew it would be Peter.

Thank you Peter, my uncle and very good friend.

Day 92: Mumbai, India

We arrived at the airport to be told that the flight was full - even though we had tickets! In actual fact, the plane was over-weight! This often happens in hot countries where the plane can get so hot that a restriction is put on the number of passengers flying. This is made worse when you have people checking in with heavy luggage and the airline would constantly be calculating and re-calculating numbers - and they were and we were at the end of the line! I was furious, with everything that had been going on over the last week - firstly trying to get tickets, then the accident and then having the tickets re-scheduled, I had had enough! After a fairly heated discussion with a number of airline staff we were told that there would be just enough room for us!

Hoorah! We were on our way across the Indian Ocean and after nine hours we arrived at Mumbai International Airport, completing 31,575kms of 'Hunter's Journey'. I was now in my 23rd country!

It was mad, completely mad outside the airport! It was 1.00am and yet there were hundreds of people all over the place! It was still very hot and there was this strange smell in the air – it was humid and smelled toxic. Things got worse after we sorted out a taxi and headed 'down-town'. It took about 45 minutes to reach our hotel, and in that time we must have seen over two hundred bodies lying against shop fronts or in bus shelters. People with no homes to go to who just made their beds along the streets! What a terrible sight - it was upsetting and made me feel sick!

Day 93: Still in Mumbai, India

Our hotel was cheap 'n cheerful – we were in the heart of Bombay, which has now changed its name to Mumbai! Something to do with trying to forget the city's past, when it was part of the British Empire, by reclaiming its heritage and losing any colonial stigma! We were situated close to the 'Gateway to India' where King George V first stepped onto the shores of India in 1911 and took claim to the land! It was a huge monument with large steps leading down to the sea, where boats still dock at the foot of the steps for tourist excursions.

After having my arm cleaned and re-dressed by my assistant (Ross) we went off to explore! What a place, it stunk of garbage and dirt, and dust filled the air. There was just no fresh air and it was so unpleasant! The streets were completely littered with everything imaginable that people just throw away. Taxis belching out noxious fumes that seemed to just linger in the air hogged the roads. **"Namaste India!"**

Looking around Mumbai was like going back in time – living conditions were Dickensian! The environment was degrading, full of pollution and sewage and an absolute public health risk! The people, however, were so happy; they were so polite and smiled whenever they spoke to you! The 'head-wobble' was hysterical, what great people they were! There was a population in the city of 16 million people and they were everywhere!

After a really good soak in the bath (and getting all the black stuff out of our noses!) we went to have our first 'Indian meal' in India. Wow - it was fantastic! The service was excellent and the food was so tasty, it was hard to imagine that I was actually in India, but tasting such wonderful food just made my day! A genuine 'chicken tikka masala' with naan bread washed down with Kingfisher beer! Mmm!

Day 94:
Still in Mumbai

"Main jab India aaya to bada khush hua. India ek loktantrik desh hai. Yahan ke logion main anekta main ekta hai! Main jab Mumbai aaya to aur khush hua. Dhanyavad!"

Well, I'm not that good at Hindi but I just wanted to share that with you! Today (after a very late start) we visited 'Shelter' a project operated by a Don Bosco priest called Fr Jose. Children left home for various reasons but many children were also dumped by their families (usually because they couldn't afford to feed them!) On

Crossing Calcutta streets was an art, amongst rickety old cars and trams. It's hard to read, but this one carries a destination board proclaiming 'Ballygunge Esplanade'. I dread to think...

the street there were hundreds of children who now faced rejection, exploitation, abuse, health hazards and insecurity. Shelter gives these youngsters a direction to move forward by offering a home to them. Here they were safe; they were given food and clothes whilst professional staff supported them through drug de-addiction, rehabilitation and educational skills to find work.

It is hard to comprehend the life that many people have in a poor country; when you make a comparison to the living conditions that I am used to, then you have pity - but these people have nothing to compare to! My concern is with young people and children who do not even have the basic things in life, simple things like clothes to wear, a meal a day and an education. An education develops a person and these youngsters have no opportunity for this - and I blame the government! You can give to charities that can support people, but in every country where the basic human rights are not provided, I think the government should be made accountable and do something about it!

Day 95: Mumbai, India

Our main task today was to arrange our tickets for the Gitanuali Express Train that would take us across the heart of India from Mumbai to Kolkata (Calcutta). Culture is everything about the way people live and it was an amazing challenge to even begin to understand how things were done in India!

Nothing here was simple; deciding what train you wanted to get determined which station to buy your ticket from; then you had to fill in a form and present yourself with your passport to the ticket office during certain hours of the day! I had left my passport in the hotel and the ticket counter closed at 3.00pm. I had just thirty minutes to get my passport otherwise we would not be able to take the train in the morning! The taxi driver was great, he beeped his horn all the way back to the hotel and many times he would take the other side of the road to jump ahead of all the traffic! We arrived back at the station

Four aboard: and no-one bats an eyelid. Look who's wearing the helmet...

counter with only two minutes to spare but we now had our tickets!

We visited the 'Gateway to India' at sunset to watch the sun falling onto the sea's horizon; it was a fast but spectacular sight of colour and warmth.

As dusk fell, the cruise ships on the water were lit up with a spectacular display of lights and a crowd of people came to watch. Once it was dark, most of the city became very quiet. We heard the news that a terrorist bomb had exploded on a bus on the outskirts of the city and although a curfew had not been imposed, the Police were stopping anyone travelling around that night and I guess for many nights to come! We went for another curry at the hotel restaurant – what can I say!

Gateway to India: people were later killed here in a bomb attack.

Day 96: The journey from Mumbai to Calcutta

A very early start and by 6am we were on the train which would take us to Calcutta. My arm was improving so well but I still needed to keep it covered up with bandages - to protect the stitches and keep it clean!

The journey began with some of the most horrific sights of the outskirts of Mumbai. Looking out of the window as the train slowly took us out of this over-populated city the living conditions looked absolutely terrible. The worst image was of the number of people who use the railway banking as a toilet, and I was disgusted!

At first I could not understand why so many people were crouching on the banking or close to the walls separating the railway banking from the houses. Then when you looked closer you could actually see that they were 'going to the toilet'! You cannot imagine what it was like to see this kind of unhygienic sanitation. I felt physically sick, the railway line was covered all around with human excrement and litter - goats and the 'religious' cows wandered around and children in school uniforms walked along the line in this early morning rush!

Ross slept for about six hours as I just gazed out of the window looking at this 'real' India! My Dad had taken this

same journey in 1945 whilst on his way to fight in Asia during the Second World War - thankfully it was all over by the time they reached Singapore.

It was a most incredible experience, the living conditions, people working on the land and the sun just burning down on everything! Each time we stopped at a station I would jump off and just stand on the open platform watching with absolute fascination the turmoil and organised confusion of people getting on and off the train. Sellers draped with all sorts of junk for people to buy! It was another era and certainly another world!

Ross and I made friends very quickly on the train (well, as soon as he decided to get up!) We were travelling first class air-conditioned sleeper carriage - this was for people with money (US$50 to travel across the whole of India) but there were no other tourists in the carriage. In fact we were the only foreigners - other passengers were mainly businessmen and a few wealthy families! They thought we were great and at one stage, they were queuing to sit and talk with us! They were such friendly people and we were having such a laugh all the time!

In the early hours of the morning we stopped at a station and as usual I jumped off to be inquisitive! A small number of the passengers in our carriage joined me and we bought some coffees from a drinks machine on the platform. There must have been a dozen Indians laughing and joking with Ross and I. The next station at about 2am was the last station until morning and only a few of us were still up. I jumped off with a passenger called Rajesh who saw the drinks machine further down the platform - we set off! The train whistle blew and it was off without us! We were now running back to the train and I managed to jump on further down the train - oh my God! This was a nightmare! We had both ended up in third class and began to walk through the carriages towards first class. As we got to the end of the fifth carriage there was a steel shutter separating us from first class. We were told it would be another two hours before the next stop when we could jump off and get back on in

Spot the blond foreigner: arrival at Calcutta.

the first-class compartment. Luckily Ross and the others had told the 'Ticket Examiner' that they thought Rajesh and I had managed to get back on the train but further down the carriages; he hoped we had, and came down to open the shutter and let us in! There would have been nowhere to stay in third class, the carriages were packed solid with people - 16 people in a compartment that was the same size as ours - but we had only four people!

Waking up and looking out of the window again to the brilliant sights of the Indian countryside was sheer brilliance! The land seemed to be farmed everywhere but looked so dry and burnt. Another strange observation was the number of women working in the fields - and everything appeared to be done by hand!

Approaching Calcutta was similar to Mumbai, litter was thrown absolutely everywhere! In Africa empty water bottles would be given to the children (to use or recycle) but when you stopped at the stations here everyone just hurled them out of the windows!

India's population is over a billion and Calcutta is home to nearly 14 million people. Renamed only recently it used to be the capital of British India. It is known as the cultural capital of India now, but as we arrived in Howrah station we were met by the absolute mad crazy confusion of hundreds of people, a culture of madness!

We found a hotel and after a well deserved shower went out to find food! Yes, another curried dish was beckoning and what better place to eat one! Mmmm!

Since Ross would be leaving the next day, we wanted to make use of what time we had left together and so we then went for a tour of Calcutta. It had many similarities to Mumbai but seemed to be a little cleaner, less litter, less dust and exhaust fumes and a few less people sleeping on the streets! It was still a very disturbing sight, especially when you see little children sleeping at the side of the road with hardly any clothes on. They need more than a

Day 97: Calcutta, India

'Evenin' all': yes, this Indian policeman is carrying a shotgun...

blanket, they need the government to get their act together and stop this dreadful life that people have to live! I'm sorry to say this because when you walk about this city and see the poverty on one side and the fancy restaurants and coffee shops on the other - the gap of rich and poor is so extreme its hard to comprehend!

Day 98: Calcutta, India

Our night at the hotel was not good, dogs barking all night and rats rummaging through litter heaped outside my window! We went to find another hotel for my next few days, which was a little more upmarket and then went for a walk. It was hot and very busy and we were not sure where we were going! I spotted a Police Station and we wandered in to check exactly where we were. The Sergeant at the desk was so funny and he sat us down and called for the 'tea-boy' to bring us drinks. We chatted for ages and then set off along the road again; this time we stumbled on a school run by the 'Missions of God' and we could see youngsters playing cricket! It was such fun to watch them and later we talked with them and listened as some played in a band and wanted to perform for us.

One rupee: this note's worth little more than 1.5p; you have to wonder if it's worth the paper it's printed on...

The day had gone so quickly and I was now at the airport saying goodbye to my nephew. It is hard to imagine what we had shared together over the last two weeks - escaping death, black townships and children sleeping on the streets. We had shared some great experiences, both good and bad, and I had really enjoyed his company. I was not looking forward to saying goodbye and so we made it fairly quick on arriving at the airport. Off he went on his journey back to Canada and I went back to downtown Calcutta.

I was staying at the Lytton Hotel and it was like a five star hotel, en-suite bathroom, air-conditioning, satellite television and a huge double bed that I got lost in! The room was huge, so homely. I watched movies all day and ordered food to my room! I really was spoiling myself!

Day 99: Still in Calcutta, India

I'd made 100 days today and felt so pleased! My arm was feeling more comfortable and I had a lovely soak in the bath. It felt strange today because I had no-one to talk to, and I really missed having Ross around - but I also was looking forward to seeing Jayne who was flying out on December 24th to meet me; it would be like something in a movie - miles apart from each other and then meeting up on Christmas Eve! It really didn't feel like Christmas for me, I'd seen no trees or lights nor heard any carols! There was nothing in any shop window, and I'd got no cards! I had a lovely walk around the city today; I must have walked miles and just absorbed the way of life here in Calcutta. I found an Internet place and so the rest of the day was spent reading my e-mails, guest book messages and getting my journal up to date!

Day 100: Still in Calcutta, India

Such poverty is all around

Day 101: Still in Calcutta

I went back to Howrah Railway Station today to see the work of the 'Don Bosco Ashalayam'; a railway children project. 'Asha' means hope and 'layam' means home; the project offers a 'home of hope' for street children but in particular to those found at the railway station. Every single day, as many as seven children were found in this huge central station, wandering completely lost and bewildered amongst the crowds of up to 10,000 passengers daily. These children, so young and helpless, were abandoned - usually by poor or sick parents who literally just put them on a train somewhere in India and dumped them.

As I sat with the workers, they had a three-year-old boy with hardly any clothes on who had been found by a guard on a train coming in to Calcutta. I was absolutely speechless as I looked at this innocent child; he

spoke very little (there are up to thirty different languages in India!) as the staff tried to communicate with him. The project had started back in 1985 when a priest passing through Howrah Station on one of his several journeys noticed many children on the platforms. They had made the station their home – a helpless and lost tribe! The project now has some 30 homes for over 500 children at any one time. They provide an education and training skills for them and support them to grow up and become members of society.

I then went on to visit Pilkhana and the home of 60 young boys who have been rescued. Many are now in their late teens and even go out to work. The project helps them to manage their salaries and move on to their own homes. It was a marvellous opportunity to see such needy work having a positive end; many of the staff are volunteers from Europe who devote a year of their life to the hopeless, rootless and roofless children in and around Calcutta.

Very late this evening after some recent e-mail correspondence from CBC Radio in Canada – I had a telephone call at my hotel and was interviewed for a radio programme that was to go on air throughout the whole of Canada in the New Year. Apparently, the story in the Sun newspaper in England had made its way to a researcher in Canada and they were fascinated with my epic journey and survival! The interview went really well, I loved it and was on the telephone for over an hour! I guess that this will give me yet another opportunity to share my experiences with other people and CBC were eagerly awaiting my eventual arrival in Canada sometime in March next year!

TAXI!: I defy anyone to ride a taxi in Calcutta without develping an inane grin like this; it's pure fear..

Day 102: Still in Calcutta, India

With sewage running along the streets and litter everywhere, this was a horribly disgusting city for me. Everywhere you looked people were scavenging, buildings were falling down and it was a constant battle to get round this overpopulated oasis of survival.

People use the sidewalks as toilets; they wash themselves and their clothes in the streets. I was becoming weary of the din and bustle, the stench and dirt and the madding crowds.

It was time to move on, so I went to India Airlines offices and picked up a bargain flight to Kathmandu. All I needed now was my visa!

The airline would not issue the ticket without the visa and so I was now under pressure - and once more racing against time, because the flight was tomorrow morning!

At the Nepalese Consulate I was greeted by two soldiers who searched me and led me to a small room. As an official entered I thought I was going to be interrogated but I was wrong - he was so friendly and took my $30 and photograph away with my passport and was back after just five minutes with my visa issued - I could not believe that things were going so right.

From the Consulate I made my way to Calcutta General Infirmary. A nurse who ushered me onto a bed after seeing my bandaged arm went to get the doctor.

He was great fun and after examining my arm decided that the stitches could come out. No messing – he pulled out his scissors from his pocket and began tugging at my arm – some really hurt and he just laughed!

The doctor left in two that were still helping the deep cuts to heal. With new bandages on, I collected my tickets and relaxed once more in my hotel!

Easier visa: getting permission to go into Nepal took only five minutes.

Day 103: Calcutta to Kathmandu, Nepal

Calcutta is a city of five laureates - including Mother Teresa - and I wanted to see where she spent so much of her life helping the sick and dying people of this city.

Before leaving for the airport I visited the 'Mother House' of the Missionaries of Charity. It was here that Mother Teresa founded her work for the disadvantaged people of Calcutta. I handed over a bag of clothes I no longer needed (and some from Ross) and the Nuns thanked me. I was then invited into a small chapel where the body of Mother Teresa is laid in a huge marble tomb. I was overcome by such a peaceful atmosphere when you consider what it was like outside!

At the airport I could not believe the security; soldiers everywhere and after checking in you have to follow a strange procedure around the terminal with immigration, security check, customs, security check, checking in your luggage for the flight, security check, boarding cards and yet another security check - I had presented my boarding card fifteen times and my passport nine times.

Since the bombing of the bus in Mumbai, there have been five bombs in cinemas around Bangladesh and a further bomb on a bus on its way to Kathmandu in Nepal. All these countries have got internal terrorist problems that we hardly hear about in the UK, but which contribute to 'global terror' - I was now entering a very unstable part of the world!

As the plane took off from Calcutta you could actually see the smog lingering in the air above the city. This was by far the most polluted city I had visited and I was looking forward to some fresh air!

Just forty minutes into this one-hour flight I was stunned by what I could see out of the window! The Himalayas - as far as you could see, mountain after mountain capped with snow. It was an awesome sight; I was looking down at the top of the world!

As we began our descent the mountain range turned to

green and there were hundreds of patches of cultivated land where you could just make out the small number of houses scattered at the edge of the mountain tops! I was wound up – it was such a fantastic view and we were still above some of the clouds! **"Namaste Nepal"**

I had an absolutely terrible sleep; it was so cold! The hotel had no heating and even with three blankets I could not get warm. This was a real culture shock for my body after spending so much time in Africa and India. The daytime temperature was very hot, but when night fell, the temperature fell too! I moved hotels to find a room with a heater!

Kathmandu is a legendary city at the foot of the Himalayas; I walked through a crowded maze of courtyards and narrow alleys filled with hundreds of bazaars and tour/travel agents. It is such a bustling place with a great atmosphere and everywhere you looked there were Hindu shrines and Buddhist stupas.

Nepal is a country of unrest and the Maoist people (a political party) are seen by the government as political terrorists! On every street corner there were Police Officers and on all the roads there were Army patrols.

Here also were many back-packers and trek enthusiasts – this brought with it the many hawkers pestering you with anything that they could sell you.

The unrest here had certainly led to a decline in tourism as many locals told me; this did not help because you were therefore bombarded all the more by these street sellers!

I was looking forward to an early night in a warm room and after a meal in one of the many nearby restaurants I was off to bed.

Day 104: Still in Kathmandu, Nepal

Day 105: Still in Kathmandu, Nepal

The 'must-see' landmark of Nepal is Mount Everest - the highest mountain in the world. So, you think I'm up for a strenuous high-altitude trek? - then think again! Early morning and I was on the back of a motorbike with Rakesh, a local guy who worked as a waiter in the restaurant I visited on my first night. We had chatted and I told him about my journey, he wanted to be a part of this and offered to take me to one of the most famous viewing points for the Himalayan mountain range, a place called Nagarkot. It was difficult to get there by car and so he suggested that as it was his day off work, he would take me on his Pulsar 180cc!

The journey was frightening at times as we climbed out of the city along narrow bending roads – passing pagoda-roofed temples, traditional farmlands and getting closer to the mountain peaks. Army roadblocks interrupted the journey as tension is still running very high since the assassination of the Royal family a few years earlier.

Nepal is a landlocked country wedged between India and China and was thrust into the headlines in 2001 when Prince Dipendra allegedly went on a Rambo-like rampage slaughtering his father, King Birendra, his mother, Queen Aiswarya and seven other members of the royal family before turning the gun on himself. This threatened the stability of a nation that has been struggling towards democracy for so long. Despite its volatile history, which has included corruption and revolution, palace coups and human rights abuses, Kathmandu is above all sacred ground, a place of ancient and modern pilgrimage. Its citizens are obsessively nationalistic and its landscape breath-taking.

Nagarkot is on a ridge on the north eastern rim of Kathmandu valley. It was here that you could get the best views of the Himalayas and climb up a lookout tower, as I nervously did, and enjoyed a 360 degree view that was unbelievable! There in front of me was Mt Everest standing at 8,484m above sea level. Wow!

I was looking at the top of the world and it was a magnificent view. We stayed for over an hour before starting our descent on the bike back to the bottom. We stopped on the way to watch some kind of Bollywood movie that was being filmed at the side of the road overlooking the mountains. Very attractive girls dressed in bright yellow and gold costumes and dancing to the sounds of 'Asian' music were being filmed by cameramen suspended from cranes that moved them high in the air. It was fun to watch and just like the occasional movie that I have seen in the local Indian take-away back home!

I was a nervous wreck by the time we arrived back at my hotel, my knuckles were white from holding onto the bar at the back of the bike but this had been a great day that I would remember for a long time! Thanks Rakesh!

Day 106: Still in Kathmandu, Nepal

I was not feeling too good today; this had nothing to do with the altitude changes – basically I spent the whole day between bed and toilet. Sorry! Early evening and I was still back and forth to the toilet and then the nightmare got worse. All the power went off in the hotel and as I looked out of the window, the whole of Kathmandu was in darkness. It is not nice being unwell when you are away from home and it just makes you feel worse. After nine hours, there was nothing left inside me and I took my emergency dehydration medication and tried to sleep!

Day 107: Still in Kathmandu

Feeling a little better today, I had one more place to visit before leaving. Durbar Square was just a twenty-minute walk from my hotel – but it was like going back in time! Filled with old temples and small palaces, it epitomizes the religious and the social life of the people. This was the real world of the people here and yet it felt like I had stepped back in time. Many people worshipping in the temples were clothed in traditional outfits and everyone appeared to have great red spots on their foreheads! The smell was exhilarating – incense sticks burning everywhere and people chanting strange noises! (I was tired and struggled to describe this weird and wonderful experience!). I really enjoyed myself and wandered back into the more modern Kathmandu just in time before night fell.

So farewell to 'Sagarmatha' – Nepalese name meaning head of the sky. Farewell to 'Chomolungma' – Tibetan name meaning Mother Goddess of the earth. Farewell to 'Everest' – English name referring to Sir George Everest a Surveyor General of India. I have now seen the top of the world and will continue my quest to go round it!

Day 108: Bangkok, Thailand

I had a terrible night's sleep with many disturbances; this was due to the number of power cuts that started in the early evening throughout the whole city making it impossible to do anything but sit in your room with a candle. I had needed to pack, shower and have a good sleep. Each time the power came back on I would begin to do something and then the power would go off again!

5am and I was up and on my way to the airport. Now, let me try and explain; I was due to travel from Nepal to Shanghai but when I visited the Chinese Consulate here in Kathmandu it was immediately apparent that I would not be given a visa.

Trying to converse with one of the staff was impossible and I knew that not having onward tickets and the fact that I was travelling from Nepal was going to make it all very difficult! 'Hunter's Journey' was a challenge after all, a global trek of the world and part of what I wanted to explore were the barriers of travel between countries. I had no tickets or visas in advance and each country's acceptance or non-acceptance across their border would be part of my experience. This meant leaving out Taiwan also and instead travelling south to Thailand.

Airport security was very strict here and as soon as you checked in you had to go through a rigorous procedure of searches that left you with no time but to board the plane. This level of security was becoming more noticeable now

- both internal and worldwide factions were using terrorism and travellers seemed to be their easiest target. I heard only that day that a train travelling across India – the same route my nephew and I were on last week - was sabotaged and derailed, killing many passengers. Southeast Asia has been hit recently with a number of bombs targeting tourists, and although I was maybe more vulnerable as I travelled through this part of the world, I also seemed to look suspect to Security Officials, the Army and the Police wherever I went!

Royal Nepal Airways was not a very modern fleet and things were pretty basic on the plane but the view never changed! A second chance to see a most majestic sight as we flew along the Himalayan mountain range. What a magnificent view looking down at these snow-capped peaks; I was so happy!

Typically Thai: outside a Thai temple.

I had been to Bangkok three years ago, but arriving in the airport today was so different. A very clean and modern building greeted you, no great long queues at immigration and no hassle when you came out of the airport. Organised taxi stands and buses took you into the city. Travelling on the bus was amazing, everything seemed to have changed, massive new 'super highways' and fly-overs allowed you to travel without sitting for hours in traffic jams. The driver told me that around three million vehicles came into the city every day and the government had certainly worked on the terrible congestion problems I had experienced previously! There were no 'old' cars on the roads either, new emission laws having greatly reduced the terrible smog I remembered. I was so amazed, this was a huge, modern and clean looking city. At last, I was in a civilized world - at least for a while!

With mobile text support from my friend Chris back in England I was able to find the same hotel that we had stayed in previously and had my long awaited shower (it had been four days since my last!). I then took a 'tuk-tuk' (an open sided three-wheel mini taxi) down town to

Patpong, just for a look of course! Nothing has changed there - girls, bars and shops! Oh, I did find somewhere to eat and enjoyed a delicious Thai dish of chicken and fried rice! **"Sawadee pated Thai!"**

Day 109: Still in Bangkok, Thailand

I met Fr Louis Phonchit today who took me to visit Savio School – with over 2,000 pupils in his charge this made it a very large school! Thailand is a Buddhist country but when it comes to education the Salesians have some very popular and highly respected educational facilities. Nearly all Thai people are born and brought up as Buddhist but for many they would not say that they actually practised the faith and were happy for their children to be educated in a Christian environment! I was told that even Christmas was celebrated by many as a time for families, gifts and parties! Sounds very familiar!

I left the hotel to stay at the Provincial House in Hua Mark, which is about 11kms out of the city, however you were still very much in the city, as Bangkok is huge! This capital city edges the banks of the 'Chao Phraya', the mighty 'River of Kings'. Passing by some of the modernistic hotels that have replaced what used to be the derelict and shanty parts of the city I got my first glimpse of Christmas trees and lights decorating the fronts of these buildings! It had become a modern metropolis of high-rises and shopping centres.

I had time to work on the computer and then take an early night, but it was hot; and I do mean hot! The daytime temperature had been 36 degrees and my body was just so confused! The air-conditioning was essential to help get a good night's sleep!

Day 110: Still in Bangkok, Thailand

After lying in until midday I was up and about enjoying the sunshine! My arm was painful; it may just be the heat but it looked as though I had better get it looked at!

That evening I had been invited to a Carol Service

involving some of the Don Bosco past pupils here in Bangkok; I was given a very warm welcome by everyone and really enjoyed myself! Listening to the Christmas songs brought tears to my eyes; I felt really homesick and began thinking of my family! It was hard being away from home for so long - I really understood the importance here of people making an effort to be with family and loved ones over this festive season!

It was Jayne's birthday today but I had waited until nearly midnight to telephone her because I was now seven hours ahead! It was great talking with her and giving her my shopping list of things that she could bring out for me next week! I was so looking forward to seeing her!

Day 111: Still in Bangkok in Thailand

Another lazy day but I had the chance to begin researching the next stage of my journey! Cambodia, Vietnam and Indonesia have all been hit by war or terrorism and I needed to think very clearly about the safest route around this dangerous and hostile part of the world! I had by now spent over half my budget so I had to bear in mind that easy options like flying would also be the most expensive!

That evening I was invited to the house of Dr Winlop who is the President of the Salesian Past Pupils Association in Thailand. Every Christmas he holds a party for his friends at his home just outside the city. It was fantastic to meet so many wonderful people and enjoy the food, wine and carol singing. Outside, caterers provided the most amazing food and I tried everything from noodles and rice to 'snakehead' grilled fish, barbecued meatballs, spicy fried pork, steamed ostrich meat and the popular Thai soup called 'kooe-teao'!

It was a feast and it was all washed down with red wine! The whole event was staged in the garden and as it was still very hot, the evening breeze was welcome. I was invited to say a few words and took the opportunity to thank everyone for such wonderful hospitality and

confirm to all the guests that Thailand truly was 'The Land of Smiles'.

Day 112: Still in Bangkok, Thailand

After a pleasant morning spent resting I was taken into the city to look for a new camera. If you like shopping there can be no better place to come than Bangkok - shopping mall after shopping mall, store after store and good price after good price!

The city was a shoppers' paradise where you were expected to bargain for everything – however, travelling around this huge metropolis is difficult. Bangkok has every mode of transport from the main roads to the two-tier highways; the taxis are everywhere, buses and airbuses (air-conditioned), sky trains and the local 'tuk-tuk'.

Dr Winlop owned a four-star hotel in the city and suggested I could book a deluxe-room at a special rate for the week with Jayne. I went to check it out and it was perfect, the room was massive with a lounge area and lovely en-suite bathroom. The hotel also had a rooftop swimming pool, jacuzzi and sauna - next week was going to be a luxury!

Day 113: Still in Bangkok, Thailand

I attended a church service in the morning, it was all in Thai and I was the only foreigner but it was a great experience as the packed congregation celebrated this last Sunday of Advent.

This evening was my fourth Christmas party with carols, wine and delicious food! It was being held at Provincial House and again was outside - I cannot get used to it being so hot, especially as it was now only three days before Christmas.

I have talked to so many people about my journey around the world over the last few days but I always finished by reflecting on my Christmases back in England. Even in a country where the majority of the population was Buddhist, they celebrated Christmas in a very similar way to my family and friends back home. The strangest thing was listening to their versions of Christmas songs, often words were pronounced differently and the tunes were slightly altered - and they all seemed to enjoy speaking English because they knew the words 'Happy Christmas' and enjoyed also the opportunity to say them to an Englishman!

Day 114: Still in Bangkok, Thailand

I attended a press conference today, which was being held to announce the beginning of a year long celebration to mark 75 years of the work of the Salesians in Thailand. The work of Don Bosco in Bangkok is very well known, the schools are prestigious and the past pupil movement is vast – they are very important to the 'Salesian family'.

I think that this is why the work of Don Bosco is so successful here, it is a family of priests, nuns, teachers, pupils, past pupils and their families and friends all supporting the work of educating and developing opportunities for young people.

Day 115: Still in Bangkok, Thailand

When I arrived at the airport to meet Jayne today, I was very excited but a little nervous too! I hadn't seen her since I left home. The airport was packed with people, mainly Scouts from all over the world arriving for the 'World Jamboree' being held this year in Thailand. I saw her in the distance and as soon as I could, gave her the biggest hug! It was great to see her and we had so much catching up to do!

When we arrived at the hotel I was eager for Jayne to open her suitcase to see what exciting goodies she had brought for me! We put some decorations up in the room, opened the Christmas cards and put them up and then it felt more like Christmas. We ordered room service and opened a bottle of wine! By midnight we had opened all our presents and had fallen asleep! I remember looking at my watch – it was now the 25th December and I turned over and gave Jayne a big kiss and wished us both a 'Happy Christmas'.

Day 116: Christmas Day in Bangkok, Thailand

Spending Christmas Day at the side of a swimming pool sunbathing was certainly different! Plenty of text messages on the mobile phone and then disaster! We had left early evening all dressed up to find somewhere nice to eat.

The taxi dropped us off in Pat Pong and we walked along the road where I thought I had seen many restaurants. We walked and walked for ages and eventually we were in the middle of nowhere! We could not find a single restaurant and eventually had to stop a tuk-tuk to give us a lift back to where we started. The driver did not speak any English and we were getting pretty frustrated and very hot! After this, we took a second taxi to another part of the city where we hoped to find a restaurant, but with no success we were left with no choice but to get a third taxi back to the hotel! It was now nearly midnight and we had been looking for somewhere to eat for over three hours. Even the hotel's three restaurants were now closed and we were back in our room ordering food from the room service menu!

That was our Christmas Day and I look forward to next year back in the UK with a roast turkey dinner and Christmas pudding!

Day 117: Boxing Day in Bangkok, Thailand

Bangkok has about 400 wats (temples) and today we took the boat on the river and got some great views of a number of famous wats.

River travel is much more interesting and far more pleasant than travelling through the city by taxi. The boats went up and down the 'Mae Nam Chao Phraya' and across from side to side to Thonburi. They were fast and cheap but could be a little scary as you got on and off – they tended not to stop properly so you needed to jump!

We eventually got off at Banglamphu and made our way to Chinatown – it was busy with people eating on every part of the sidewalk and the road was congested with traffic! We found a restaurant and ate with chopsticks, but eventually I conceded and asked for a spoon!

Day 118: Still in Bangkok

Back in the tuk-tuk today for a whistle-stop tour of the city. Wat Pho is the temple of the reclining Buddha and it is the oldest and largest wat in Bangkok. The statue is over 46m high and looks down on you as you creep forward to touch one of his huge gold-painted feet! After visiting a couple of wats and admiring the stupas we decided that when you have seen one Buddha - you've seen them all!

We then went to visit the Grand Palace, paid our entrance fee and arrived at the gate. We were informed that you couldn't enter if your footwear showed your toes or heels! This was crazy; in every building we had visited that day you had to take your shoes off, but in the Palace, you had to wear shoes, and sandals were not allowed! We got a refund!

Temple viewing: Jayne and I in Bangkok.

The tuk-tuk driver had stayed with us all morning but he insisted that we visit a number of shops where he could collect petrol coupons for bringing tourists. We played along and had a great deal of fun pretending that we might buy gems, rings and fitted suits!

That evening we went to a Japanese restaurant and the food was wonderful, it was really tasty and I ate all my vegetables!

Day 119: Still in Bangkok, Thailand

After today, many of the shops and all offices and banks will close until January 2nd. I had not been able to arrange for a visa to Vietnam and could not risk trying to get one at the road border crossing. I also realized that I may have difficulty at the land border crossing to Cambodia but would be all right at the airport. This left me with only one option for the moment and that was to get a cheap flight to Phnom Penh at the same time that Jayne was returning to the UK. I was now running a week behind my schedule and would need to get back on the road promptly in the New Year.

Later we visited one of the largest open-air markets in Asia at Chatuchak Park. If you wanted to shop until you dropped, this was the place to be – it was quite literally massive with stall after stall of everything you could imagine for sale! After three hours we were done in! I had done very little shopping whilst travelling and now I was happy to do no more! I did enjoy doing the bartering and feeling good when you thought you had a good deal, but no more shopping please Jayne!

It was a very hot day, and the humidity made it quite uncomfortable. It was time to relax with a jacuzzi and then an afternoon sleep!

Day 120:

The sleep continues!

Day 121:

Yet again, time to relax – Oh! and sleep…

Day 122: New Year's Eve in Bangkok,

We had made no plans for New Years Eve, but after sunbathing most of the day, we were ready to 'hit the town' by 7pm! We left the hotel and in no time we came across a Japanese restaurant that looked quite inviting! We enjoyed a lovely meal with Singha beers! We left the restaurant and passed an open-air bar just outside our hotel and as the band was playing we decided to sit and have another beer! We stayed here all night, the band members joined us for more beers, and I assisted them in the countdown to the start of 2003. Here however, they were celebrating the year 2545 as they recognize a different calendar year to the Christian world!

"Sawadee Pee Mai" to you all!

Now, I was not drunk - I had been thinking all week (and in fact for months beforehand) of asking Jayne to marry me! We had stayed together so well during my time away and we were having a fantastic time this week and I decided that I should wait no longer!

So, minus a ring, I asked the question and she said 'Yes'. I was so happy and will let you know the big day!

Cartoon travel: the tuk-tuk gets its name from the noise made by its traditional two-stroke engine.

Chapter 5:

Foreword

by Greg Chappell, M.B.E.,
former Australian Test cricketer

It was a great pleasure to meet with Peter in Adelaide as he made his way around the world. I was amazed at the epic journey he was undertaking and very interested in his experiences of the world before arriving in Australia. Who would be mad enough to undertake such a journey? I have heard about 'mad dogs and Englishmen' but this was something else!

Ever since I was a boy I have been fascinated with the game of cricket. My dream now is to assist young people in becoming better players and I encourage them to make cricket their journey as the game has many great rewards.

What a life changing journey this has been for Peter. The experiences and knowledge he has gained from the trip will no doubt have a positive effect on all those people he meets as well as on his work in the future. Once again we see what can be achieved by one person who is prepared to follow their dream.

I wish Peter well now that he is safely back home. I know that his journey will continue to touch many people and I hope it will inspire them to follow their dream!

www.chappellway.com

Day 123: Bangkok, Thailand

After some last minute sunbathing, Jayne was packed and we were at the airport for her return flight to the UK. It was very hard for us to say goodbye and we were both very quiet! After she had checked in we hugged each other for ages but the time had come and off she went through passport control.

I left the airport with tears in my eyes and returned to the hotel. The same band was playing outside again and I sat down for one last beer before bed! The band members, Boss, If, Sit, Axe and Ding were good company for me, as I felt really lonely. They were such good guys and cheered me up so much.

When I got back to my room, I packed ready for my departure to Cambodia later the next day and then went to bed.

I could not get to sleep and was still wide-awake at 4am. I had spent all week with Jayne and we had had such a great time together and suddenly I was on my own again. 'Hunter's Journey' means a great deal to me, the experience of travelling around the world, meeting so many people, exploring the cultures of so many countries and having such great opportunities of sharing the work of Don Bosco all over the world.

By the end of next week I should be in Australia and I would be passing the halfway point in my journey. I needed to focus again on that journey and move on to my next country!

Day 124: Phnom Penh, Cambodia

The staff in the hotel had been so hospitable over the last week, the Thais are such happy and friendly people and I was sad to leave. Boss and his girlfriend collected me and took me to the airport - they must have felt I needed some support and it was so nice of them. I was now on my way to Pochentong International Airport in Cambodia, my 26th country. We flew in a small propeller-driven aircraft and it was a very bumpy and hair-raising flight, but we landed safely!

It was very hot; the sun was scorching and the heat was very intense, the sky was completely clear and there was a slight breeze. It really was hot, such an amazing difference in just a two hour flight!

Leaving the airport I was astonished at how different it looked - it was back to a third world country of wooden huts (many suspended on stilts) and dirt-track roads. The dust was terrible on the road to the Don Bosco School on the outskirts of the city. I was given a great welcome and was amazed at how big the school was.

After Pol Pot's terrible evil in the 1970's, many Cambodian children were left homeless and orphaned. The school is a vocational technical training centre for many of these children where they can begin to break the 'circle of poverty'.

It is an educational facility that will contribute to the development of their country. Providing training skills in machinery, welding, mechanics, printing and electronics, the school caters for nearly 1,000 students and 60% are orphans who are boarders.

My room was like a sauna when I went to bed - I put the air conditioning on full power and sprayed the entire room with an insect repellent! It was my worst nightmare - the room had hundreds of insects all over the place, in the air, on the walls, around the lights and crawling or running on the floor.

It was horrible, the lizards and mozzies I had become accustomed to, but all the other creepy crawlies were making me shiver inside! I just could not get to sleep and eventually I wrapped myself completely in the sheet and pulled it over my head!

Day 125: Still in Phnom Penh, Cambodia

In the morning (6.30am) I jumped out of bed, dressed and left the room! I was absolutely shattered but was departing at 7am to assist in the delivery of some food parcels to a village school across the Tonle Sap River. We left in two trucks to make the hour long journey to the river where we could then take the short ferry service to the other side and a school called Preataroat. People just turned up from the wooden huts at the side of the riverbanks and we began to unload the food parcels and some school desks onto the boat (we could not transport the vehicles across!).

This school was made up of corrugated iron huts erected in the centre of the village and I was absolutely appalled at what I saw and at the same time overwhelmed by the children and villagers. Most of the children had never seen foreigners before and I was mobbed by nearly two hundred curious youngsters - many wearing very little clothing, all of which was dirty and torn, most had nothing on their

The faces say it all: just 30 children from the 200 in this school were to be given food parcels. Imagine how I felt...

feet and most - in fact all of them - looked pitiable! They were unkempt but their smiling faces made them shine through the basic simple living conditions they had. This was truly a third world community relying on aid from the outside if they were to survive.

We were invited into a classroom where 30 children were lined up to receive their food parcels. Now, with over two hundred children in the school, the Don Bosco Children's Fund had enough supplies to provide some food, soap, exercise books and a small amount of money to only thirty! My heart sank as I then realized that these children standing in front of me were the poorest of the poor in this village! I was feeling absolutely sick that only these kids could be supported this month. I had never seen anything like this before; how could you select the poorest from the poor? These children were aged between 7 and 10 and when you saw their faces light up on receiving their parcel – well I just wanted to cry! It was disturbing to see how giving a child their own exercise book for school could be all they ever wanted. I left the room.

After bringing myself together I turned to look at the children still mobbing me outside! I began filming these happy smiling faces, so innocent because they knew nothing different! I turned the video monitor round so that they could see themselves and you should have seen their reactions!

The teacher told me that none of these children had ever seen a television before, let alone seen themselves on a screen! They loved it and every time I said anything they would repeat it like parrots! None could speak any English but they just copied everything I said. I even got them to say 'Leeds United'!

Our mission was over, but I was invited to see where some of the children live; many of the parents had come to the school to collect the parcels from their children and I was a celebrity. They wanted me to see where they lived, probably hoping that I would be able to give them something more! I was escorted down to the river bank and allowed to peer inside a number of very unstable looking wooden huts with virtually nothing inside! This was their home – nothing! It was far more primitive than many houses I had seen in Africa and India. They were like tree houses that I played in as a child! They were just so primeval; they had very few personal possessions and with no wardrobes I guessed that the only clothes they had were those they were wearing! No electricity, no running water and no bathroom! The kitchen was the

These Cambodian children smile, but their poverty moved me to tears. We had enough aid to help only 30 of about 200 - and all of them were poorer than Western standards can comprehend.

ground under the house that was supported by the wooden stilts. These were desperately poor people.

The sun was now beating down and I was very hot; I needed to get into the shade and it was decided we should leave. I wanted to stay and look around more, but in reality I had seen enough.

Day 126: Phnom Penh, Cambodia

I must have some tasty blood; I was bitten eight times last night and again got very little sleep! I spent the morning visiting Phnom Penh and my guide was Sotaea. He was a past pupil of the Don Bosco School and was now a teacher in charge of the mechanics department. He spoke very good English and we had a great time exploring this most remarkable city.

It was crowded with motorbikes everywhere; most were taxi bikes and you would be astonished at the number of people they transported at once! Most of the people wore those rimmed hats that you see on those American movies in wartime Vietnam. What I liked the most was that every time I looked at anyone, on a bike, in a car, on the sidewalk - they would always smile. They are the smiliest people possible and I was making loads of friends! I was told that it is like a duty to smile and I wished it were compulsory all over the world.

Suffer little children: these young people have precious few possessions, and not much more hope...

Driving through the city we passed a huge monument in the centre of a roundabout. It was a handgun and stood nearly 10m high! It represented the recent amnesty for a weapon that made this country very unsafe. This, added to the serious landmine problems, has meant that this country has had to work very hard to attract foreign visitors.

Cambodia is still recovering from the conflicts over the last thirty years and the regime of the Khmer Rouge who are estimated to have massacred over two million people. Most people know of the 'killing fields' made famous by the film and today I went to visit the place where many of the innocent victims of Pol Pot were interrogated, tortured and then killed.

In 1975 Pol Pot transformed Tuol Suay Prey High School in the centre of Phnom Penh into a prison called 'S21'. It was completely surrounded by a large double fence made of corrugated iron and laden with dense electrified barbed wire. The ground floor classrooms were turned into torture rooms and the upstairs rooms made into rows of narrow wooden cells.

Several thousand victims, mainly engineers, technicians, intellectuals, professors, teachers, students, doctors, Buddhist monks and ministers were imprisoned and exterminated here with their wives and children.

I was shocked at what I saw as I entered a classroom where the blood still stains the floor, chains are fixed to walls with shackles and torturing devices unimaginable are still in place. It was a disturbing site of absolute cruelty as you made your way around this school looking into the tiny cells where small iron buckets were still attached to the floor and into which prisoners had to defecate.

Many classrooms had wall to wall photos of the innocent victims and a number of rooms displayed hundreds of human skulls dug up around the site and displayed in glass cabinets; but I was traumatized by the final classroom and what I saw.

A large wooden box placed in the centre of the room full of skeleton bones, skulls with bullet holes through the top and at the side, a pile of old blood stained clothes and personal belongings! These were the remains of human beings slaughtered by other humans.

It is totally incomprehensible to think that people could be so cruel and that I was looking into a box of innocent, slaughtered victims whose only crime was their intelligence! It seems that if you were intelligent Pol Pot's regime did not want you in society - you were seen as a threat and that was the end.

Day 127: Still in Phnom Penh, Cambodia

I can't believe I slept last night; I was still upset at my experiences of yesterday. Nevertheless, I was up at 7am and although the school was closed today there must have been over 300 children playing in the field and yard.

These children were 5-10 year olds that do not go to school. They are from poor families in the villages near to Don Bosco School and every Sunday they voluntarily walk to the school for an opportunity to have some basic and free education. They were such joyful and contented youngsters and it seemed that Sunday mornings were the highlight of the week for many of them! Most of the schools in Cambodia are operated by NGO's and cater for older children including the Don Bosco School but as Sunday is a day of rest, these schools were utilised to offer opportunities for the younger boys and girls in the community.

Later I was taken to see the Royal Palace and home to the King; it was not open to the public but is a spectacular sight! I then passed the FCC (Foreign Correspondents Club) that became infamous for many years as a safe haven above a hotel used by journalists to report on the war and famines of Cambodia that made news around the world.

I had really enjoyed visiting Cambodia despite the awful poverty and evidence of past atrocities that I had witnessed. It had been a short visit and although I hated the nights – only because of the horrible insects and mozzies, I felt a real sense of welcome here.

It is significant that an organisation such as Don Bosco founded so many years ago in Europe has made such an impact with its work in Cambodia today. The people enjoyed smiling and that made you happy! I was now returning to the airport and on my way back to Bangkok to catch the train to Malaysia.

"Chob m roaom!" and now it was time to leave!

Day 128: Back in Bangkok, Thailand

The flight back to Bangkok had been super – a new 717-200 jet with just six of us on board! After a good night's sleep I awoke today back at the Provincial House feeling refreshed and focused. I now had a few days planning to do.

I was feeling so much more confident here in Bangkok to use the public transport and off I went on a bus 93 that would take me downtown (about twelve kms) where I could then get another bus to take me the shorter distance to the Australian Embassy. I was concerned about my entry into Australia because a British Citizen does need a visa - which is simple if you are flying from the UK - but since I was hoping to arrive in Australia via Indonesia and probably travelling from East Timor, I knew that I needed to be fully prepared!

It took me three hours to get to the Embassy, and this had included three buses and a trip on the BTS Skytrain. This elevated rail network is actually pretty cool but you need to climb loads of stairs to get to it and it goes very slowly - looks good but is really quite ineffective! Most of the problems in travelling around the city centre were down to the sheer volume of traffic. Bus lanes were useless and taxis could make your journey expensive - mainly because you were paying to sit in the congested traffic!

I arrived at the Embassy at 12.15pm; I could hardly believe my eyes when I saw the notice, which read 'Visa section open 8am to 12noon ONLY'. What a bloody nightmare. I would just have to get up early and try again tomorrow!

I went for a coffee; well I ended up in a traditional 'raan kaa-fae' a Hokkien-style coffee shop, where I had some luscious cake and filtered coffee while I composed myself!

I could not arrange my transport to Malaysia until I had everything else sorted out and so having some free time on my hands I decided to risk a 'Thai' haircut! Yes, I found somewhere and for only US$6 had my hair bleached, cut, washed and then a free head massage was given! Wow! I just wanted to sleep!

Day 129: Bangkok, Thailand

I was at the Embassy at 9am this morning (I had taken a taxi!), collected a form and received my ticket with the number 127 – this was my serving number and they had just shouted out 'Number Eight!' Anyway I filled in the form and waited. Still waiting after an hour I went to the reception to check out the situation. I wanted to go for a drink and to the toilet – I could not understand the number sequences as they had become really messed up! They were not being called in order any more. I was told I was at the right place and that they were just busy!

Now, let me share this with you. There were 155 people in the waiting room, only 34 were white, the rest were all Thai. All the 34 white people were men and all had a Thai girl with them! Now, I know I'm surmising, but it is most probable that these Thai women were probably applying for immigration visas – OK, I can say that I was pretty much told this by a number of people whom I spoke with whilst waiting! It is becoming more and more popular for 'western' men to come to Thailand and find a bride to take home! (I'd already found mine!).

Four hours I waited before my number was called! It took just three minutes to issue my visa and I was out of the Embassy; well, I was gobsmacked! I knew however that it was better and safer to be prepared! ('Be Prepared' is the motto for the Scout movement and today was the closing ceremony of the 20th World Jamboree, which had been taking place here in Thailand!).

Day 130: Bangkok, Thailand

Up early again and reading through my e-mails. It was amazing the correspondence I was receiving from people in South America asking when I would be arriving; I was running behind schedule but should catch up over the next two weeks! I booked my ticket to take me to Malaysia; it was actually faster to go by bus (12 hours) rather than by train and as I was running low on funds, I knew I must try not to fly unless I had to!

So **"koobkun Samrab wanwelatidee-dee naimaungthai"** and it's off to Malaysia tomorrow!

I arrived at the Coach Station in Bangkok with plenty of time and we departed at 7.00pm for Pakbara (or so I thought!).

Sitting very high up on this air-conditioned coach, I was able to get a birds-eye view of downtown Bangkok for the last time! It was a very big city with skyscrapers and hotels almost everywhere! 'Dunkin Donuts', '7eleven' and 'KFC' were everywhere and people - hundreds of thousands of people. It was strange to consider that even with so many people it was nothing like India. You did not see homeless people, people begging or just hanging about the streets!

You did see the smog, something you don't really see in the UK but clearly visible here - with the sheer volume of traffic it wasn't surprising! I was told that there are over 4,000 taxis and I was now leaving this 'City of Roads' in one of 16 lanes of buses, cars and taxis! HELP!

It was nearly five hours before we stopped and I just relaxed in the reclining seat watching the world go by. We were at a so-called service station, but it was just at the side of the road and was not very clean at all. I was hungry, but was not keen on what there was on offer!

At 5am we stopped again in Suratthana and I thought we were making good progress until I was told that our journey would continue by minibus! After two hours swapping from one minibus to another I was finally on my way to Hatyai. This took us five hours and we were still not at the border! I was really frustrated and annoyed that we were not being told anything. After a thirty-minute wait I was on another minibus which took a further two hours and at last I finally arrived in Pakbara!

Then I was given my final blow! The boat service did not operate from here any more - I don't swear much but if you've got to practise then now was a great opportunity.

Day 131: The journey from Bangkok to Santun, Thailand

Ticket from Bangkok - even though I can't read it!

After much confusion talking with some of the locals, I was offered a lift on a motorbike to the next town where I was promised there would be a taxi to take me to Satun!

Now, I was in the middle of nowhere, completely on my own and absolutely knackered. I had no choice but to accept, and when I arrived at the next town my 'taxi' turned out to be a pick-up truck! However, it got me to Satun in one piece!

Day 132: Satun, Thailand

After 23 hours travelling, I had made it to Satun. This was a small town on the south western border of Thailand and Malaysia. I could not take the ferry today, but tomorrow I would be able to travel to Lankawi (a small island that is part of Malaysia) and meet up with some friends who are from my home town in the UK and who have a holiday home there. Each year they spend six months in their other home where it is surely much warmer than England! For now, I had booked into a hotel and by 7pm I was fast asleep!

Day 133: Lankawi, Malaysia

I slept for 15 hours non-stop. On waking up I rushed from my room just in time for some breakfast in the hotel restaurant! By late afternoon I was on the boat to Lankawi; I was now in Malaysia and one more hour ahead!

Alan and Maureen (friends from my local pub in England) have a fantastic house on this island and were entertaining other locals from the pub who had come over for a holiday. They were all at the port to greet me and I was overwhelmed at the welcome!

We went out to eat and then sat at Alan's own bar that he built in his garden! The beer was free and flowed until six in the morning when the talking stopped and we all collapsed in our beds!

Day 134: Lankawi, Malaysia

Today we went to hire some motorbikes and take a tour of the island. I was a little nervous about riding, as I am not very good; however, I jumped on the bike from the hire shop and went for a little test drive down the road. As I reached the junction I forgot which order to do the gears, front brakes and rear brakes and couldn't stop. Oh no! I ended up in the middle of the main road after panicking and my heart was pumping faster than ever!

After taking the bike back to the hire shop feeling a little shaken, Alan suggested I ride with him instead. I decided it was crazy for me to try and ride the bike when I was not confident and certainly did not want any more road traffic injuries!

What an amazing island Lankawi is; there had been a huge development programme over the last five years and I think they were preparing to make this a real tourist attraction for the future. It was a beautiful island and only about 30kms from one end to the other. The roads were all good and the scenery was awesome!

We travelled to the cable car station in Machinchang and climbed over 700 metres to get a really fantastic view of the whole island and the Andaman Sea. It was spectacular as we glided up through the rainforest looking down on the Telag Tujuh waterfall and we even saw monkeys on the ground.

It felt very humid at the top and it was actually a little difficult to breathe! With a 360 degree view, I was so impressed with it all; you could see lots of development projects for new hotels and in one bay where a new hotel was being built, they had actually created two man-made small islands in the sea with the foundations from the building site. You would never know they had not always been there. Malaysia was a mix of natural beauty in jungles, beaches, mountains and rice fields and it seemed that Lankawi had it all!

Sunset over Lankawi was simply breathtaking.

145

Day 135: Still in Lankawi, Malaysia

Up early today and by late morning we had left the island seaport on a catamaran to tour the smaller islands. You've got to have contacts and then you can enjoy the life of the rich and famous! I was on the 'Day Dreamer' sailing on blue water seas in a natural paradise, basking in the sun and drinking beer! At one stage we all jumped into the water and held on to a huge rope net that carried us through the waves. It was so cool! Eventually we anchored off a remote island and took a small dinghy to the shore. It was just what you see in the travel brochures

but it was actually becoming too hot for me - my neck and shoulders were beginning to burn and after another swim in the sea we were on our way back to Lankawi. This coastline is one of the most unspoilt parts of Asia and with white sandy beaches it is certainly an idyllic holiday destination.

It was fun spending time with some friends from my local pub in England but it was time to leave and go back to the mainland of Malaysia and begin the journey down to Kuala Lumpur.

Day Dreamer: I had fun with my friends in Lankawi

"Selamat Jalan Bahasa"!

Day 136: Kuala Lumpur, Malaysia

I took the ferry back to Kuala Perlis on the mainland and looked around for the bus station. This was a small town and I was struggling to find anything. It was very hot! I was dripping all over with sweat, my back was hurting with the weight of my rucksack and the straps were rubbing on my shoulders that were stinging from the sunburn! I was a wreck - hot, lost and tired! No-one seemed to speak English and I just couldn't stop because the sun was scorching me!

After an hour walking around this town (and I must have done it all!), I found the bus station - opposite the FERRY TERMINAL! I had walked right past it without seeing it, and every time I had asked somebody where the bus station was, they had pointed back at the ferry port and I had thought they were telling me to get a boat.

I then waited for over an hour before a bus arrived and took me to the main town of Butterworth (three hours away) where I could then catch the express coach to Kuala Lumpur, another five hours drive!

Kuala Lumpur is known as 'KL' and is a really cosmopolitan city. After finding a cheap hotel opposite the bus terminal I went exploring - it was a colourful kaleidoscope of sight, sound and taste. I was in Chinatown and it was the start of celebrations for the new Chinese Year (of the goat by the way!) and it was unbelievable! Lights, decorations and people everywhere - and food!

I was really hungry and feeling confident... I sat down at one of the many Chinese restaurants to eat. Most of the seating spilled out on the streets and it was such a great atmosphere. I enjoyed honeydew chicken and flaming rice noodles. Mmm! It was delicious and I was really enjoying the experience here, but unfortunately I would have to leave tomorrow.

Day 137: Singapore

The bus terminal in Kuala Lumpur was quite an experience. There were rows of small stands representing each bus company and basically they operated all over Malaysia, Thailand and Singapore. You just had to walk up and down each aisle and pick the one who shouted the loudest selling a seat for your destination! It could be very frightening and you were really put under pressure to make a quick decision about a journey that was actually going to take you all day and you wanted to know that the bus would be decent and not break down. Once a bus was full, off you went!

No Onward Ticket

We left at midday on a full size bus with only twenty seats - this was because it was an executive style bus and you could drop the seat almost to a sleeping position. Wow! I slept for nearly three hours before we made our first stop. It was at this stage that things began to go wrong! The air-conditioning stopped working and we had to complete the final four hours in terrible conditions!

It was very hot and humid and these buses were designed so that you had no windows that you could open! As we hit the traffic approaching the border control for Singapore I was feeling pretty ill and was glad to get off when we had to take our passports to immigration.

At last, I was in my 28th country and arrived safely at the bus station. I began walking to find a hotel and I was immediately shocked by the difference in prices from the rest of Asia. Singapore is one of the most affluent countries in Asia and certainly the cleanest and most organised. Public transport is elite and there is no traffic congestion - but it is expensive!

Well, I was now lost and becoming very frustrated! I saw a young couple walking along and asked if they could help me. They were so kind; they took me on a bus to find a cheaper hotel and then took me for something to eat. We had a great chat and I was able to learn a little about Singapore and its people!

Eileen and Chris were actually of Chinese descent; their family came to Singapore some 60 years ago and at the same time many other families were coming over from China, Malaysia and India. This was the first time I was seeing two totally different cultures living together in one country and as I was told, they were all very friendly and respected each other and their religions! They all spoke English as a main language but when they were in their own groups they would often speak Chinese (called Mandarin), Tamil or Malay.

The bright lights of commerce in Singapore.

They shared so much with me about religion, the economy and more interestingly the 'Police State', that Singapore is often referred to as. Over the next few days I saw evidence of what they meant. There were signs all over about what you could and could not do, where you could and could not walk, when you could and could not eat, drink, smoke, skateboard, stand and even where you could not read newspapers or study! Chewing gum was banned and drugs could still carry the death penalty! The crazy thing was that

Dining out in Singapore: anyone care for another chicken's foot?

over the next few days, I saw no Police or Police cars, no people begging, no tramps and no elderly or disabled people. This was truly a very interesting place where the cost of living was akin to that of Europe, crime was unheard of and cleanliness was the law!

Day 138: Singapore

This morning I met with Heidi and her two friends who had just arrived in Singapore to go backpacking around the world for eight months. They were from England and lived in my home town. They told me the weather was pretty cold in Wakefield, but I would happily have gone home just to cool down for a few days! I had been in the heat for almost three months now and so often it was unbearable!

Later I met with my Singaporean Chinese friends who took me to the University to meet some more of their friends and also do some filming. I wanted to know more about what the young people thought of their country and its 'rules'! The National University had over twenty thousand students and the campus was so big that it had its own bus company to take you around.

With only two weeks to go before the Chinese New Year, in the evening I visited Chinatown with Heidi and her freinds - it was totally decorated with colourful lights and displays and was a fantastic sight. My choice of food tonight included grilled chickens' feet and they were... pretty awful!

It was good to be in a country where people spoke English, sorry 'Singlish', but I did manage to learn just a little Mandarin! **"Wo hen gao xing lai clao xing jia po, zhe li de ren hen qin qie. Huan jing hen zhen jie, duo duo bao zhong!"**

Day 139: Jakarta, Indonesia

From Malaysia or Singapore there is no safe route to Indonesia unless you fly and thankfully the price of the airline ticket was very cheap. It was a little strange when I went to get my ticket - you now had to pay an additional fee for 'war risk' - well, at least I would be covered!

The airport in Singapore was unrecognisable since my last visit there three years ago; checking in, immigration, passport control and boarding the plane were all so convenient and simple. The security staff were invisible and everything was so smooth. I was on the plane and on my way to Jakarta and you could even watch the take off from your mini TV screen! That was pretty cool - with a camera fixed to the pilot's windscreen you got a super view of both take off and landing! We had a pretty awful two hours in the air however, a storm ahead was right in our flight path!

Indonesia is a long chain of islands stretching over 5,000kms across the Equator. Jakarta is the gateway to the five main islands and another very hot place! Having just passed through the Equator the seasons here were hot and VERY hot! The heat was uncomfortable and I don't know what I would have done without air conditioning!

Finding a cheap hotel was another nightmare; Indonesian people did not appear trustworthy to me when I arrived at the airport and I was convinced I was going to get stitched up! I had no idea where to go but hoped that I had negotiated a good deal at the airport (which is an hour's drive from the city) and took a taxi to my hotel.

The taxi driver was explaining to me about the Government's recent rise in petrol taxes (over 20%) and that people had been demonstrating and even rioting!

Today, in Jakarta, the Police had fired warning shots to disperse hundreds of people protesting. Several had been injured, a number of buildings had been burnt and tyres had also been set on fire. As we drove into the city the Police were everywhere, but it was now quiet.

My impressions of Jakarta were not good and I was glad to get to my hotel. I was feeling very scared and I was not really sure why. I was also feeling very homesick; I was a long way from home and really felt like just giving it all up!

Got plenty of sleep before taking a taxi to visit the Salesian school nearby. Well, I say nearby, but what a nightmare! No sooner had I got into the taxi than we were in the middle of a huge demonstration and there were Police everywhere. This was the third day now (explained the taxi driver) of protests against the government and it would probably turn into another riot and probably account for more injuries among the people and it was all a little scary for me!

Jakarta was a mad city, a little like Mumbai or Calcutta - no rules about driving and thousands of vehicles blasting horns and driving like crazy! They had their own version of the tuk-tuk called the 'budgie' and it was so funny seeing them dodging through the traffic - they actually look like budgies on three wheels!

The taxi driver took me through dozens of back streets and over humps, bridges and one-way streets before eventually arriving at the school almost two hours later! It cost me 90,000 Rupiahs and I'd been had!

I enjoyed my visit and was well fed before being taken back to my hotel by Fr Lil (one of the school staff) - and the journey took just ten minutes, which showed that my taxi fare should have been about 8,000 Rupiahs! (US$1)

I really did not like Jakarta. These were my first impressions as somebody arriving in a strange city on their own and I did not want to stay here! My whole

Day 140: Still in Jakarta, Indonesia

journey was about my experiences arriving in a country with nothing pre-planned and I had allowed for a similar amount of time in each place, but Jakarta was not for me!

Day 141: The journey from Jakarta to Bali, Indonesia

I was taken to the bus station in the centre of Jakarta to get the overnight coach to Bali. The system was quite simple - you picked the coach you liked, went to the ticket office representing that coach company and bought your ticket. Once that coach was full it would depart. There are loads of coaches and minibuses travelling all over Indonesia from there and it was the maddest place to be!

We departed just after 2pm for what would be an estimated 26-hour non-stop journey to Bali, including the short ferry ride to the island. I was happy to leave Jakarta; I just did not feel very safe at all!

By late evening the only vehicles on the road were the coaches and wagons but that was more than enough. It was like a convoy of coaches each one trying to overtake the other and then take on the wagons! It was a nightmare! We had three drivers who took it in turns and I was chatting to one of them who told me that the current driver was 'the best in the company'. It became obvious after a while that this was a race between the different companies to get to their destinations first! We were suddenly in our first hold-up; a coach had overturned and many of the injured passengers were lying or sitting at the side of the road - covered in blood! The Police had not yet arrived and whilst I felt upset and frightened I hoped it would make our driver slow down a little!

Day 142: Bali, Indonesia

Our coach was very comfortable with all the usual facilities; it even had a cubicle at the back of the vehicle with two seats and ventilation! No, this was not the toilet but the 'smoke room'! Unbelievable eh? We had now been on the road for 15 hours and passed our fifth road traffic accident - each incident involved a wagon, a coach or both! The roads here were very narrow and climbed through the valleys and forests of Indonesia with no side-barriers and most of the time - no road markings!

The coach did stop for food, it was all part of the ticket price, but as I am writing this just a few days later - I have been suffering quite badly with my bowels and wishing I'd not tried the local cuisine!

I met some great people on the coach - no tourists, just Indonesians visiting family or travelling to and from work. Before the end of the journey I was talking to everybody! These were executive coaches similar to the one I took to Singapore. It was the size of a full coach, but only had 25 seats inside, so it was very spacious and you could actually walk about. You could also sleep as the seats reclined to an almost full bed position.

Ground Zero, Bali-style: the pain from one night of terror is still being felt here.

Some of the scenery was spectacular and as we followed the coastline the sea looked beautiful. We went over so many bridges that I lost count - there was water everywhere!

At the port to take the ferry, the coaches and wagons were packed on like sardines as the passengers went on to the top deck. The ferries were very old and rusty and they didn't seem very safe at all to me! However, I went to the captain's deck for a chat and got a great view of our crossing to Bali!

Bali is one of about 17,000 islands of Indonesia and you did not need to show your passport on arrival but security was ever present! It was just three months since the terrorist bombing in Kuta that killed 200 people and injured over 300 more. It took a further four hours to arrive in Denpasar and here I got a local taxi to Kuta. It was pouring with rain and I was happy to find a hotel and rest!

Day 143: Bali, Indonesia

With a reputation as being one of the most beautiful and diverse tourist spots in Asia, here I was in Bali. I was experiencing a real tropical climate being so close to the Equator - it was now the rainy season and it was very, very hot. It was also unbearably humid and made you feel constantly tired!

Bali is an island of Hindu people and having just had the full moon, flowers and incense were laid out in front of nearly all the shops, restaurants and hotels; but there were no people! It was a ghost town; all the streets were deserted, and the shops, restaurants and hotels were empty! My hotel had 125 rooms and only ten were filled! Everywhere I went the locals would be desperate to sell to me; with the island's whole industry reliant on tourists and the effects of a terrorist bomb - Bali has become a very sad place to be!

I went to the site of the bomb blast; it was an horrific mess of half demolished buildings and rubble everywhere! 'Ground Zero' was a completely flattened area and I felt overcome by what had happened here just three months ago. Nearby shops were gutted from the effects of the explosion and as I just stood and gazed, I began to cry; it was a devastating mess of destruction - a terrible tragedy.

Murder in paradise: there is no doubt the locals in Bali are suffering because of the terrorist attack there.

It wasn't long before the rain started again and I was wading through 25cms of water back to my hotel. Kuta used to be a major hustling and bustling resort town, with its hundreds of hotels, bars, restaurants and shops - but not any more!

Day 144: Bali, Indonesia

I took a walk down to the beach this morning and was very disappointed. It was littered with garbage, driftwood and seaweed washed up by the tide; apparently with no tourists the beach is not getting regularly cleaned and I was not very impressed! The sea was very warm as I waded in to my knees, just a few windsurfers in the distance but no sunbathers!

I spent the rest of the day visiting travel agents trying to arrange a ferry to Kapang; from there I would take the eight-hour bus to East Timor. It seemed that nobody wanted to go to Timor! The border crossing from West Timor (Indonesia) to East Timor (now independent) was still quite dangerous and the advice from people was to travel only by air! My next problem was that all flights to Dili were very expensive, so I was left with a dilemma!

To be honest, I'd had enough of Asia; the heat, culture, language and food had now become too much for me and I really needed to get to Australia. I knew that East Timor would be a fantastic experience for me and I was so close but after nearly five months of travelling - I needed to change my environment! Yes, I really missed home and yes, I was beginning to find the whole experience tough going, but if I was going to get right round the world then I needed to move on to my next continent! I was not liking Indonesia at all; Bali was making me very frustrated because of the people desperate to sell all the time - there were no deals and whilst I really felt sympathetic for the people I made a conscious decision to book a flight directly to Darwin. No travel agent would accept credit cards, they wanted only cash, which proved to be a serious problem for me. Each bank I visited was reluctant to allow a transaction on my card. This was crazy! I was feeling desperate! I then saw a small HSBC logo on the window of a bank, and my luck was in! I would be leaving tomorrow night!

"Tiang polih pengalamon becik ring Bali!"

Paradise lost? This conventional view of Bali is a world away from what I found.

Day 145: Bali to Darwin

I didn't sleep very well last night - I seem to find that the day before I was due to travel I never slept well! This sleep problem was compounded by the fact that I was on the move every three or four days.

Anyway, I went round the town once more and onto the beach before going back to my hotel for an afternoon sleep! I felt lost! It was so hot and yet by 4pm the heavens had opened and it rained for the rest of the day!

Late afternoon I packed my bag and joined Howard (an English guy travelling on to Australia to work) for some food in a restaurant owned by an Aussie couple! Super food!

Shortly afterwards I was sitting in the airport waiting for my flight which was not until 2am tomorrow! I couldn't wait to get to Australia - here I go again! Planes, trains and automobiles!

Day 146: Darwin, Australia

I flew out from Ngurah Rai Airport in Bali at 2am and arrived in Darwin and yet another time zone three hours later. This was my 17th clock change since I left the UK.

Australia has very strict quarantine laws and I was screened and examined by the Customs Officers for nearly an hour. There were no problems - I was thrilled to be in Australia, halfway round the world and this inconvenience at the airport was nothing compared to other immigration and arrival border controls that I had endured!

I now had to begin learning about another country - a new continent; and understand the massive distances that I would have to cover to visit any contacts I had.

I originally planned to take the bus from Darwin to Alice Springs. This would take 21 hours and then a further day would be needed to get to Ayres Rock. A train from there would then get me into Adelaide 24 hours later. It became apparent that Australia was a big country! The journey straight down the middle would take me the best part of a week and that same distance in Africa would take me through four countries! Still exploring the options, I found that I could take a flight directly to southern Australia and it would be cheaper than travelling by land! My decision was made. I would stay in Darwin for 24 hours and then head directly to Adelaide.

The humidity and heat in Darwin was as bad as Bali; I had hoped it would be cooler here, but it was hot!

I walked for most of the afternoon around the centre and it was a great feeling to be in a Western culture again. For the first time I also saw Aboriginal people whose history dates back in Australia long before any white man 'discovered' this continent! I was a little stunned at first because Aborigines do not look like Africans, Indians or Asians - they have their own distinctive features and this was a new experience for me!

As I came to the end of the shopping precinct I noticed a Police car (more like a pick-up truck) and two officers who were speaking to a group of seven or eight Aborigines sitting on the ground. After an exchange of words and confrontational body language, the officers placed two of them in the back of the vehicle and took them away! This was a disturbing sight for me and unfortunately my first impression of Darwin!

Later, I went to find the local cinema since this was my first 'English' speaking country for a long time and I hadn't seen a movie for five months! Unfortunately, the late showing was too late for me (early flight in the morning!) and I was walking back to my motel when I met Len and his son who were on holiday from Brisbane. We began chatting and Len offered me a number of contacts that may be useful for me on my way around this vast country. I had now lost a whole night's sleep and was shattered - my flight was at 5am so it was back to my room for an early night!

Day 147: Adelaide, Australia

Climbing up into the sky this morning I was heading for my 70th destination and was in my 28th country - and I was now halfway round the world! The view was fantastic as we flew over the Tanami desert towards Alice Springs. The landscape was deep reddish in colour, flat and just went on for miles. Australia seemed so remote from the sky; I had not seen anything like it and as we passed Lake Eyre I thought I was looking at another planet!

I was a little disappointed that I was missing out on seeing Ayres Rock but - Hey! I can't do everything!

As we approached Adelaide we hit a hot stream of air and the aircraft shook from side to side so we immediately changed our direction in order to make our approach from a different angle! Those last ten minutes in the air were pretty frightening and I was glad when we touched down! Another time zone and another change in temperature; it was 44.1 degrees centigrade (113F) and bloody hot!

Greg (a friend of Len's whom I had met in Darwin) met me and instead of just assisting me with finding some cheap accommodation, he spent the whole day taking me on a whistle stop tour of the city! He first took me to Mount Lofty and the view from there down onto the city was awesome. Whilst we were there, ABC News were filming to cover a news story on the possible threat of the bush fires reaching parts of Adelaide. They were going up to the top of the bush fire lookout tower, and I was invited to join them! It was out of this world - the tower looks out over the whole of Adelaide and beyond.

South Australia like many areas of Australia was on RED ALERT today because of the soaring temperatures! I could see the effect of the fires hundreds of miles away as the smoke lingered over the skies. This actually makes things difficult to even spot nearby fires but what else can they do?

Australia had been in a heat wave for the last six years and the seriousness of the fires around the country was incomprehensible; I mean this was a disaster that was out of control!

Adelaide is an elegant city; with traditional stone architecture and wide encircling parklands - it is such a wonderful place and so spacious. It was designed by Colonel William Light in 1836; he laid the city out on a square mile grid pattern of wide streets and airy squares and lots of green parkland. It is one of the only cities of Australia that was not designed to house convicts but instead, the wealthy overseas trippers who settled here!

I was exhausted with the heat by the time Greg took me to my hotel; a pub on the beach with a window view room of the sea, Wow - this is Australia!

Day 148: Still in Adelaide, Australia

Today was Australia Day and a bank holiday weekend; it was also the end of the 'summer' holidays, as the climate would soon change to autumn! It was strange to be experiencing the opposite climates in January!

News today was all about the bush fires still, many roads connecting major cities were closed and fire-fighters (many of whom were just volunteers) were losing their lives whilst trying to save others.

Other news today was of a bus crash in Indonesia - the same bus company and route that I had been travelling on just a few days ago! The bus had smashed into a house and a drum of oil had sparked a fireball that incinerated all 17 passengers, trapped when it had become engulfed in flames! I still know that my nephew and I are lucky to be alive after our car accident in South Africa; this just makes me think all the more!

Greg took me downtown to watch a cycle race, (the Jacobs Creek Tour Down Under) the final leg finished in Adelaide and was a great experience to see. It was an extraordinary display of colour and excitement; speed and endurance, sweat, tears and triumph! The crowd made for an enthralling atmosphere and the soaring temperatures made for a tiring afternoon.

Late afternoon and I had the opportunity to meet Peter Smith at the Next Generation Tennis Club; from an early age he was Lleyton Hewitt's tennis coach and now helps to promote and support opportunities for young players from all over the world who come to Adelaide.

In the evening I had the chance to wander along the jetty from my hotel and I was fascinated by all these people 'crabbing' - dropping baskets of raw meat into the sea and catching 'blueys'! I ended up chatting with three local guys who called me 'dude' and insisted I try a bottle of Coopers draught! (Cheers dudes!)

Day 149: Still in Adelaide, Australia

Where I was staying was so much like I had imagined Australia would be - very laid back, hot weather and great beaches! Adelaide itself was so 'England'; it was one of the only free settlements in Australia, as most were penal colonies. People here were so friendly and life seemed so much in the slow lane! There was a sense of space too in Adelaide; it had remarkable parklands that let the city breathe! (and me!)

Time for me to relax, sleep, use the Internet, make phone calls back home and have a swim in the warm Aussie seas!

This was my first English-speaking country for a long time and it was great to meet and chat with so many friendly people! Everyone calls you 'Pommie' and it just made me laugh!

Aussie English is so funny, they have loads of crazy words like 'Shonky' and 'Troppo' and 'Bunghole', which means cheese!

So, is Australia **"Hay, Hell and Booligal?"** Maybe not!

Day 150: Still in Adelaide, Australia

30 countries
47,050 kilometres
418 hours travelling
18 time zones
24 trains
15 planes

8 boats

11 buses

5 cars

45 stamps in my passport

39 Don Bosco projects/communities/schools visited

36 hotels

74 cash machines

and....ONE HUNDRED AND FIFTY DAYS!

Day 151: Still in Adelaide, Australia

My highlight of the day today was meeting Greg Chappell (Aussie cricket captain when England used to be good competition!) Thanks to Len in Darwin and Greg here in Adelaide, they arranged for me to meet their pal who is now State Manager of Cricket for South Australia.

We met at Adelaide Oval regarded by many as the most picturesque test cricket ground in the world - and this was my first visit to a cricket ground anywhere! It was so good to have Greg show me round and give me an insight into the extensive history of the Oval.

He was more interested in my epic journey and told me that I was a great inspiration to people and that I would be able to share so much with so many. He was just pleased to see a Yorkshireman too I guess; he commented on some memorable times visiting my home county and gave me some supportive words of encouragement for the second half of my journey!

Cricket legend: Aussie Greg Chappell was the scourge of English cricket. He's the one on the right!

What a humble and sincere man Greg is. I was so pleased to meet him and he sent his best wishes to the people of Yorkshire!

Later I visited 'Tandanya' - the National Aboriginal Cultural Institute in Adelaide. Tandanya is actually the name given to the area of Adelaide by the Kaurna (Aboriginal) people. 'Tarnda' means red kangaroo and 'anya' is the place of.

I saw displays of some of Australia's most influential and progressive indigenous art and craft along with the infamous didgeridoos! It was also very interesting to get the views of local aboriginal people on what 'Australia Day' meant to them when you consider that their land was actually 'invaded'.

It is important for me to explain that Australian people are working very closely with many Aboriginal tribes, recognising the need to live together in peace, respecting many issues of land ownership etc.

I was then treated to a demonstration of the didgeridoo and showed off my talents as I made rude sounds through this hollow 'tree trunk'!

Day 152: Melbourne, Australia

Having found the Don Bosco School in Adelaide, I met the Parish Priest (Fr Bernard) who was planning to travel to Melbourne today and asked if I would like to share the driving as he was travelling by car. Well, this was great as I would be able to see a bit of Aussie countryside!

The journey took eleven hours, but it was a fantastic experience of remarkable contrasts. From rolling vineyards, pristine coastlines, sandy beaches, the legendary Australian Outback and National Parks. Sadly, I saw so much barren and dry land too - the road went on for ages, but so did the scorched landscape that looked very similar to parts of Africa.

We chatted all the way (not just me!) and stopped in small towns for food and drink.

Roos cruise: I spotted these white kangaroos on the 11-hour drive to Melbourne.

The best thing was that I got to see kangaroos - they were magnificent and they just stared at me for ages before jumping away, probably wondering why I was so excited! They were white kangaroos but I wasn't racist!

We eventually arrived in Melbourne; I was tired but had enjoyed the journey into another time zone and another State - Victoria.

It was the feast day celebrating the Saint 'Don Bosco' and I was now in Sunbury visiting a Salesian College just outside Melbourne. Unfortunately the school was still on summer break, but the staff were willing to show me round and take me up to the main building called Rupertswood. This Victorian mansion had been converted into a hotel but was once the main school building and was still owned by the Salesians.

It has a famous story to tell, the 'Birthplace of the Ashes'. On the 29th of August 1882, an Australian cricket team, to the astonishment of all (none more than the English), defeated an English team on English soil. A witty tongue-in-cheek obituary in the 'Sporting Times'read:

"In Affectionate Remembrance of English Cricket, which died at the Oval on 29th August 1882. Deeply lamented by a large circle of friends and acquaintances. R.I.P. N.B. The body will be cremated and sent to Australia."

Later that same year an English team came over to Melbourne and was invited to play a game at William John Clarke's lavish home - Rupertswood. They won the game and Lady Clarke burnt the stumps and placed the ashes in a small urn to be presented to the English team! The 'Ashes' are housed at Lord's in England, but I enjoyed visiting one of the Salesians most famous schools!

In the afternoon I took the tram into Melbourne and met Angie and Mark, who were from Wakefield and had emigrated here in 1990. I had been on the road five months and they had invited me to stay with them in Geelong about an hour away from Melbourne; here I was going to have an opportunity to 'recharge' myself before travelling on to Sydney.

So, welcome to Geelong and time for a rest!

Day 153: Geelong, Australia

You just never know who you might meet...

Chapter 6:

Foreword

by Malcolm Cameron M.B., Ch.B., B.Sc., F.R.C.S.
retired neurosurgeon

In 1993 I met a young Yorkshireman by the name of Peter Hunter. He was brash, extrovert, gregarious and an energetic guy; with a touch of naivety and brown skin!

Always industrious in educational and social welfare matters he served the local community well and was always at home talking to the young and the disadvantaged; even then I believe he knew that he had a mission in life but how to fulfil it?

Having spent 20 years in Yorkshire I came back to New Zealand in 2001 to find some things change and some don't: one that hadn't being Pete.

Thus this man arrived into the Whakatane Airport with backpack and camcorder and without about a stone and a half of bodily weight. OK mate we'll fix that says me and all the belligerent brown blond bugger wanted was a soak in a natural geothermal hot pool: Yep OK Pete and so that was done.

Spent six days with me he did, and supped a few cold Kiwi ales, devoured good Kiwi kai (food), rested, recuperated and recharged the inner engine but through that time an inner light kept shining through. Comes the time to depart New Zealand en-route to South America - clothes washed and dried, hair re-bleached, new tapes for the camcorder and back to the airport, only to fall into the clutches of a gaggle of Maori girls wanting to extract life blood for no cost. No sweat that for the intrepid Hunter. I met one of the Maori Amazons several weeks later to be told she thought he was a sweet nice boy!

He has fulfilled an ambition that few of us dream about and even fewer attain. Fulfilment is born of desire, courage and grit; Peter embodies all three. May young people the world over be energised to strive to communicate and break down artificial barriers - Peter has done this against the odds and in peril of his own life.

I was happy to help Pete and meet him again. He had a dream and made it to the end of his rainbow: you who read his book have courage and conviction to do what you dream of but at the same time do no harm.

The World should be one big caring community and we must all contribute - Hunter did his bit; now go out and do yours!

Day 154: Still in Geelong, Australia

It was so good to meet and stay with Mark and his wife Angie - a real chance to relax and catch up with things! Their generosity was extraordinary as they made me feel so much at home!

Unfortunately, I was having serious difficulties getting a flight from New Zealand across the water to Chile. This was always going to be the most expensive and longest trip I would need to take and waiting until I was in Auckland could make things problematic! My best chance was to try and book tickets ahead from Australia to New Zealand and then on to Chile. I visited the 'Flight Centre' and established that the long haul flight to Santiago only ran three times a week - and they told me that they were all fully booked with no flight available until March. Oh no, I thought!

However, with determination and persuasion, luck and 'looks' I had seats booked on the flights I really needed! So, now I could enjoy the rest of my time in Geelong and what better way to start; a kangaroo dish washed down with a 'flat white'. Mmmm! Not really! It was a very dark meat and quite rich in taste - maybe I should have tried koala, emu, wombat or even dingo instead!

In the evening it was time to sample Aussie beer in a local pub; here I was surprised to see a couple of guys all dressed in white! Well, not completely surprised as I guessed they had been playing cricket - but I went over to chat with them and they were true Aussie locals! We all had such a laugh and when I told them I had met Greg Chappell - they were so pleased for me! They knew everything about cricket - every Aussie seems to love cricket and tennis! (What about Leeds United?)

I was really enjoying Australia; the people were very friendly and seemed to like us 'pommies' so much - they had to be careful I guess, so many had relatives all over the UK!

Australia was a very relaxed environment, and everybody seemed to have 'No Worries' - so why should I?

This was the first time I really felt like I was back in England - it was just a real 'lounging' Sunday and I did very little! All my washing and ironing was done (thanks Angie!) and we had been invited to some friends for a barbecue in the evening.

The day went very quickly; in fact the whole weekend went so quickly and before I knew it, I was packing and preparing to leave very early in the morning for Sydney.

I took the early morning bus from Geelong to the airport in Melbourne. I was feeling a little sad as I had said goodbye to Mark - I had enjoyed a relaxing weekend with no rush to do anything and no filming! I enjoy filming but sometimes it was so good to just leave the camera behind and enjoy things without worrying that I needed to capture them on film!

I was taking the flight to Sydney because the roads and railway lines east of Melbourne were affected by the bush fires. I had wanted to go to Canberra, but again this was awkward because of the bush fires; travelling around these states at the moment was going to be more convenient by air and amazingly, so much cheaper!

The budget airline 'Virgin Blue', owned by Richard Branson, is a huge success in Australia. Fast, no-ticket flights booked on the Internet take thousands of people from all the major cities to and from work every day. I have never seen anything like it; simple, modern and so convenient and before I knew it, I was in Sydney.

Well, what can I say - I was now in Australia's largest city, but for only 24 hours and so off I went exploring!

The CBD (Central Business District) of Sydney has some of the most impressive natural and architectural features that I had seen anywhere in the world (so far!) and the pedestrian precincts are a hub of activity - buskers, people, shops and more shops! I walked through the town towards the harbour and whilst I enjoyed the atmosphere, I was feeling a little tearful. It struck me that I was now so

Day 155:
Still in Geelong, Australia

Day 156:
Sydney, Australia

Sydney: one of the world's most recognisable cityscapes.

far away from home, in such a magnificent city and on my way to see the most famous landmarks of Australia - and I was on my own! I really wanted to be sharing this experience with other people but I had nobody with me; as the tears ran down my face I knew that I just had to keep going!

My first stop was to Macquaries Street; I had been informed that a row of houses built on this street was named 'Horbury Terrace' after a William Holt from Horbury (a suburb of my birthplace in the UK) who emigrated to Australia in 1878. Sure enough, I found the heritage plaque fixed to the wall of a row of terrace buildings and felt proud to be from Horbury!

I then continued my walk through the Royal Botanic Gardens and on to Mrs. Macquarie's Point where I saw the magnificent harbour showcasing the twin icons of the Sydney Harbour Bridge and the Opera House. It was spectacular, absolutely amazing and I just stood and gazed for ages at a view I would normally only ever see on the television!

Sydney sights: the bridge, the Opera House; what a view. I'll be back...

I set my camera up to get the perfect pose, with me (of course!) and those two great structures. I then asked a passer-by whose name was Chloe to assist me with the 'photo shoot'! At last, I was here in Sydney and I now had the evidence to prove it!

Walking back through the gardens I saw this great big tree - well it was big and old! I can't remember the name of the tree but it had a story! In earlier times people believed that certain trees contained spirits and that you could make a wish by touching the trees or walking around them three times forward and then three times backwards. This is how the idea of 'wishing trees' and the saying 'touch wood' originated. I walked round the tree three times forward and three times backward, made my wish and then just touched my head!

I loved Sydney, it was a shame that I was here for only 24 hours but I knew I would come back!

Day 157: Brisbane, Australia

After a good 'Aussie' breakfast (which incidentally was bacon and eggs!) I was on my way to the airport yet again. This time, and because it was far cheaper than using the train, I was flying to my final destination in Australia - Brisbane.

I had awoken this morning feeling really tired and had a horribly stuffy nose! Although the flight was good - Virgin Blue had impressed me yet again - when we came in to land my ears were so painful with the change in altitude and wouldn't pop! I was coming down with a cold and as a result flying could be so uncomfortable - I was feeling ill!

I travelled into the city and collected the tickets that would take me to Auckland on Sunday and then went to find an hotel. It was late and although I had people to contact - I was feeling desperate just to lie down!

Having found a great hotel, cheap and very clean - I went to bed and slept!

Day 158: Still in Brisbane, Australia

I felt so bad today, in fact I felt like shit (sorry!) I did not know what to do - what do you do? I just wanted to be at home - this was only the third time I had really been ill in over five months of travelling, but I was on my own and didn't know what to do!

I fell back to sleep and awoke at around 2pm. My nose was running like Victoria Falls (not sure why I'm plugging Zimbabwe!) and I was coughing like a heavy smoker on his deathbed! Yeah! I was really feeling sorry for myself and did not feel like doing anything! However, feeling the need to be up and doing something, I forced myself to get up and go for some food and drink.

I walked out of my hotel into the downtown hub of Brisbane and the core of all things happening, vibrant and savvy! The Queen Street Mall was amazing, although it was an open precinct, it was filled with dozens of canopies giving shade from the sun - and music was playing from outdoor speakers all over the place. It was a fantastic atmosphere of recreation, retail, dining, culture and

entertainment. I was starting to feel a little better and after eating in one of the many food courts, I decided that rather than going straight back to bed, I would go and see a movie! Yep! My first visit to the cinema since leaving home and better than sitting in my room for the afternoon. I sat in the movie theatre for nearly three hours and enjoyed the sequel to 'Lord of the Rings'.

Having gone through a box of tissues (for the runny nose!) I was back in my hotel and in bed!

Day 159: Laidley, Australia

Still not feeling great but I needed to get on - I met Len (the guy I'd first met in Darwin two weeks earlier) and he invited me to stay with his family in Laidley, an hour out of the city.

Len was so good to me; first we toured Brisbane by car - just to get a feel of the place. The city was established as a penal settlement in 1823, but by 1839 it had grown rapidly as an industrial centre and is the home of the famous XXXX beer! All the streets were named after boys and girls and designed on a grid system. It was really quite fascinating - if you drive along George Street from the south of the city to the north, all the side streets are named after girls (Alice Street, Charlotte Street, Mary Street etc). I thought it was so funny but we never found Peter Street - it was a dead end!

After visiting the notorious 'Valley' area we went down to South Bank. Just minutes from the CBD and there you were on the beach with sand, swimming pools and ice cream! This was unique and was what made Brisbane such a 'cool' city for me! We then drove up and out of the city to Mt Coot-tha (Aboriginal name) and here I got a superb view of the whole of Brisbane and the Brisbane River that meanders for miles with such distinct bends to its estuary.

Arriving at Len's home, I was shattered but kept going. I had been invited to meet with Di and Ces who lived in this small 'gathering of houses' in the middle of the 'bush'! Di was the Principal of the school that I was visiting the following day and it was great to meet with her and Ces (her husband) and we had a great chat.

I was certainly ready for my bed again and as my head hit my pillow - I was out!

Day 160: Back in Brisbane, Australia

I had now been travelling for 23 weeks and had been very lucky to visit many community projects, missionary projects and schools. Australia has some very small schools in remote areas of the country. Isolated by distance, few and poor roads and a lack of transportation - many early settlers established local schools and the fight to keep them open is a constant battle.

However, community spirit and determination has kept Ropeley State School running since 1890 and with an average of only ten pupils at any one time, I wanted to experience the life of such a small school.

The school was situated about 85kms south west of Brisbane in a rural area called the Lockyer Valley. It was a predominantly farming community with a large selection of fruit and vegetables being grown in the area.

They were suffering badly from the effects of the drought and the land was very dry.

The school relied on tank water for personal use and very salty bore water for the gardens. The following is an extract from the 'guestbook' of the website and sums up the day!

"I would like to thank you for a wonderful day we had at Ropeley last Friday(7th). The students were enthralled with your stories and you have inspired us all with your enthusiasm for what you are achieving. The morning tea, bbq lunch, the students singing Waltzing Matilda, staff, parents, past pupils and the media was something we will never forget. I get paid to work here - that's a bonus"

I had a fantastic time meeting and talking with the pupils (nine children aged 5-11yrs) and sharing my experiences with them and learning about life here in a small part of Australia. They grilled me with questions, and this reminded me that what I was doing was a dream come true with memories that will be with me forever! Thank you, Ropeley kids!

Day 161: Brisbane, Australia

Yesterday evening, I came back to Brisbane and was greeted by my second cousin Margaret and her family. I was only ten years old last time she saw me but obviously I was still recognisable (even with the blond hair!).

Today I was going to visit my great uncle Maurice aged 85 and his wife Val who is 80! This was a great day for me, meeting up with my Mum's oldest living relative and the last of that generation. We talked and talked all day and looked at photographs, giving Maurice and Val the opportunity to reminisce. Since my family is so large, I was amazed at how many people they remembered! He

Fabulous family: great uncle Maurice and great aunt Val, a wonderful couple and so kind to me.

reminded me so much of my late Grandma (after all, he is her sister) and still has the British military clipped accent, although it was some 50 years ago since he had emigrated.

In the evening we went out for a meal and shared many stories; I met both my second cousins and their families and it felt so special to be talking about my family. This was a short visit, I knew that, and I wanted to spend more time with members of my family so far from home. We were all very tired and it was time to rest - it was time to say goodbye to my great uncle and aunt and I could see the tears building up as the old man gave me one last hug! I was feeling very lost, I missed my family so much and having spent all day talking about them - I was filling up with tears also.

Day 162: Auckland, New Zealand

After a long wait at the airport check-in, I was finally on my way out of Australia. Two weeks had seen me visit five of the seven main cities of this vast country. The Aussies were such friendly people and having not been in an English speaking country for a long period since leaving home, it had been good for me. Well, I did struggle with some of their crazy words and in particular the phrase 'no worries'! They seemed to use it for everything and it just kept making me think if I actually did have any worries!

One thing I had noticed over the last few weeks was the build-up to the 'War on Terrorism' and the 'War on Iraq'. People were talking about it everywhere and because I was travelling I got to hear lots of people giving their thoughts and feelings on the situation.

We flew on a 747 aeroplane with almost 400 people on board across the Tasman Sea into my 31st country, and I was now 13 hours ahead of GMT - the furthest time zone away from home! Arriving at the airport, I missed the domestic flight to Whakatane (the 'wh' is pronounced 'f' which highly amused me every time I tried to say it!) and so I booked into a small motel nearby. The owners were

fascinated by my journey so far (I was telling everyone!) and invited me to eat with them that evening. They were very generous to me and I had a lovely room which incidentally they charged only NZ$10 for instead of the usual rate of NZ$90.

New Zealand is known as 'Aoteoroa' by the Maori people which means the 'land of the long white cloud'; I was still full of cold and when my head hit the pillow, I was immediately 'in the clouds' fast asleep!

Day 163: Kawerau, New Zealand

It would take four hours to drive from Auckland to Whackatane but only one hour by plane and also far cheaper! The flight was in a propeller driven Beech 1900D, which was a very small aircraft with only nineteen passenger seats. The view was spectacular as we descended into the Bay of Plenty on the east coast of the North Island. The forested hills and fertile soils passed by my window on the approach close to the washed golden beaches and sparkling sea! Wow! My thoughts turned to a virgin landscape that was awe-inspiring!

The runway was in a field and the terminal was smaller than my house! In the terminal Malcolm was waiting to meet me and take me to his home just 20kms away. He is a retired neurosurgeon and having worked for twenty years in Wakefield, England, he had come back to his homeland New Zealand and to the town of Kawerau in the Bay of Plenty.

It was great to meet him again and I knew that I could relax and prepare myself for the final stage of my journey - the Americas.

The cold I had picked up in Australia had now gone to my chest - my throat was very sore and it was now time to take antibiotics. Since there was now a 'doctor' in the house, I could be 'looked after', rest and get well!

Day 164: Kawerau, New Zealand

The oldest and most famous sailing race in the world hit the waters this week - the America's Cup yacht race was at the weekend and the fever of it was gripping New Zealand; although I would have left by then and thankfully wouldn't be caught up with the thousands of spectators beginning to arrive on this small island!

After a good sleep, I had the chance to experience a natural geo-thermal spring near to the town. It was in a very isolated and non-tourist area and with Malcolm and his brother, we were the only ones around. It was unbelievable!

After filming the great clouds of steam coming out of the ground (something to do with natural gases escaping from the Earth and mixing with the atmosphere to become steam!), I was in my swimming shorts and slowly I lowered myself into this great pool of hot water. It was hotter than a bath, but although it was a 'medicinal' hot pool you had to be very careful not to drink the water and in fact I would not put my head under! It was an absolutely amazing sensation; I had always wanted to experience the natural hot springs in New Zealand and this was brilliant!

I felt so refreshed when I got out although my skin felt like it had been covered with a thin soapy solution. I was immediately attacked by 'sand-flies' and got dressed quickly! I felt exhilarated and a jug o'ale was the order of the day! We visited the 'Corner Bar' and I had a chance to meet some of the locals; the community was made up of a 50/50 split between Pakeha (white) and Maori. There was still some on-going friction but I did not feel this in the bar.

Later I returned to the town and picked up some fish and chips from the local shop - I was beginning to feel at home!

Natural luxury: you just can't believe how good it feels to relax in this hot spring water.

Day 165: Still in Kawerau, New Zealand

I had stopped up late to watch the World Cup cricket on TV, so I did not surface today until lunchtime! I had an appointment with the local hairdresser called Lynne who did a great job making me look blond again!

An interview with the local press had been arranged at 4pm, after which I just relaxed! I was beginning to feel better but my cold was still with me! So, after some time on the computer reading my mail and the 'guestbook', I had an early night!

I found this little verse in a book written in 'Te Reo Maori':

"Ki mai koe ki a au,
he aha te mea nui tenei ao:
He tangata, he tangata, he tangata."
which means:

"If you should ask me what is
the greatest thing in the world,
the answer would be:
It is people, it is people, it is people."

Day 166: Still in Kawerau, New Zealand

I did nothing today; I really had so much to prepare for my next continent and wanted to re-pack my rucksack and collect my thoughts!

I also needed to work on my journal, eat plenty of food, watch a little television (and the build-up to the war), charge my camera and mobile phone, shave and get some rest!

Tomorrow would be the longest day of my journey around the world, as I would be flying from Auckland for twelve hours to Santiago in Chile. Less than two hours into the flight I would cross over the International Dateline and put my clock 13 hours back; when I arrived in Chile, I would have to then put my clock a further four hours back. This would mean that I would be in the air for half the day and when I landed, the time would still be earlier than it was before I took off!

Day 167: The journey from Auckland to Santiago, Chile

I said farewell to Malcolm at Whackatane Airport (the runway in a field!) and took the short flight back to Auckland. I now had six hours before my flight to Santiago and so I took the bus into the centre of Auckland for a look around! I had met a guy called Dan in the airport; he was a Kiwi fisherman going to meet his friend for the weekend in the city. He joined me on the bus and showed me some of the sights of New Zealand's largest city. I have been so lucky - I seemed to meet with somebody everywhere who was prepared to give a little of their time to show me around! We had lunch down at the famous Harbour where the Americas Cup races would begin tomorrow - it was busy and full of wealthy high-class looking folk!

I did not like Auckland too much, sorry! Even the airport was not very 'user friendly' and when I returned there I had some real problems! Basically, they would not let me board the plane to Santiago because I had *no onward ticket*! I explained that the whole purpose of my journey around the world was to travel from country to country with no advance tickets or visas. I was (in case you've forgotten!) trying to see how much of the world was one community by challenging the system of access! When I asked at the check-in to speak to a senior officer, I was able to explain and give evidence of my journey since September 1st, 2002. He was very impressed and after about an hour of discussion and telephone calls, he wished me good luck for the rest of my journey and handed me my boarding card!

In the air again: leaving New Zealand

I then had to go to another counter to pay my departure tax, then on to immigration! They were so slow at the airport and I was just standing in queue after queue whilst my name was being called out as the 'final' passenger required to board! The whole thing was a nightmare and I was bloody annoyed!

Finally, we left New Zealand in the glare of the late afternoon sun cruising at 595mph, 36,000 feet in the sky with an outside temperature of -67°F. At last I could relax!

For the next 12 hours, I was sitting next to a German guy who spoke no English, but we managed to communicate and had quite a laugh! He was on his way to the Antarctic but I'd no idea why! It was just so funny as we both had our meal and kept ordering wine (a lovely Chilean red. Mmmm!) - I was beginning to get drunk and he just kept ordering more! Eventually I fell asleep! Such great 'in-flight' entertainment!

When I awoke, some eight hours later, we had passed over the International Dateline and it was now Friday morning all over again! How strange, I had left New Zealand on Friday afternoon and we had been in the air almost 12 hours and yet it was still only Friday morning! Not only was this the longest day of my life, but it was also St Valentine's Day! Would Jayne have managed a 41-hour St Valentine's Day with me?

On our approach into Santiago - still high above the clouds, you could see the peaks of the Andes range and it was very exciting! As we circled over Santiago I was amazed at its size. With a population of around four million - it would be one of the smallest cities I had visited.

I had no problems at all on arrival, I was issued with a visa and it was free! American, Australian and other citizens had to apply and pay for a visa but British citizens were exempt! This was due to the fact that Chilean travellers had to pay in their countries and so it was basically tit-for-tat!

I had no problems at the tourist office and was given a free taxi downtown and on to a lovely hotel in 'Providencia' - a safe part of the city! It seems that in the evening some parts of Santiago could be a little bit risky and so until I had got an idea of where I was, I wanted to be safe!

It was still early evening and after a little walk I went to bed, I was very tired and feeling very disorientated!

I had a terrible night! I just could not sleep! I was totally exhausted but unable to actually fall sleep! I was hungry and was the first one down for breakfast at 6.30am, hoping that afterwards I could go back to bed and sleep!

The day went from bad to worse; fatigue, insomnia, anxiety, loss of appetite and totally impaired concentration were, between them, making me feel really bad! My throat was still very sore (and I had finished the antibiotics!) and my nose still blocked! I was an absolute wreck! I knew that lack of sleep was the main problem, but I could not believe that the jetlag could affect me so much!

I had another walk around the area where I was staying and visited a small supermarket. I began talking with the owner who was called Mario and who was very helpful, giving me ideas of places to visit and useful information on land travel to Buenos Aires. Eventually he actually mentioned that he was from Argentina and had worked in Australia (that's why he spoke English!) for a while before coming to live in Santiago. What was funny for me was the fact that I had been having such a great time talking with this guy and it didn't matter that he was Argentinean! I went to bed very early again but at 10pm I awoke feeling very hungry and ordered a pizza from a local shop. Unfortunately, I was unable to eat it when it arrived and was becoming very frustrated with myself!

Today, I met with Fr Andres Morales who had been following my journey since I left England. He took me to the Don Bosco House in Republica where I would be staying for a few days. It was the summer holidays at that time and all the schools including the huge Don Bosco College were closed. In fact, the city was very quiet, as many Chileans had taken off to the coast for their holiday breaks!

Chile is a very Catholic country and there are churches everywhere! A strange contrast for me having spent so much time travelling through India and Asia where

Day 168: Santiago, Chile

Question of style: old rubs shoulders with new in Santiago.

Day 169: Still in Santiago

temples and mosques are everywhere! I visited one of six Don Bosco parish churches in the city and I realised that the work of Don Bosco here in Santiago was huge!

I had the opportunity to meet with so many people today - it was great! Most people prefer to forget the 'golpe de estado' (coup d'etat), the 16 years of General Pinochet´s dictatorship when some 4,000 people (including foreigners!) 'disappeared'! The people of Santiago were among the friendliest people I had met around the world - they are not 'hot peppers'! (the name Chile comes from an indigenous word meaning 'place where the land ends').

Not surprisingly - as the Andean Peaks shadowed over this clean and vibrant city, it was an awesome sight! Every time you looked to the west you saw those huge mountains climbing high up into the sky and to the east was the Pacific Ocean and hundreds of miles of coastline.

Day 170: Still in Santiago

Responding to an email from a student in Santiago who offered to show me around the city, I met with Maria at the Metro subway. The underground rail network here in Santiago is the best I've seen; clean, efficient, uncrowded, simple, safe (security guards at every station), cheap and beautifully decorated with locally-painted murals on many of the walls.

In another example of the luck I seem to have, Maria was prepared to spend the whole day with me and show me as much as possible of the landmarks of Santiago. We began at the Plaza de Armas and home to the Cathedral; European history dominated much of Santiago and you could easily mistake parts of the city for Italy!

People were constantly coming into the church to pray and light candles. It is estimated that 98% of the population were Catholic and when we then visited the Templo de San Agustin there was a constant rush of people praying at the altar of Saint Rita (the advocate for the impossible!). This church was built during Colonial times and during an earthquake many years ago, the crown of thorns was brought down around the neck of Christ and legend says that when people tried to dislodge it, the statue's face bled!

The ´Mercado Central´, one of the main markets was in fact built in England in 1872 before being assembled here in Santiago and it actually reminded me of the market building in Halifax (England) although everybody spoke only Spanish!

Shadowing over the city is Cerro San Cristobal - a huge mountain with a gigantic figure of the Virgin Mary at the top, which is illuminated at night and looks spectacular! We took the cable car up to the top, some 860 metres above sea level and here I got a view of almost the whole city. This was certainly the best way to see Santiago!

I thought Santiago was great, I never knew what to expect but having visited so many capital cities, this had to be the best!

Model citizen: street theatre in Santiago.

Day 171:
Still in Santiago

Today went very quickly. I went to get a ticket for the bus journey to Mendoza - this is on the other side of the Andes and one of the first main cities of Argentina. It was in the direction of Buenos Aires, but since the journey time to get there is around twenty hours, I decided to have a stopover!

After time on the Internet, I was invited to join Fr Andres and the community for an evening meal. Speaking no Spanish could be difficult around the table but Fr Andres was a great translator and I was able to do my usual after-dinner speech!

I was still not feeling great and the journey was becoming very hard for me; I had become very lonely although I was with people. New Zealand had given me a chance to rest but since I arrived in South America I just couldn't seem to feel as motivated! It was tough, and maybe I could never have prepared for being away from home for so long, as well as constantly being on the move! Every night I looked at my maps and thought about my route; I

calculated my budget and stared at the same things in my rucksack that I had been carrying for almost six months!

It was time to pack my belongings and prepare to leave one of the longest and narrowest countries on the planet, where I had met with the friendliest of people in one of the world's southernmost places. It's another world!

Day 172: Mendoza, Argentina

Another goodbye and I was on the bus to Mendoza. As we left Santiago I felt a little sad but also very excited at the prospect of travelling over the Andes!

It wasn't long before we were surrounded by the fertile wine-producing valleys that made Chilean wine famous! It seemed like hundreds of miles of vineyards and then they disappeared and the view changed.

The nature of the land became dry and arid; we were now slowly climbing up into the Andes mountains and the view was mind-blowing! We had now been travelling for nearly three hours and there was nothing in sight but rock, mountains, barren land and the odd cactus! They were unusual, as they stood high from the ground isolated by the dry and rough terrain. Looking high above through the window I could see the snow nestling on the peaks, particularly where they were hidden from the sun.

Long and winding road: twists and turns took us up the mountainside.

As the bus began the main climb to the top, we would drive up the steep road for about 500 metres at which point a sharp bend would turn us in almost the opposite direction and we would drive another 500 metres. This went on for what seemed like ages and with each sharp turn we climbed further and further towards the top. It was absolutely amazing, bend after bend and as we got higher I could see below the path of the road running criss-cross along the edge of the mountain. A sign at each bend counted the number we had negotiated and as we reached the top I read the sign '26'!

Wow! What can I say, I had never experienced anything like this before - we were now at the top of the road that led to Argentina! The view below was awesome and the view ahead was of dozens of snow-capped peaks that looked almost edible!!!

It had been a very slow journey covering only a short distance as we finally reached the border control buildings. It was like driving into a huge hangar in the middle of nowhere and as we got out of the bus it was bitterly cold. All the passengers were Chilean or Argentinean except me! "Welcome to Argentina" the police officer remarked and stamped my passport without even a question!

As we drove out of the hangar there was nothing around us for miles, just mountains and snow and one solitary road to take us on our descent into my 33rd country - Argentina.

Almost four hours later we arrived in Mendoza - predominantly a tourist city for Chileans who came here because Argentina was now so cheap! One year ago it was almost one US Dollar to the Argentine Dollar (pesos), and now you got three pesos!

At the bus terminal I was lost. Staff at the Tourist Information Centre were unhelpful and apparently all the hotels were full! I was exhausted and did not want to take the bus immediately on to Buenos Aires, as this would take a further 12 hours!

A taxi driver approached me who said his name was Louis and he spoke English - he knew I was lost! He offered to telephone a number of hotels and check on a room for me - he was great!

He found me a hotel (only 30 pesos!) and also helped me to book my ticket for the overnight bus to Buenos Aires the following day. He took me to the hotel (2 pesos!) and pointed out a good restaurant at which to eat. Again, I had found a friendly person to help me! Every time I arrived in a new place it was daunting - you would think I would have got used to it , but you really needed people like Louis sometimes "Gracias Louis!"

Food and bed!

The road just seemed to go on for ever - but as the crow flies, the top wasn't far from the bottom.. and this was Argentina (below)!

Day 173: The journey from Mendoza to Buenos Aires, Argentina

I had only the one day to explore Mendoza and I was amazed at how busy this town/city was! In fact, it was the busiest place I'd been to since Asia and yet it was not a capital city! Lots of Chileans were just coming over the border for a holiday!

I had real difficulty finding somewhere to eat; fast food takeaways were everywhere but I wanted some healthier food! I enjoyed a stroll around the 'central mall' and had coffee near to a pavilion where local singers and dancers were entertaining the folk gathered nearby; my first experience of the local tango and it was fun!

The Tango was born in Argentina in the late 1800's as a cultural expression. It is not known if this 'emotion to dance' was an original creation and there are various theories but it is known that it is a combination of native urban music and immigrant traditions. I was invited to join this 'dance in the mall' but unfortunately I had a bus to catch!

I had no idea what to expect on the bus to Buenos Aires and when I saw the bus I was amazed! It was the size of a double-decker but the lower deck was fitted with only nine huge seats that each reclined to the size of a bed! I thought that must be First Class and I had no idea that Louis (who helped me to purchase the ticket) had booked me on seat number nine!

The cost of the ticket was only US$9 for the 14-hour journey and I had expected a normal coach! It was great - hot food was served, drinks and even a game of bingo! I couldn't stop laughing; I had to quickly learn some numbers in Spanish - but I didn't win! I met Alberto who was a print machine engineer who had been working in England for a year. He spoke very good English and assisted in translating so that I could speak with all the passengers sharing the lower deck! Then a movie was shown and I pressed the buttons at the side of my seat and I was horizontal!

The road to Buenos Aires was flat all the way and dead straight - I had a good sleep and when I awoke, we were in Buenos Aires. Alberto helped me to find a hotel, as the tourist centre was unhelpful yet again!

The high rate of the US dollar had turned Argentina into an excellent tourist destination and I was staying in a four-star hotel right on Av 9 de Julio; the road is the largest 'avenue' in the world with 22 lanes; but is not a highway - halfway along is the 'Obelisco' and all the way are shops and hotels on either side! To cross is a nightmare, no subway, just traffic lights and fast walking!

My first impressions of the city were of very friendly people who just wanted to help you when they saw you studying maps at the road junctions! It seemed that Buenos Aires had lots to explore and after a good rest that was exactly what I was going to do!

Day 174: Buenos Aires, Argentina

Here I am in Buenos Aires! I spent the day wandering around and admiring some fascinating European-style buildings! As I turned down the main street towards the Government buildings, I stumbled across a huge crowd; thousands of 'Argies' were demonstrating about something and the Police were equipped for what looked like a potential riot! I did a little filming (I stood with a number of camera crew from TV companies who were obviously covering the event) and then began to ask a few passers-by what the demonstration was about. I could not make out what they were saying and decided that things were beginning to get a little 'hot' and that I ought to leave!

I found a restaurant that had been recommended and when I went inside, the place was empty! It was open but apparently the locals did not eat until after 9pm. However, I was starving and could not wait another two hours! I enjoyed the best 'bife de chorizo' ever - I have never, ever had such a wonderful steak! It was massive, tender and bloody tasty!

What made me laugh was that since I did not speak Spanish, the waiter had brought me the English menu but

when I gave him my order - he did not understand English! We just kept laughing for ages as his colleagues joined in and I attempted to explain what I wanted to eat and drink!

It was a first class meal in a first class restaurant with such great staff; and as I was leaving, the place was filling up rapidly and I knew I had come to the best place in town and I had paid less than US$6 for the privilege!

Buenos Aires was huge: the Avenue 9th July had 22 lanes!

I wished I spoke Spanish and yet I couldn't speak any other language and so my experience of the language barrier was the same as in any other non-english speaking country! "**Buenos Noches**".

Day 175: Still in Buenos Aires, Argentina

Think I already mentioned it, but my hotel was fantastic and I was beginning to feel so much better. I still could not believe I was actually in South America - so far away from home and such a different part of the world! I couldn't explain why, but it was such a great place! I think that the people were just so friendly! Anyway, enough of that...

I spent the whole day exploring the town. I was unable to plan my journey ahead because all the travel centres were closed at the weekend, so I made the most of seeing the sights of Buenos Aires and visited the Catedral Metropolitana, the Casa de Gobierno and the Estacion Retiro - or the 'Railway Station'. This was another building in South America that was similar to the architecture of 'British Colonial' style! In fact, it was surprising how much of the city was 'European' but with far friendlier and helpful people.

The one thing that did surprise me was the number of Police Officers everywhere! It made me feel safe as I wandered around on my own and must have made such a difference to the crime on the streets. I spoke at the hotel about this and I was reminded that Argentina has gone through turmoil in the last year and with the country nearly bankrupt, many people had recently lost their jobs and were desperate! Street crime had grown rapidly in the preceding months and with regular demonstrations turning to riots - the government needed to make the city safe for all its people!

I enjoyed another fantastic 'bife de chorizo' but it was no fun eating on your own - I really did feel pretty lonely and what made it all the more difficult was the language barrier!

Day 176: Still in Buenos Aires, Argentina

After a bacon and egg breakfast I went back to bed and watched CNN and BBC World! It was interesting to keep up with 'world affairs' and with the threat of war and many terrorist incidents around the globe, I needed to be as up to date as possible! Venezuela was still not safe, Columbia had never been safe and I suppose that with the language barrier I must be sensible about where I should actually go!

Most of the movie channels played films in English with subtitles and so I kept flicking through the 65 channels to see what to watch! Unfortunately the TV guide was in Spanish so it was difficult to know what I was watching, or even find a movie that was just beginning!

A real lazy day and an early night!

Day 177: Still in Buenos Aires, Argentina

I left the hotel first thing to find a 'Travel Centre' - it was amazing, I really struggled to find one! Eventually I came across a small shop advertising flights and they were very helpful. It soon became apparent that I would have difficulty just flying into Brazil without an onward ticket! Yes, the same old problem! I found the office of Aerlinius Argentina but they would not sell me a one-way ticket anywhere!

I had spent the whole day trying to buy a ticket out of Argentina and was having an absolute nightmare! I found the office of Varig (a consortium of small airlines including Pluna - the Brazilian Airline) and explained the situation to the staff. They were great - we planned a route from Buenos Aires to Montevideo (Uruguay), then on to Rio de Janeiro (Brazil) and finally to La Paz (Bolivia). The price was good and I went ahead! It was suggested that I travel by bus from La Paz into Peru via the Inca settlements!

So, at last I had a plan for a while! Visas were not the problem for British citizens visiting South America - it's just that Immigration Officers wanted to see onward tickets and I wanted to get round the world country by country without them!

A whole day of trying to buy my ticket and I was shattered! Tomorrow I would take the flight to Montevideo - not far from Buenos Aires, but it was simpler than taking the boat!

Day 178: Montevideo, Uruguay

Taking the flight to Montevideo was probably crazy, but certainly convenient! We were in the air less than thirty minutes and I spent longer waiting to check in! I was given a very warm reception at the tourist office and then took the local bus into the city. It was fun; people kept suggesting I take the taxi, but I felt that I had hardly travelled from Buenos Aires so I should at least take a bus and make the journey to my hotel a little more of an adventure!

Montevideo was founded in 1726 when settlers arrived from Argentina and the Canary Islands. Its streets are 'blocks' set out in a simple Northeast - Southwest orientation and at right angles - who could ever get lost!

My hotel accommodation was arranged by the staff in Buenos Aires with a good discount and so I was treated to another four star room overlooking the Cagancha Square - where the old and the new cities meet.

Uruguay is recognised as being one of the safest countries in the world and so I was tempted to have a walk around Montevideo and find somewhere to eat - although it was now dark. I was recommended the Las Brasas restaurant and when I found it, I was keen to have some 'bife'! The kitchen was open-plan and consisted mainly of a huge wood-fired grill where various meats were sizzling away!

Now, I have visited 34 countries and tried most traditional foods in each one; I am not into 'gastronomy' but I had the best meal ever tonight! It was the most tender, mouth-watering, tasty 'bife de chorizo' I had ever tasted and served with a great portion of fries and salad. It was the best! I needed to walk around the city afterwards because I was so full and would not be able to sleep!

I took the bus out of the city to the Don Bosco school today. Unfortunately, just like the rest of South America, everybody was on their summer holidays and the schools would not reopen until the middle of March! I was invited for lunch at the Provincial House and we discussed (in broken English!) my arrival in Rio de Janeiro and the problems I was going to have! All the Don Bosco projects were closed in the city of Rio over the Carnival weekend! Can you believe it; I left England six months ago with no pre-booked tickets and would arrive in Brazil (and Rio!) on the busiest weekend of the year when the largest Carnival in the world would be taking place!

The only places open in Rio would be shops, restaurants

Day 179: Still in Montevideo, Uruguay

and hotels! The problem was that I couldn't even find a hotel with rooms available! At the travel agents in Montevideo they were unable to find a single hotel with availability and I was beginning to get a little worried!

The bus back into the city took me past the Centennial Stadium, where the first football World Cup took place in 1930! This is the Uruguayans' national pride!

The city was a combination of so much; immigrants have produced a culture with so many customs and with indigenous remains, colonial buildings and traces of the 'gaucho' life - Montevideo has so much to offer but it can be seen in a day!

Enough sightseeing - I was going back for another meal at Las Brasas!

On my return to the hotel (full!) I chatted with Francisco who worked there; he had always wanted to travel and was fascinated by my trip! He spoke very good English and it was nice just to have this conversation with him. Travelling through South America was exciting, but I had so few contacts here that I was meeting far fewer people - especially people who actually spoke English!

I admit that I was beginning to get very tired of it all; how much could you actually take in? How much travelling could you physically do before it became exhausting? And how much time could you bear to be away from home?

Day 180: The journey from Montevideo to Rio de Janeiro, Brazil

My flight was in the afternoon, but after breakfast I went to the front door of the hotel and found it was absolutely pouring with rain, so I went back to my room, laid on the bed and fell asleep!

The airport in Montevideo was something else! It was packed with people but there were only three flights due out over the next five hours! I spoke with a man in the queue who told me that about 80% of the people in the airport were friends and relatives coming to say 'goodbye' to folk! Going through the departure gate, I was struck by the sheer number of people saying farewell to someone! Tears and cries in Spanish and you would have thought they were never going to see one another again! Apparently, Uruguayan people get very emotional when a loved one is leaving the country and such scenes of hysteria were not at all uncommon!

Climbing high above the clouds that had been over Montevideo all day, I watched the most spectacular sun setting on this part of the earth; the colours reflecting on the thick white clouds were something else!

Now, trust me to end up in the world's busiest city this weekend! Welcome to Rio de Janeiro and home to over 10 million people - beaches, samba, football, beer, cachaca (sugarcane rum!), beautifully browned and gorgeous women and the Carioca Carnival. Nearly one million additional Brazilians and foreign tourists have come to help the 'Cariocans' celebrate in style in this city named 'River of January'.

Immigration was easy at the airport and after collecting my luggage I went immediately to the 'Touristo Informacia' and asked about a hotel! The lady just laughed and I joined in! We both laughed as she reminded me what was happening this weekend! As if I didn't know!

After numerous telephone calls and an hour of praying (by me!) the lady was smiling and talking so fast that the Spanish sounded more like Japanese! Unbelievably, she had found a hotel for me in Flamengo near to Copacabana and the Centro! These were all just names I had heard in the movies, but now I was actually there! As the taxi took me to downtown Rio, I was so giddy! I could see high above that massive statue of Jesus looking down on the city that you see on any brochures of Rio and I felt really happy!

So, the good news first! My hotel was four star and yet was only costing me an inflated price of US$40; I had been given the only room available and it happened to be the

Everyone was looking forward to the Carnival in Rio, including me. I couldn't believe I'd arrived here by accident for just the right weekend!

executive suite! Oh my God! It had a private jacuzzi and a sauna leading off from the bathroom! It was unbelievable, but there was only one problem - the room was available because it was already reserved from Saturday for five days and therefore (since the Carnival was from Saturday to Tuesday) no-one had taken the room! I could have the room for two nights (Thursday and Friday) but would have to leave on Saturday. My flight to Bolivia was on Sunday... Well, maybe I should worry about that later!

I went for a walk although it was getting late and I was bewildered by what I saw! Homeless people seemed to be sleeping in nearly every shop doorway whilst on almost every street corner, people were drinking beer around temporary bars with plastic chairs! It was another world! I was very nervous, it was a little bit like Mumbai and yet there were loads of people just enjoying themselves whilst homeless poor men, women and children were systematically going through sacks and boxes of garbage! It was disgusting!

Some people were simply begging, but I was keeping my head down; I kept on walking and decided that I'd had enough! Being on your own made it far more difficult to walk the streets of one of the most dangerous cities in the world - especially at night!

Day 181: Still in Rio de Janeiro, Brazil

Walking out of the hotel this morning it seemed a totally different world from the one I saw last night! It was very, very hot and I had lots to do! Standing at the bus stop - I was burning from the morning sun! The heat was intense (36 degrees centigrade) and I tried to stand in the shadow of the lamppost to keep out of the direct sunrays! I must have lost so much weight, I was so thin!

Public transport in Rio was generally reliable although most buses and the metro were not air-conditioned. The bus was like an oven and I was glad to reach Cosme Velho to take the twenty minute train ride to the top of Corcovada; on this 710 metre peak stood a 38-metre statue of Christ the Redeemer looking over the city with his open arms. It was the most powerful icon that I had ever seen! Now, the statue was one thing but the view was then something else - I climbed the last few steps (220 altogether), dripping in sweat and struggling to breathe with the high altitude and heat; I turned round to look over the whole of Rio and it was incredible. The business district toppled over the stunning beaches across the Guanabara Bay. The largest of these was Copacabana and my next stop! I could also see the ´Maracana`- the biggest football stadium in the world with a capacity of 110 thousand spectators! I knew I had to move on, but being here was fantastic!

Using the metro disappointed me. I was confused that such a modern, big city could have such a primitive, slow and infrequent, hot and stuffy underground rail network. I arrived at Copacabana, the most famous and populous part of Rio and went for a walk on the beach. It was over 4kms long, curving sinuously along the road and was just packed with people! Wow, Brazilian women were well known as the prettiest in the world and beside one other - I would have to agree! Elegant, exotic, refined, brown beautiful bodies and they were everywhere! There was an overwhelming mixture of races here in Rio - both men and women were all nicely tanned, just like me! In fact, I really blended in well and most people presumed I was Brazilian!

The beach was bustling with activity. I have never experienced such a busy place of near nakedness! Sunbathing, swimming, surfing, football and partying everywhere! It was just the most amazing place and I wished so much that I hadn't been alone! I paddled in the warm water and chatted to a few 'locals' and then headed on. I was totally stunned by Copacabana; there was a real atmosphere and everyone was just having fun; there seemed to be a complete lack of small groups, or couples just sun-bathing, everybody was just partying together! With a lack of concentration I had to leave; I guess it was the sun!

I arrived in the Centro district downtown and was amazed to see that although it was packed with people, all the shop windows and banks were being boarded up in preparation for the weekend activities! In fact, most people were on their way home from work as the city was about to turn into the world's busiest party!

The sights of
a bustling
city, as seen
on a postcard.

Chapter 7:

March

Foreword

by Peter Brown
host, That Saturday Show, CBC, Canada

I had sat in a dimly-lit radio studio, listening to a voice of loneliness and uncertainty from half a world away. The voice belonged to Peter Hunter, whose mission you know well by now.

Peter had hit a run of bad luck – he'd recently survived a terrifying car crash in the middle of the night in South Africa. As Peter sat recovering in a hotel room in Calcutta, he talked about his fear, his doubts about the trip and the powerful sense of purpose that drove him on. He sounded terribly alone. I remember feeling honored that he spoke so openly and what began as a five-minute radio interview turned into an hour heart to heart.

At the end of many interviews, I often say "take care". It's a casual remark, just a way of saying thanks and goodbye. But I've never meant 'take care' more than I did that day. I promised to buy Peter a pint when he arrived in Canada. It felt important to me to make a gesture of faith in Peter's trip and in the universe in general. It should have been something more impressive than a drink, but that was the deal we'd made. Peter Hunter's part of the bargain was simply to make it to Vancouver, Canada in one piece. To be honest with you, I wasn't sure he'd make it.

And then, suddenly, there he was. Months later, he appeared at the front door of the radio station in Vancouver. Younger than I expected, still bearing some scars from his car accident, but in much better spirits. He showed me his map of the world, a solid black line looping around the globe from England to the west coast of Canada. And with a beer, our promises had been kept.

I really do wish I'd promised something grander than a drink. It seemed such a small thing to honour a great spirit. Such a small way of saying thank you to a man who had showed me (and many others) what you can accomplish when you refuse to give up on yourself or the world.

Day 182: Still in Rio de Janeiro, Brazil

I had to check out of my room this morning and the hotel staff tried desperately to find me a bed for my last night here in Rio, but with no success. So they agreed that I could sleep on the couch in reception, as I would be leaving at 6am for the airport and my flight to Bolivia.

The city of Rio puts on the largest popular festival in the world and it is all part of the Catholic peoples' preparation for Easter.

In fact, South America (predominantly Catholic) recognises the forty-day period before Easter Sunday (Lent) as a time of fasting and so the week leading up to the beginning of this period (Ash Wednesday) was a time of partying!

I went to the downtown area of Rio Branco that was now fully prepared for the next few days as all the shops were shut and boarded up, roads were closed, beer stalls were set up along the streets and 'floats' were lining up everywhere! The Police and Army were on every street corner and the atmosphere was beginning to get really exciting! I met a Japanese guy who showed me where to go to see some of the activities.

Carnival: Rio's streets were packed with noise, colour, and excitement; it was a huge party that seemed to be everywhere.

During the pre-carnival period and the four days of 'merry-making', local cariocas dance through the streets behind carnival bands, clustering into informal groups and by nightfall it was just one big party everywhere! The main area of the Carnival competitions was ticket only, but it seemed that the real party was just everywhere! I had never seen anything like it before and such masses of people made me feel very scared! So many people were drinking and dancing and bumping into me and I had my camera with me!

I took the metro back to Flamengo and could not believe my eyes; there was partying and parades up and down the streets and I was overwhelmed by it all!

Eventually I found a restaurant with a perfect view and enjoyed a meal watching the best party events going on all around me! There was a general explosion of 'Carioca' joy, emotion, colour, sound and lots of fancy costumes. The samba rhythm, drummers, flag carriers and beautiful girls, all just having fun!

Peace, love and tolerance - this was the Carnival's musical message, (I was told!). It had neither frontiers nor nationality and its philosophy extended throughout much of Europe, Africa, China and even Israel! It was very sad that since I left the UK the news had been dominated by preparations for war, terrorist bombings and demonstrations leading to violence, looting and killing all over the world!

Everyone parties!

I didn't get much sleep last night but at least I was in a safe place and at 6am I left the hotel and arrived at the airport. It was very quiet, nobody was travelling anywhere today except me. The flight included two stops before eventually arriving in La Paz, Bolivia and my 36th country.

Day 183: La Paz, Bolivia

I was unprepared for the huge change in temperature; La Paz is nearly 4,000m above sea level and the first thing to hit me was how cold it felt! Since Nepal (three months ago) I had constantly been in temperatures of around 32-36 degrees centigrade and suddenly I was experiencing a mere 11 degrees - I was shivering and desperately needed to find a hotel with heating!

La Paz was amazing! It was actually similar, in its way, to Kathmandu, but with the Amazon rainforest nearby. The city is perched along the Andes with most of its inhabitants living in small red-bricked houses all along the mountainside! The taxi took me down into the city

and to my hotel. I was feeling very strange and lethargic. The high altitude was affecting me almost immediately; the lack of oxygen made me breathless, I was feeling nauseous and had this instant dry irritating cough.

This was a real test of a person's physical strength. The hotel staff advised me that this was common for visitors arriving in La Paz - something to do with the make-up of blood cells and oxygen reaching the brain! I decided to stay inside and rest.

Day 184: La Paz, Bolivia

I had the most awful hangover this morning and yet I had drunk nothing last night! I felt terrible, headachy and dizzy! This is what they called 'altitude sickness'. I knew I needed to go outside and after breakfast I attempted to wrap up warm with what few clothes I had and went for a walk.

As I walked up the main street I saw a huge statue and thought to myself that it looked familiar. As I got closer I realised it was a statue of Don Bosco. I had no idea that the Salesians were working in Bolivia and yet right in the heart of the capital was the huge Don Bosco University! Unfortunately it was closed for the summer break, but it cheered me up! How could this be summer though? It was cold, damp and raining and I was so frozen and out of breath walking around the city that by early afternoon I was back in bed!

High living: that's Cecilio Guzman de Rojas looking back at you from a Bolivian banknote. He was probably used to breathing air with very little oxygen in it, but it made me ill.

People here were preparing for their 'carnival' and by late afternoon I could hear the drums as the parades began. I have never experienced such severe altitude sickness and knew I had to find something to eat. I walked back into the centre and saw Ivan (whom I had met earlier in the travel agents) and I asked him where I might go for some good food! He spoke good English and offered to show me a restaurant along the road. We passed the statue of Don Bosco again and I commented on knowing who it was! He was really excited and told me that he was very much involved in the work of Don Bosco in his church. He ended up joining me for a meal and we talked for ages about my trip and experiences of the work of Don Bosco around the world. I felt better after eating, but walking back to my hotel I was clearly out of breath and felt as if I was floating! Lying on my bed, I knew I needed to move on and so I began planning a route that would take me by bus to Lake Titicaca and across the border into Peru. I would have to stay overnight in Puno and take another bus to Cusco (near to Machu Pichu) and the ancient Inca region. Another bus would then take me to Lima a day or two later, where it would be back to a warmer climate!

A local in La Paz.

Well, I was still suffering today and feeling cold and frustrated. I just felt totally knackered and couldn't seem to get motivated. I chatted with Emilio at breakfast. He was a doctor from Spain who was working for an NGO in northern Bolivia. He had come to La Paz on business, but was also taking a few days break. We had a great chat and he gave me advice on my altitude problems.

Most of the shops were closed today as Shrove Tuesday is a public holiday - I just wanted my pancakes!

La Paz was not a very wealthy or commercial place compared to other cities of South America; I was very surprised and it felt more like one of the third world countries I had travelled through earlier. The people also looked very different from those in other places I have

Day 185: Still in La Paz, Bolivia

For sale: market day in Bolivia.

visited; they had their own features that could not be described as Indian, African or European!

This was a special day for Bolivians when they 'consecrated' their houses, shops and cars! Yes, I watched in amazement as a ritual using 'bangers' (a sort of firework!), flowers and alcohol were used. First they laid the flower petals around the area, then they lit the bangers and stood back! Afterwards they poured pure alcohol over the area and drank beer together. Even the beer was poured around the area as part of the tradition!

In the evening I walked into the old part of the city with Dr Emilio and saw the celebrations taking place all over. These were very poor people but very happy as they celebrated the start of Lent. Everybody appeared to be outside and it was freezing cold! My few days here in La Paz were all about people and culture; everywhere was closed but the place was a hub of activity. I couldn't find any trace of Butch Cassidy though!

Day 186: Puno, Peru

Early morning and I was on the bus to Puno. The climb out of La Paz was steep and very slow but eventually we were approaching Lake Titicaca; this is the largest lake in South America and almost 170kms long, it is also nearly 4,000m above sea level nestling high in the Andes. It was a fantastic sight!

We had to leave the bus and cross the lake by boat whilst the bus was put on a small raft-like thing and taken across. I kept looking and thinking it was going to sink! Back on the bus we followed the lake to a town called Copacabana (nothing like Rio!) and took another bus to Puno. At the

What a way to get a bus over a lake - I was pleased not to be aboard!

border we had to get off the bus again and have our passport stamped in a very primitive office. Finally we were back on the road and now I was in Peru!

It had been a long journey and I was glad to arrive in Puno and get to an hotel. It was still a cold and wet place and I just felt miserable! After finding somewhere to eat I walked around the main street for a while but as the rain was coming down I was keen to return to my hotel and go to bed.

Puno, Peru

The bus left Puno in the early morning and it was a long and slow journey to Cusco nearly 400kms away. A number of times we just stopped for what appeared to be engine problems, but eventually we were climbing through the Peruvian mountains and part of the Andean range.

Day 187: Cusco, Peru

Peru is where the Amazon river begins and is the third largest country of South America. It has three distinct regions - the coast (where I wished I was!), the Andean Mountains (where I was!) and the Amazon rainforest (that I could see in the distance!).

For most of the journey the roads were pretty poor; the hills were very steep and it was raining! The on-board video entertainment was all in Spanish, and I was still suffering from the changes in altitude.

However, the views were spectacular - mountain after mountain topped with snow and blankets of rich green land running down their sides. It was the vast panoramic landscape of Peru and it was fantastic!

Puno in Peru.

As the rain continued I began to feel as though I was in England and travelling across a very large-scale version of the 'Yorkshire Pennines'!

Peru is a very devout Catholic country and at the side of the roads, by rivers and mountains and in some remote places - simple crucifixes could be seen - I was quite amazed at the number. Peru is not just the Andean

mountains and jungle, it is an immense archaeological treasure and for many people the journey to Cusco was a stopping point to visit Machu Pichu. The conquest of the Inca people took place in 1513 by Spanish explorers; now 500 years later tourists flock to Machu Pichu to explore the ancient abandoned ruins that were once homes to so many people. I was not travelling to Cusco for this reason, in fact I was finding it difficult to believe that so many years ago a community could be murdered and wiped out completely. Today, the area was just a mass of tourists!

Cusco was very similar to Kathmandu - tourists, climbers, shops, cafés and restaurants! My only different observation was the number of children selling things as you walked through the town. They stood in the freezing cold, wrapped in handmade wool garments from head to toe with just their eyes showing - I felt so sorry for them!

Day 188: Cusco, Peru

I needed to get out of here! It was freezing cold, wet and I was still suffering with the altitude - Cusco is 3,346m above sea level.

Still pondering on why all these tourists were here, I could see that Cusco was certainly one of humanity's legacies - a story of bloodshed, rebellion and extermination and now tourism! However, the main square was a picture postcard. Two great buildings sat side by side. The Cathedral and the Church of Jesus, both great masterpieces and the architecture was superb. I met Alvero and Lauren – Alvero was a Peruvian, now living in the USA - they were staying in the same hotel and we found a great café overlooking the square and sat watching the world go by! (and talked a bit).

OK, so my next job was to find the quickest way out of here. I booked a flight for the following morning to Lima and hopefully a warmer climate!

Later I joined Alvero and Lauren for an evening meal. It gave me the opportunity to sample 'lomo saltado' - Peruvian steak! Mmm! Another great tasting dish with beef, coriander, tomatoes, onions and rice!

Day 189: Lima, Peru

My hotel was great and had a balcony overlooking the entire town of Cusco; I could see the thick clouds coming towards us and felt the damp cold wind on my face. No, I was not in England but really wished I could be! It was now that I was feeling really lonely, but I hoped that the warmer climate in Lima would make me feel a little better!

The airport was primitive; modern technology had not yet reached this part of the world and when the flight was delayed, we were informed by an airline supervisor standing on a wooden box using a megaphone! This was the first time one of my flights had been delayed but two hours later we were flying over the Andes and above the clouds. The mountain peaks appeared though the clouds covered in snow and looked spectacular!

Landing only one hour later I found that the temperature had jumped to 35 degrees and I was stripping off!

When I booked this flight I'd been offered a deal to take the flight on to Mexico City the following day. This would give me only 24 hours in Lima, but as I had seen a good part of Peru whilst travelling across by bus - I took it.

I found a hotel in the district of Miraflores, which is supposed to be the safe part of the city - many people had told me that Lima was not a safe place, particularly during the night, but I wanted to see as much as I could and so would need to walk around a little after sunset!

In the early evening I took a walk to the Parque Central and it was wonderful - hundreds of people and an atmosphere that was unimaginable! This pedestrian square was huge and even had an amphitheatre in which people were crammed together watching some traditional pantomime.

Everyone was out enjoying themselves and according to people I spoke to, this was what happened every weekend! I liked Lima, but unfortunately it was to be a short visit. As I walked back to my hotel I kept thinking somebody was following me, but I think my mind was

playing games! It was a strange feeling to be in such a warm climate again but I wasn't complaining!

Day 190: Mexico City, Mexico

I arrived in my 38th country and the world's largest metropolis, jam-packed with over 22 million people. Abbi and Luis met me at the airport. Abbi had been a student living in Canada with my sister two years ago and always said that if I came to Mexico she would love to meet with me! Well, here I was and it was great to see her again!

Luis (Abbi's boyfriend) invited me to stay with his family in the heart of Mexico City and I was given a great welcome at the family home. I met so many of his family and we talked for hours about my journey and experiences around the world. I was exhausted and as soon as my head hit the pillow - I was fast asleep!

Day 191: Still in Mexico City, Mexico

Mexico City was mad! I had never seen so many people, cars and more cars. The taxis were the same as the 'Herbie' car and there were hundreds of them. Ivan (Luis's brother) took me to enquire about buses that would eventually take me to the border with the United States and as we drove about I was just overwhelmed by the traffic!

I spent most of the day meeting members of the family and relaxing; it was great to feel so welcome and the hospitality was first class! I was amazed at things that they told me about living in Mexico. Schools had to operate on a shift basis due to the number of children in the city. Pupils choose to attend school either from 7am to 1pm or from 1pm through to 7pm. It was incredible to imagine but with so many people, everything operated like that, including the universities! The smog over the city was terrible and you lived in constant fear of an earthquake - but the people were happy, friendly and so kind!

In the evening I sampled Pozole, a traditional Mexican dish and Nopales, a type of cactus! Mmm! I don't think so...

Day 192: The journey from Mexico City to Torreon, Mexico

Tonight I would be taking the overnight bus to Torreon - over 1,000kms north, as I needed to keep going! I wanted to see the 'real' Mexico!

Today I explored downtown Mexico City and it was crazy! I have visited over 40 major cities around the world but Mexico City was a nightmare! With so few people who spoke English, I just kept getting lost!

I began at the Alameda Central, a promenade of greenery, fountains and people - yes, people. I then spent most of my time admiring huge buildings (most were museums) and churches. It was just a big, mad city and I was going mad!

By 8pm I was on the bus and trying to get out of this huge city. In just less than half an hour, I had counted 15 Police cars just driving around! It may be the most dangerous city in the world, it may also be the largest city in the world, but for me it was just a mass of people and cars!

Day 193: Chihuahua, Mexico

I slept really well on the bus and when I awoke all I could see was desert and cacti dotted around the landscape.

I arrived in Torreon Bus Terminal and was immediately stopped by a Police Officer who wanted to see some identification. The terminal building had no information for tourists and when I began asking for advice - NOBODY spoke English! Aaaagh!

It was crazy; I just did not want to stay here! I went to the ticket office and enquired about buses going north and found that I would be able to take a bus to Chihuahua in just twenty minutes!

This was to be my shortest visit anywhere and after stocking up on food, I was back on the bus that would take me a further 500kms north - nearer to America, I thought!

There was just nothing in Torreon for me except folk

wearing cowboy hats. Adios Torreon; Hola Chihuahua!

Six hours later I was in another bus terminal struggling to find information for tourists (about hotels etc) and anyone who spoke English! I was only 300kms from the American border but still having a nightmare!

I managed to communicate with a taxi driver and found a hotel - but when I then went out to find somewhere to eat... impossible! Everywhere was closed by 8pm and I was too late. I walked around for over two hours and eventually found a pizza take-away open. I was maddened and so wound up that I had spent the evening in search of food.

Walking around this deserted town made me realise that it would be better for me to take the bus the following day to El Paso and hopefully a user-friendlier civilisation.

Day 194: El Paso, America

I had been told that a bus left Chihuahua every day at 1pm bound for El Paso; this included the journey through border control. This morning I awoke with that plan - however, I also awoke with terrible stomach pains and after my first visit to the toilet I was back and forth for over two hours!

I spoke with my brother Giles back in the UK who suggested I take some tablets to calm things down and get on the bus! Hopefully I could survive until I reached the US - things would obviously be better for me then.

The bus was a non-stop express to the border and we drove through mostly barren land and desert for almost five hours. We did stop a number of times at checkpoints and twice we had to get off the bus, show our passports and have our luggage checked.

Eventually and quite by surprise, we were in a huge traffic queue (six lanes) packed with hundreds of cars! I couldn't work out where all the cars had come from, as the road had been pretty quiet, but it was amazing! All these cars were in line to cross the border into America over the International Bridge. The US military and immigration officers were everywhere, searching vehicles and checking passports. We had to disembark and enter a small terminal building with our luggage - just like in an airport. I was unsure where to go and nobody on the bus spoke English.

I joined the queue for non-American citizens and it took me over two hours to explain the purpose of my visit to the US and have my papers checked and stamped. It was not easy, especially since I had *no onward ticket* out of the US but eventually I was cleared and on the other side of the barriers.

My bus had not waited for me, but fortunately a Greyhound bus travelling to El Paso picked me up and I was quickly on my way over the bridge and into my 39th country - the United States of America.

I was excited and relieved when I eventually checked into a hotel and could get some rest.

Small ticket; major step. This scrap of paper took me from Mexico to America - even if the bus did leave me behind and I had to finish the leg by Greyhound.

Day 195: Still in El Paso, America

Straddling the border of two nations and three states, El Paso lies in between arid desert, green valley and rugged mountains. Looking out of my window last night I could see the huge 'El Paso Star' high on the mountainside. Nearly five hundred bulbs light the star, which is almost 500 feet high and 300 feet wide.

El Paso was a big city and I was surprised at the size of the population - over 650,000 . The slogan on a billboard near to the hotel described El Paso as 'The Sun City' with a diverse culture, climate and history! I would describe it as dead, boring and with a small mentality. I had been so excited about 'coming to America' - mainly because I had struggled through South America and Mexico with the language barriers. El Paso might look like America, but its culture and language were definitely Mexican! Yes, it was a diverse multi-cultural community but one with 'nothing to do'!

At 8pm, all the restaurants were closed; there were no Internet facilities in the city and by nightfall nobody was

walking the streets. It was like being back in Chihuahua, except that here the biggest building was the US Court office.

Come early evening I was trying to find a takeaway for some food when, walking through the town centre, I could hear loud banging and shouting. I turned a corner and saw about 100 demonstrators who were protesting against the threat of military action in Iraq. I was standing there watching when a guy called Simon came over to talk with me; he was originally from England and worked now in El Paso with refugees and homeless people.

I did some filming of the protest and talked with Simon about his work there in El Paso. He invited me to share dinner with his family and we took the short walk to his home.

Storm clouds gather: Bush goes to war; El Paso didn't support him.

The NGO that Simon and his wife both worked for is Annunciation House; the building served as a house of hospitality for the undocumented and refugees who come north to the border areas in search of food, employment, survival and some way to support families back home. Their work is tough, the hours long, but the rewards are great.

Walking back to my hotel I was lost in thought, reflecting on experiences and stories I had heard all over the world similar to the problems I was now hearing in El Paso.

Stories of poverty; stories of malnutrition and of hungry children; stories of cardboard houses and poor sanitation; stories of no work; stories of bombed communities; stories of fear; stories of torture and death - unfortunately I had seen all of this too and just at that moment it felt like it was time for me to go home!!

Day 196: The journey from El Paso to Los Angeles, USA

Here we go again, another overnight bus for the 14-hour journey to Los Angeles. I was glad to be leaving El Paso, but extremely nervous about going to Los Angeles. My whole journey had been tough, but especially so when I had to arrive in a big city with no contacts – which was often. It's a scary feeling when you have no idea where to go and what to do until you arrive – especially when you're travelling on your own as I was!

The journey north had been gruelling; I did not have any of the luxuries that I had been used to on overnight buses through Asia, Africa and South America. No, this was just an ordinary, boring, even primitive bus full of Spanish-speaking folk filling every seat!

After very little sleep, dawn was breaking and I got my first glimpse of America's largest city - Los Angeles.

Day 197: Los Angeles, USA

We arrived at 7am in downtown Los Angeles and I had no idea where to go. I approached a man standing at a bus stop who suggested I walk three blocks to 'Broadway'. I did and Oh my God, it was a nightmare. The only people walking about were the homeless, many pushing supermarket trolleys with all their possessions mixed in with garbage that they were collecting from the bins! A few came up to me asking for money but I politely apologised and told them that I had nothing. I was beginning to feel that if I did not walk faster somebody was going to push me over! (I mean this literally because my rucksack was so heavy and I was so tired) - what the hell was I to do?

The place was a dump! Now, I understand that all the shops were still closed, but was this really Los Angeles?

Walking along Broadway I suddenly noticed a group of people talking to a Police Officer and it turned out that they were closing off a road to film a movie! I asked where all the hotels were and was immediately laughed at! It seems that 'downtown' Los Angeles is not where I should have been - I was told I should be in Hollywood! OK! Sounded good to me - I'd forgotten about Tinseltown and so I was now on my way to the Metro Station.

Nearing the station I was approached from behind by a guy wanting to sell me a ticket - I was so bloody nervous! He looked at me, I looked at him and then he smiled and told me that I was not in a very safe part of town! He turned out to be my 'Guardian Angel' and assisted me in finding my way to Hollywood Boulevard. He gave me a token for the subway and joined me on the train. I really did not know what to think, but 25 minutes later I was safely in Hollywood and on my own!

It was still early and the first thing I saw was a Starbucks and off I went for a coffee! The next person I met was a guy sitting outside the café who introduced himself as 'Toothless Wolf' and I could see why as he opened his mouth to speak! Oh, this was turning out to be quite a day - my nerves couldn't take anymore!

I was now walking down Hollywood Boulevard, in the entertainment capital of the world, the home of glitz, glamour and the Oscars! Then, I just happened to look along a side street and high up on the mountainside was the renowned Hollywood sign! Wow! It was amazing to see it with my own eyes, something you saw so much on television and there I was standing just gazing at it!

Street cred: anyone who's anyone has their name in a star in Hollywood; but I don't think they mean my sister and her family!

I then noticed something else; I had been walking on the 'Walk of Fame' - right under my feet were the names of all those famous stars! I had been walking along and hadn't realised! This had to be the most famous sidewalk in the world and I was just walking along it! Phew! I needed to find a hotel and then I could explore!

"Now, how do I get to Beverly Hills"!

Day 198: Hollywood, USA

There are over 2,000 stars on the two and a half mile Walk of Fame, completed in 1961 and with around 15 to 20 new stars being added annually I just walked and walked and walked all morning! I found Elvis, the Beatles, Marilyn M, Michael J, Frank S, Tom C, Louis A, Bob M, Charlie C, Whoopie G, Jimi H, Mickey M, Barbra S, James D and the Simpsons - but no Peter H. (work them out then!)

I had such good fun and finally made my way to the Kodak Theatre where preparations were under way for the 75th Academy Awards that were taking place that week. I spoke to the staff at the Information Centre who were so helpful and assisted in my little bit of filming that I wanted to do - including walking the famous red carpet up the huge stairway to the auditorium. Unfortunately the red carpet was not down yet but who cares!

Later that day, the first of the huge statues had arrived and a crane was lowering it into position! Could I be nominated for my film next year? Maybe not!

Wandering around Tinseltown was like walking along a movie set - it just didn't seem real. Suddenly I was stopped by the LAPD. The Police car had pulled up against the sidewalk and the officer asked if I spoke English! "Why?" I asked. He then reminded me that walking across the road when the 'red man' was standing was an offence - jaywalking or something! I would have thought that the LAPD would have had enough things to be worrying about when you saw the statistics regarding the number of shootings that took place every year! Anyhow, I got the message.

Hooray for Hollywood: this was to be the scene of the Oscars the week after I'd left.

Day 199: San Francisco, USA

I awoke today to the news that the Federal Government had implemented the tightest security throughout the US since the 2001 terrorist attacks and raised the threat level to 'high' in the face of war with Iraq. We were now on 'Orange Alert' and travel across the US was going to be a little different.

Hollywood Boulevard was a different place today; Police cars were everywhere, officers were out on horseback, roads closed and generally things felt tense.

I left the glamour and wacky atmosphere of Tinseltown and headed north on the Greyhound bus to San Francisco. Even along the highway, patrol cars seemed to be everywhere! America was preparing for the worst I guess; it was in the grip of terror!

Following the west coast of California north from Los Angeles I saw acre upon acre of vinyards, the home of their famous red wines!

We stopped at a motorway services and I was gobsmacked when I walked in and saw that French Fries had been re-named 'Freedom Fries'!

San Franciso

When I left the UK I could never have planned exactly where I would be and when! I was in Palestine when the Israeli tanks moved back in; I was in Bali just after the bombing of a nightclub; I was in Phnom Penh, Jakarta, La Paz and Buenos Aires whilst protests and demonstrations were taking place in which people were actually killed; I was in Australia during their worst bush fires on record; I was in Rio de Janeiro in time for the Carnival and now I was in the United States just when they were about to go to war with Iraq!

By late evening I arrived in San Francisco - I was surprised by so few people walking about but was told that it was not safe to walk downtown after dark! This was another dangerous big city and I needed to find somewhere to sleep!

Lying in bed, approaching midnight I mused on the fact that tomorrow would be my 200th day travelling the world.

39 countries

78,795 kilometres

554 hours travelling

27 time zones

24 trains

26 planes

9 boats

21 buses

6 cars

64 stamps in my passport

41 Don Bosco projects/ communities /schools visited

56 hotels

103 cash machines

and... TWO HUNDRED DAYS!

Europe, Asia, Africa, Australasia, South America and now the last leg of my journey through North America! It won't be long before I'm back home safely in Wakefield, England.

Day 200: San Francisco, USA

San Francisco was amazing - hill after hill, the world-famous cable cars looked so small in the distance, but soon they were at the top of one hill and on the way back down another. It was just so different from Los Angeles; cleaner and plenty of famous named shops and smart buildings!

Again, the Police were everywhere - I had just come out of a coffee shop and suddenly six SFPD cars were surrounding the coffee shop and rushing in with batons and guns! I was gobsmacked and quite frightened - what went on here was like being in a movie!

Eventually, and since I heard no shooting, I was on my way to visit the Provincial House of the Salesians where I would be staying for a few days.

I spent the rest of the day catching up with my e-mails and journal before hearing the news that war had now begun in Iraq.

My thoughts and prayers were for the innocent people in this conflict and of course for the US and British Armed Forces. Having travelled through countries still suffering from totalitarian rule and tyranny and seeing the human remains that shocked me in Cambodia, I firmly believed that nobody should suffer under a Dictator! Every person on this Earth has rights and we have no idea how lucky we are! (sorry for the speech, it's just the way I feel!)

Day 201: Still in San Fransico

By early morning I was visiting the famous Golden Gate Bridge stretching across 4,200 feet of ocean, connecting San Francisco with Marin County. It is one of the longest suspension bridges in the world and pretty 'awesome'! Unfortunately as America was on such high security alert it was impossible to get very close just then (unless you were actually driving over). In fact, San Francisco was bracing itself for huge anti-war protests that day and I got caught up in it all later!

Gazing at the bridge I was bewildered at the strange orange-red colour of the metal construction contrasting with the gleaming expanse of water below. To my left was the infamous island of Alcatraz, but I wouldn't have time to visit this former prison known in Hollywood as 'The Rock'!

Open up that Golden Gate: here comes Hunter.

When the Salesians first arrived in America nearly 100 years ago from Italy, they came to San Francisco and built the church of St Peter and St Paul. Today I visited both the church and school. The church is magnificent, with Italian design and marble interior. The school was built above the church - unusual but again quite amazing!

I had the opportunity to talk with both Grade 7 and 8 pupils who were just fantastic; on the day when everyone was closely watching the news as the war began in Iraq it

Seventh graders at St Peter & St Paul School in San Francisco.

was a great chance for me to talk about my journey around the world, my experiences of a 'global community' and how the work of Don Bosco was so strong and rewarding to so many young people educated in schools all over the world!

The pupils were great company for me as we chatted throughout the morning about life in San Francisco. Crime was an everyday thing here and in fact murders were not generally reported on the news until they reached landmark numbers i.e. the 100th murder of the month etc! I was amazed at the life and culture of young Americans here who have so much love for their country and ambition to live a good and rewarding life!

Once again it was time to take my leave, but I was desperate to take the cable cars up and down some of the many small hills separating the 'blocks', so I waited at the stop near to the school and took the cable car downtown. We had only travelled three blocks (or three hills) when we were stopped by the Police who had blocked the road! Thousands of people demonstrating downtown had forced the Police to close the roads leading into the centre and we had to walk!

In the centre it was pretty frightening watching so many people protesting and sitting on, or just walking along the roads - many seemed to be hoping that they would be arrested for blocking the roads (I guess this was jaywalking!) but the Police were very well prepared.

Since they had closed the city centre roads it seemed that the protesters' aim of causing disruption to commuters

was unsuccessful! Only the tourists like me seemed to be affected - but then it did lend some drama to the day!

Day 202: Berkeley, California, USA

American people make me laugh! The language was just like in the movies - and then I remembered that I was in California, the home of the American film industry.

I visited the Salesian High School in Richmond today and had a great time with the students talking about the diversity of American and British culture! The different language kept us all amused and I was really enjoying being on this side of America.

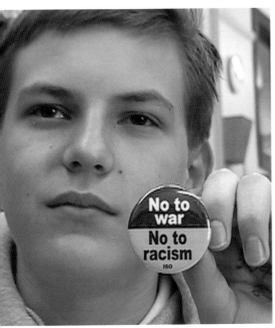

Clear message: young Americans know what they want.

Watching the television had also been an amazing experience - with adverts constantly bombarding your screen and then the coverage of this war on Iraq! I could not believe the way the US TV companies had live cameras on the tanks as they were driving and then firing into Iraq! Was this a war for freedom or virtual reality Hollywood style?

As demonstrations continued in downtown San Francisco, I had very mixed feelings about military conflict in the Gulf and hoped that the Western world could handle the inevitable retaliation for many years to come.

Well, onward bound tomorrow, with a cheap flight up to Seattle. This had worked out far more economical than a 14-hour bus journey and it also meant that I would be very close to the Canadian border and my next country so much sooner!

Day 203: Seattle, America

This was my first chance to experience 'U.S. security' at an airport and I was quite surprised! I arrived at the airport in Oakland (just outside San Francisco) and had my luggage immediately taken from me to be 'security checked'. Then it was my turn! They seemed very interested in my boots and had them taken away for examination!

With my boots back on my feet (apparently they weren't a terrorist threat) I was on the plane heading for Seattle. Sitting on the plane; I couldn't help laughing to myself at the crazy Americans! They were loud, brash and often quite annoying! I know it is usually a minority of people that can give you an impression of a country, but Americans are truly different!

I remember watching the television and seeing crazy adverts like the new portable water-jet tooth cleaner, or, the tablets that you could take to stop you visiting the 'washroom' when you were out in the park playing with your children! What was happening in this world? How can I compare that to the school children in Uganda who had no fridges in their homes or the people in India who used the side of the railway track as their toilet!

Seattle was cold - it was raining, cold and damp and brought back memories of my homeland, but I was not happy and just did not want to be here!

I had difficulty finding a cheap hotel, it was only 4pm but the city was very quiet! Demonstrations both for and against the war have been causing problems throughout America today and most places were closed.

After seeing the Space Needle - which stands at 185 metres and is the landmark of Seattle, I was more interested in finding the Greyhound bus terminal and booking my ticket to Canada!

Day 204: Vancouver, Canada

I had a really bad night - after walking around Seattle in the cold rain, I eventually found somewhere to eat and returned to my hotel. The television stations were all covering stories on the war in Iraq and each channel allowed you to select live cameras positioned on Army vehicles with combat troops or naval ships! Live pictures of Baghdad, Kuwait and everywhere else in the world allowed you to see so much and it became addictive but also pretty sad!

After two hours on the bus, we were at the border with Canada and I was so excited! At the Passport/Immigration desk, the officer was very interested in my quest to go around the world and commented that if I could get all this way, how could she not let me come into Canada! At last, after almost seven months I had reached my 40th country! (don't forget I have included Sudan in Africa where I stopped on my way to Ethiopia and the Vatican City - a country all on its own inside Italy!).

So, how did it make me feel? I felt so happy to be in Canada because it is my favourite country, added to the fact that I was now nearly all the way round the world!

The bus took the final route over a long bridge into Vancouver and looking out of the window across the river I could see thousands upon thousands of logs. They reminded me of the TV programme called 'Beachcombers'! The way they were floating in the water in such huge masses and then moved along with rope and tugboats was truly amazing to see!

I was now in Vancouver and it was so cold! I had followed summer almost all the way around the world, but Canada was only just coming to the end of its winter and it was 'bloody freezing cold'! "Aarghh!"

Day 205: Vancouver, Canada

Since I first planned this journey around the world I had always hoped that in Vancouver, I could treat myself, and travel across the whole of Canada on 'The Canadian' the Western Transcontinental Railway between Vancouver and Toronto.

I visited the station to book my ticket and was introduced to the marketing manager - Mark Pradine. He seemed truly amazed by my efforts to get round the world and I cannot believe what followed...

I was presented with a free ticket to travel first class with Via Rail on the three-day journey to Toronto. My ticket would include all meals, sleeping accommodation, a toilet and shower! Wow! I was 'Gobsmacked' and really did not know what to say. Mark wanted me to enjoy my journey across Canada and I was so grateful - "Thanks Mark, thanks Via Rail".

'The Canadian'.

Later, I met John Coughlan who is a friend I met from Kingston, Ontario whilst on a previous visit to my sister who married and emigrated there 29 years ago.

He is an Irish-Canadian and his accent was just so funny! Sorry John! We had such a great time on a whistle-stop tour of Vancouver before food and some drinks in an Irish-Canadian Pub!

Can't remember much else!!

Day 206: The journey from Vancouver to Toronto

I had a walk around Vancouver in the morning; I was enthralled by the spectacular backdrop of snow-capped mountains surrounding the city and was so happy to be in Canada. The people were so friendly and although it was cold, the sun was shining and I was feeling very happy.

I made my way to the CBC Radio buildings where I met Peter Brown, a DJ who had interviewed me by telephone shortly after the accident in South Africa when my nephew and I survived that horrific car crash! He had always promised me a beer if I made it to Vancouver and he kept his word! He interviewed me again and I was able to share more of my experiences on this journey around the world. I have so enjoyed the opportunity to share my journey with so many people in the schools, newspapers, radio and of course on the website!

No Onward Ticket

First class view: the sights from the observation carriage aboard The Canadian were just one fabulous vista after another.

By late afternoon I was on board 'The Canadian' and about to embark on a voyage of discovery that would allow me to experience Canada (well 4,500kms of it!). I was so excited as I found my private sleeping compartment with toilet and shower. I went for a walk to explore the fancy stainless steel cars and found the domed observation carriage with its panoramic views high above all the other carriages and was absolutely thrilled at my home for the next three days!

After a first-class meal in the restaurant carriage, it was almost midnight and I climbed the stairs to sit in the 'sky-train' and watched in awe as the headlamps from the front of the train shone out into the unknown! Wow! It was pitch dark all around except at the front and I could see the way the train was bending as the track carved its way into the 'Rockies'. I was eager to sleep so that I could see the view in daylight and so I retired for the evening!

Day 207: Still aboard The Canadian

I looked out of the window this morning and was so excited; I dressed and went for breakfast! The view outside was awesome! As I sat eating my 'Fruit Loops' I was gazing at the Rockies - they were almost overwhelming and nothing short of magnificent! They truly are rocks but they are huge and topped with snow! The clear blue sky was just a bonus this morning and allowed us to get a great view of Mount Robson, the highest peak in the Rockies. At almost 4,000 metres it was easily recognised and was often referred to as the 'Monarch of the Canadian Rockies'.

As we travelled through Yellow Pass into the town of Jasper, we passed through the border of British Columbia with Alberta - and the first of three time zone changes! This whole journey was a dream come true for me and I was just buzzing with excitement all morning!

We arrived in Jasper, which was said to be among the country's most photographed places, so I took my camera and off I went! Oh my God!! It was absolutely freezing cold! Brrr! My fingers froze and my bones began rattling and my whole body shivered!

This small town was surrounded by a spectacular backdrop of the Rocky mountain range and was just so picturesque! Our stop was only thirty minutes and I was glad to get back on the train to warm up! As we left the station, I was looking at some of the world's most beautiful scenery - untouched, unspoilt and unbelievably beautiful!

Jasper: the most photographed place in Canada?

The other passengers were so friendly and as we were living together for the next three days, I began to get to know them all as we shared stories and told each other what we did! It was like the Agatha Christie novel, 'Murder on the Orient Express'! I was amazed at some of the things people told me about their lives and it was such good entertainment! Just like me I guess, people were interested in my quest to circle the globe and the envy of travel was offset against some of my more difficult moments! The staff were just brilliant; they were so kind and hospitable and wanted the passengers to be relaxed and comfortable as we journeyed in such luxury!

By late afternoon the landscape began to change, as we left the breathtaking mountains and snow and entered

Prairie Province, the heartland of Canada. The landscape had been shaped by the glaciers of the Ice Age, which had left a legacy of deep rivers and flat, yes, very flat, rich tablelands! From the foothills of the Rockies I was now gazing at a massive flat land of desert and cacti!

I could see across the plain for what seemed like hundreds of miles and again I was in awe. This was truly a fantastic experience!

Day 208: Still aboard The Canadian

Seeing double: how often do you meet a TV stunt double on a train? This was Tiffiny Lynn, and who knows, I might have watched her on television without knowing.

I had a really good sleep and woke once more to the sight of the Prairies. We had changed time zones by one hour again, each day losing one hour, getting closer to GMT and closer to home!

We made one early stop this morning for a number of passengers to disembark. I said goodbye to June, who had shared the same carriage as me for the first half of this journey. We had laughed so much as we gossiped about our fellow passengers - in a nice way, I might add! The friendship made in such a short time with people on the train was so incredible and being probably the youngest traveller in first class, it was nice to be 'looked after'!

Our main stop today (and officially half-way) was in Winnipeg - the crossroads of Canada. It was not a long stop and although this time I had wrapped up warm, I was still very cold and only made a short walk around Union Station gazing up at the massive dome in the centre, the interior of which was delicately plastered in pink and white, all designed by the same architects who created New York's famous Grand Central Station.

ALL ABOARD! We were back on our way! I met a very interesting passenger in the sky train this afternoon - female, petite, middle-aged and attractive! Her name was Tiffiny Lynn (stage name!) and can you believe it, she's a stunt-woman and some years ago had been in Charlie's Angels, Hawaii Five-0, Six Million Dollar Man and Magnum P.I., to name but a few! How cool! We chatted for ages and she allowed me to interview her for my film! Just to remind you, I had been filming every day since I left

England - three main themes, Me (of course!) as in video diary, the journey (selected footage of my actual travel mode from one country to another), a school or community project from each country and a person of interest in every country!

After a very busy afternoon it was time once more for our third meal of the day! 'Food Glorious Food' washed down with a red wine and finished off with dessert; I had been fooled into thinking that the mousse was moose and thought I was trying some real Canadian food! Say no more!

No mountains today; but this view had its own majesty.

As the sun started to set on this 'big sky county', I began to look back on some of the most incredible sights of the natural world that I had seen over the last few months and the people I had met. 'It's another world!'

I was awake very early this morning. I think a freight train had woken me but I had wanted to get up early to watch the sunrise! (I had missed it the other two mornings!).

Bleary eyed, I walked down to the sky train with my camera like a drunkard (come on...48 hours on the move!!) and was greeted by one of the staff with a cup of tea! He asked what I was doing up so early and I told him. Then he just laughed and said, "Look out of the window!" Nightmare! For the last three hours we had been travelling through a snowstorm and all the windows were just covered over! "You won't see no sunrise today, dude" said a voice coming from the bar!

During the course of the morning the snow began to clear and I realised that the landscape had again changed completely. Overnight we had exchanged the Prairie Province landscape of undulating grain fields and complete flatness for the forests and lakes of the Canadian

Day 209: Kingston, Ontario, Canada

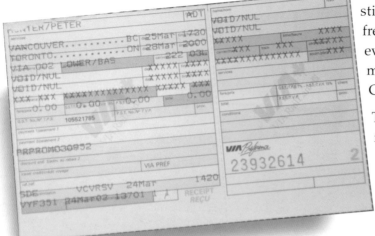

Shield. All the lakes were still frozen and with the fresh snow covering the tall evergreen trees it was, for me, a scene straight out of Christmas!

The stunning views of huge forests and large open spaces of frozen water were just an amazing contrast to the first days on board the train.

Dream ticket: I'd been to some places and seen some things, but this ticket really did fulfil a dream.

The day was going too quickly and as we travelled further east, the snow had disappeared and with the ice on the lakes now melted you could see the clear water and such wonderful reflections of the beauty surrounding them.

This was Ontario, the richest and most populous Canadian province - the word Ontario means 'shining waters' and with the countless small lakes we passed today I would have to agree that this was the best day of travel throughout the whole world! It was just fantastic - brilliant, unimaginable, stimulating and out of this world!

By early evening, we began our approach into Toronto and I was so excited. I was going to be with my sister who lived only a few hours from here in a place called Kingston. I climbed back up into the domed car and saw the slender CN Tower in the distance growing steadily larger.

I began saying my goodbyes to the people who had shared with me one of the greatest experiences of travel and had become such good friends. This train journey had not just revealed the great landscapes of Canada, but created a home for a few days, and friends that would last forever. I had experienced the soaring granite mountains of the Rockies, the vast expanse of 'nothing' called the Prairies and the lakes and forests of the Canadian Shield in just three days. It was just the best!

I was feeling very emotional as we finally arrived in Union Station and saw my brother-in-law waiting in the great hall - I dropped everything and hugged him for ages before realising that my sister Ioene was waiting with him! I turned around to embrace her too and began to cry! I was tired of course and shaking with emotion but to be with family after so long was over-whelming and such a relief! It took three hours to drive to Kingston and I never stopped talking or wiping away the tears in my eyes! We stopped for coffee at one of the famous Tim Horton's coffee shops and my whole body was swaying from side to side! My feet were back on firm land but after 78 hours and 4,600kms, I was exhausted!

My Canadian relatives.

After a late night of talking and family gossip I slept like a log, but did not want to sleep all day! I was keen to see my nephew Ross who I had not seen since India.

Day 210: Still in Kingston

Ross had joined me in South Africa and if you remember, had been in the car with me when we were both involved in the accident that nearly killed us! Seventeen countries had passed since that awful day and not one had gone by without me thinking how lucky I was to be alive!

Seeing Ross today was just fantastic - we had lots to talk about and time to reflect together on the nightmare that we had shared!

Day 211: Still in Kingston

Pancakes and maple syrup for breakfast and a belated turkey Christmas dinner in the evening with my Canadian family! What more can you say?

Day 212: Still in Kingston

I think today could be summed up as sleep followed by shopping and then sleep again!

My other niece who lives in Whitby (ONT) arrived today and so I had now caught up with my entire Canadian family.

The CBC Radio had broadcast my interview across Canada and messages on the guestbook from so many listeners had me all excited and feeling like a celebrity. I was so happy!

Chapter 8:
April

Foreword

by Mark Bradley
Deputy Editor, Wakefield Express

PETER Hunter's reputation travelled before him as he set out from Wakefield on his gruelling round-the-world expedition. He had already played an important part in bringing about a regeneration project and a new community centre for the Eastmoor district of the city and was never backwards in coming forwards with views on how residents' spirits could be lifted.

It was no real surprise, therefore, when the Wakefield Express learned of the task he was taking on. It was also no great shock to discover that hours after setting out on his journey he was a passenger on a ferry to mainland Europe which had caught fire!

The newspaper charted Peter's progress throughout his time abroad and many readers took great enjoyment in tasting a little of what he experienced.

He also provided us with a few good stories – whether it be meeting famous folk or being involved in further unfortunate accidents. The Express has always been keen to pay tribute to any of the city's residents who go the extra mile to help their communities and try to benefit the lives of others.

There can be little doubt that Peter has taken that extra step, or two, whether in Wakefield or in another far-flung continent.

We now wait to discover what is next on Peter's agenda, this time a little closer to home.

Day 213: Ottawa, Canada

I travelled to Ottawa today to visit Sacred Heart School; an old family friend called Nora who taught at the school had invited me. I spent the day giving three talks with different year groups and it was so rewarding for me, and certainly the feedback from the students showed that they enjoyed it too! I really did enjoy this public speaking - a chance to share my experiences with other people and inspire others to fulfil their dreams! The cold weather here in Canada was really getting to me. No matter how many layers of clothing I had on, I was still shivering inside!

Day 214: Back in Kingston, Canada

Being in such demand(!) I spent the morning at another school, this time back in Kingston. In fact, this was my nephew and niece's old school so it was nice to come here! The students at 'Regi' were just fantastic, eager to ask many questions and really showed such great interest in my journey. Just as we completed the lesson -

the fire alarm went off in the school! Now, come on, I thought - what's happening? We've had the boat, train and bus, but thankfully this was not going to be the school, it was a false alarm!

In the afternoon I visited my brother-in-law's workplace and met some of his colleagues. How strange it was for me to meet people who knew all about my journey around the world as they had been following all the news on the website. As they asked questions I found it so funny, because they would refer to the events I had experienced around the world that they already knew about!

Warm welcomes in a cold country: Sacred Heart in Ottawa (above) and Regi in Kingston (below)

It was now time to think about moving on... it seemed that my original plan of going to Greenland was not going to work - the water from Baffin Bay in the north of Canada was still frozen with icebergs and in fact the ferries

running from Iceland to Scotland did not begin operations until May! The other problem was that all flights leaving from Canada's east coast had a change or pick-up in Boston or New York and did not fly direct to Greenland at all!

Well, I needed to re-think my plans. This journey had always been prompted by the events of 9/11 - it was on that day when many of my friends back in the UK had suggested that it was not going to be a good idea to try and go around the world in the new present climate of 'World Terror'. But I believe that terrorist activities should not stop people from doing what they want to do, and in fact, the terrorist would win if we did not do what we wanted to do because of them! I decided that I should pick up my flight from the U.S. to Iceland, as this would give me the opportunity to pay tribute in New York to the people who lost their lives when the Twin Towers were brought down on that fateful day - I was going to 'Ground Zero'.

Day 215: Still in Kingston, Ontario, Canada

I had confirmed a flight from New York to Reykjavik in Iceland for Monday evening and planned to take the overnight bus from Montreal to the U.S. tomorrow!

A chance to rest, catch up with e-mails and watch the weather forecast - a snow storm was heading across the east of Canada and was due to hit Toronto tomorrow!

Day 216: Journey to Montreal

Chance to pack and relax before Ross and Ioene were going to take me to Montreal. From here, at midnight I was due to connect with the overnight bus to New York.

The snowstorm had now hit Toronto and was travelling east towards us! Now what could go wrong?

Well, firstly I was beginning to feel a cold coming on - not SARS as you may be thinking...! Secondly, Highway 401, the main route from Toronto to Kingston and beyond, was becoming highly dangerous with the heavy snow. This was serious and we decided it would be too risky to take

the car to Montreal. My sister and I rushed to the railway station (VIA Rail) to enquire about a train to Montreal to connect with my bus. We were informed that the only train that evening was running three hours late!

On to the bus terminal and we were too late for the bus to Montreal, but I could take a bus at midnight and pick up a connecting bus to New York at 7.30am from Montreal! (still with me?!?!).

The snow was getting worse, but for me, it was just like Christmas (I wish!). The roads were all covered over and I was worried about what was going to happen, but I purchased my ticket and went back with my sister for a Tim Horton's coffee and doughnuts. I knew that I must leave tonight and continue this epic journey of the world.

It was nearly midnight and time to say goodbye to Ioene, Jim and their student lodgers - Dan, Ian and Shi Ting Lu! Most upsetting was a final farewell to Ross, who shared with me the unforgettable experience in South Africa and without whom I could never have got so far. I know we would see each other for many years to come, but the hug was emotional and I had tears in my eyes.

Day 217: The journey from Montreal to New York

Most of the snow had cleared by the time I arrived into the bus terminal in Montreal. It was 4am and I now had a three-hour wait. Can you believe it - the midnight bus to New York had been postponed, so if I had got to Montreal any earlier it would have made no difference!

The snowstorm had now moved and was affecting travel into New York. Just minutes before our departure, we were informed that the bus would not be able to travel due to the severe weather conditions en route. I was mad - this was turning out to be a nightmare journey and I really needed to know from the bus company if I was going to be able to get to New York today!

I was very tired, cold and hungry. The staff on duty promised that the 10.30am bus would leave and so I went to let the other passengers know. I had been chatting to many of them whilst we had been waiting, and had shared with them what I was doing and how important it was to go back to the U.S. My announcement was greeted with relief and I suggested we should all go for some breakfast!

My brief tour in the centre of Montreal had me thinking I was in France. Even the menu at the café was in French, but I understood 'café au lait' and 'croissant'!

I met some very interesting people this morning including a French girl living in Montreal and a man from Uruguay who worked for the U.N. and could speak eight languages!

We were now on the bus to New York and after two hours had arrived at the border with the U.S. The Immigration Officer was not very happy with me! He took away my passport after asking me numerous questions about why I was coming back into America.

I began to think that this was what they now called in America - 'racial profiling' as the officer was clearly confused about my ownership of a British passport, where I lived, where I was born, my occupation and why I had visited 40 countries around the world and wanted to return to America. After a very long wait and with no smile on his face I had my passport stamped and I was able to board the bus across the border and on into New York.

This whole journey on the bus was so incredible and everyone was talking to each other. We had all been part of the delay caused by the snow and although I had caused further delays at the border, nobody seemed upset! The banter was very friendly and I had not experienced it so much on any other bus journey!

The approach into this great big city was awesome! For miles all you could see was the fresh white snow covering the winter tree branches along the highway but the roads were clear and we arrived safely downtown almost 24 hours after leaving Kingston, Canada.

As I walked out of the Port Authority Bus Terminal it was just awe-inspiring. I had been to New York over 15 years ago and loved it and here I was again walking along towards Times Square. The sidewalks were huge and packed with people, the skyscrapers so tall that as you looked up it made you dizzy - this was New York, the city that never sleeps but certainly a city unnerved by War!

Day 218: New York, America

Last night I had found a hotel on 41st Street (called Hotel 41) where the manager and staff were just fantastic. I was given a huge discount and invited to the restaurant for a free meal! They were proud to support me on my personal effort to visit New York as part of my journey around the world - I was here to pay tribute at 'Ground Zero'.

It was the day our world changed forever. Manhattan, New York was changed irrevocably on September 11th 2001, when a terrorist attack resulted in the tragic collapse of the twin towers of the World Trade Centre.

Most of us remember what followed - the courage, the strength and the determination of those that recovered the lost people as the world began to face the true meaning of 'terror'!

I recall watching the horrific events unfold in my local pub back home as people suggested that my already planned trip around the world was probably not now a good idea! I will never forget that night and my determination that terrorists would not - and should not - stop people from fulfilling their dreams!

Englishman in New York: a goal realised after 85,000 kilometres.

I arrived at 'Ground Zero' today after travelling almost 85,000kms through 40 countries and knew that I had done it! What was important for me was to recognise and pay tribute to the thousands of people around the world affected by 9/11, and reflect on my truly amazing dream that had become a reality.

It was once one of the busiest places in New York; today it was a huge construction site and very quiet. It was a very strange feeling to be overlooking a huge hole in the ground shadowed by the jam-packed skyscrapers that survived the attack. The profound absence of the WTC towers is marked by a simple cross erected using two twisted and burnt pieces of steel. A Stars and Stripes flag hangs over a building still waiting to be demolished and the main area is fenced, although designed to be a viewing wall that allows you to see this mass opening of devastation.

I prayed silently for a few moments and then my eyes were drawn to huge panels attached to the fence with the names inscribed of all those who died in the terrorist attacks. The whole area remains tasteful and respectful even though work at the site has begun in an effort to develop and move forward.

Zero hour: how can you explain such devastation? I had a tear in my eye as I prayed silently at Ground Zero in New York.

Just to the side of 'Ground Zero' is St Paul's Chapel, which witnessed the events of 9/11 and became a centre of comfort to the hundreds of rescue personnel in the weeks that followed. As I entered the chapel I saw the tribute banners, cards and pictures that covered the walls. At the back of the chapel, tables were covered in used first aid kits, buckets of sweets and bottles of water. There were scuffmarks on the pews from the boots and belts of the weary workers who had used them as temporary beds. The chapel had been sanctified in a new way - a place set apart from grief, toil and exhaustion. It was here that the workers ate, slept and I'm sure many cried! You could feel the sadness as you walked around the chapel that now commemorates those men and women who worked tirelessly as the world looked on.

I set my camera up back at 'Ground Zero' to film and mark this important stage in my journey around the world. I had set myself the challenge and was determined to circle the world as a personal quest, an inspiration (I

hope) to others that they too could fulfil their dreams - and an act of defiance that terrorists were not going to stop me! I looked at the camera, switched the remote to record and said: "I've done it Bin Laden, I've gone round the World!"

Day 219: The journey from New York to Reykjavik

I spent most of the day doing what most people like to do in New York, shopping! Not that I could buy very much - it has been difficult to buy anything whilst travelling as I would need to carry it - so it was more of a window shopping exercise!

The snow had now arrived in New York City and was settling fast, more than eight inches in four hours. I was feeling very homesick today - I just wanted to be at home! It was like that feeling as you near the end of your vacation and have the journey home to make - you just want to speed things up and get home!

I decided to leave the hotel early to get to the airport, conscious that the snowstorm was affecting flights in and out of JFK and that America's homeland security was on 'high' alert and that I should be prepared for anything at the airport...

Winter blues: eight inches of snow fell in four hours as I prepared to leave New York.

I was still full of cold and was not looking forward to the journey tonight. My overnight flight to Iceland was six hours and at the same time I would lose another five hours on my time zone with the U.K.

The airport was so quiet when I arrived and although the snow had stopped it was looking very bleak and wintery. Checking in my luggage was simple and I was through security in no time! I was amazed that of all the airports around the world, this one seemed so relaxed!

After waiting almost two hours, I was so bored and decided to go back out of the airport terminal and film the planes taking off! Within just a few minutes Security Police came over and began watching what I was doing. They looked closer at my camera and I politely showed them that it was just a camera! They told me that they had received reports of a man holding an 'object' on his shoulder and pointing it towards planes in the sky!

I went back inside the terminal building and this time when I went through security I was stopped, searched and questioned!

The snow had stopped, but as it was now late evening, it had got very cold. We had boarded the plane and we were waiting for a slot to take-off.

We had been waiting over an hour when the pilot announced that we could now take off, but the plane would need to be de-iced first! Now this proved to be quite something. In the dark of the night at the side of the runway laden with snow, appeared these huge cranes.

As they got closer, high at the top, I could see a man holding a large hose. He began blasting the plane and although my nose was blocked (a cold, not SARS!) I could smell the de-icer from the air vents. The plane was sprayed with the de-icer and we immediately taxied for take-off, nearly three hours behind schedule.

At last - we were in the air and on our way to Iceland. The flight was the worst in my entire journey. We had turbulence almost the whole way and even as we landed in Reykjavik, a rainstorm and a very wet and windy runway greeted us.

Day 220: Reykjavik, Iceland

I was feeling very tired as I had slept very little on the way. The airline staff had struggled most of the time due to the constant turbulence and I imagined a terrible ending to my journey on this flight!

The airport had very little business at this time of year and after a nerve-racking landing we were all on the bus from the airport into the city of Reykjavik. It was now 3.30am and I moved my watch forward four hours to the local time! This was the 32nd time zone and I was really feeling it!

The journey on the bus took an hour and I asked the driver to take me to a hotel in the city that was reasonably priced! I was amazed at the prices here; all the hotels were priced far higher than anywhere else I had been to! I arrived at Hotel Leifur Eiriksson, located in the centre, a quiet part of the older city and opposite the spectacular Hallgrims Church.

Luck was on my side yet again though - the manager agreed to a huge discount as a way of supporting me on my final leg around the world!

In fact, he offered me breakfast immediately and suggested I visit one of many thermal pools close by in a bid to make me feel better! I had a lovely room overlooking the church and decided to lie down for a short while to rest!

Reykjavik is the northernmost capital in the world and has a plentiful source of green, geothermal energy that ensures clean air and unpolluted water.

Iceland is a hot spot of volcanic and geothermal activity; post-glacial volcanoes have erupted in the past century these provide natural hot water supplies to 98% of the population. What amazed me was that the natural supply of hot water to the houses and hotels included the heating too - and the streets! Yes, hot water is piped under the roads to prevent snow from settling! Can you believe it? Now, that does not mean you can walk about in bare feet but it is a bloody good idea!

I took a walk outside late afternoon and it was windy, wet and bitterly cold. In fact, the wind was so blustery an umbrella would have been useless. I was wrapped up with all my warm clothes and found the public thermal spa. I had no idea what to do when I went in but was met by a friendly Icelandic lady who showed me round and then left me in the changing rooms to strip!

I walked outside in my shorts and my bones began shaking with the cold! Oh my... it was so, so cold. There were three pools; warm, hot and very hot! I chose the middle one and began to walk down the steps and into the lovely heat. As the water reached my chest I sat down and experienced the most incredible satisfaction and the hot geothermal water soaked through my skin and made me feel warm and relaxed.

A fluttering of snow was actually settling on my head but I felt nothing but heat - hot mineral salt water covering most of my body making me feel so good, I was in tranquillity. I took a shower for almost 45 minutes using more of the natural water that had now made my skin so soft and clean.

As I left the spa, I was in heaven. I did not feel cold any more but my legs were like jelly as I struggled to get back to my hotel and lay down.

Day 221: Still in Reykjavik, Iceland

I slept for ages, but awoke still full of cold. After breakfast I went back to bed until lunchtime!

In the afternoon Ragnar, the hotel manager, had offered to take me for a sightseeing tour of part of the island in his four-wheel drive Land Rover - because we would be going 'off-road'.

A bit of history first. The first Norsemen came to Iceland in the ninth century and throughout the period of settlement, everyday life in Iceland was very difficult. The weather was not friendly and the land was still volcanically active. With eruptions, earthquakes, avalanches and other natural catastrophes - I could not

believe people would want to stay here but my mind was soon to be changed.

After a drive around Reykjavik we stopped off at the harbour before making our way up into the mountains and the real Icelandic countryside. A gentle sea breeze was blowing onto my face as I stood looking at the coast. In the distance, I could see steam rising into the air from the hot springs as the cries of seabirds drowned out the roar of the waves.

Somewhere in all that snow is a Land Rover - and it's stuck...

We took the highway up and out of the city until we suddenly turned off the road and onto the soft wet mountain-grass and began the most amazing journey, steep and very bumpy. I was trying to film but the camera was just up and down as we climbed higher dropping in and out of huge holes, sometimes awkward and difficult situations but with the aid of the vehicle and such an experienced driver we were quite safe. Well, not exactly!

Reaching the top I was looking down on the whole of Reykjavik and beyond, across the North Atlantic Ocean. What a magnificent view! Turning round, I could see more rough terrain much of which was covered in snow. We continued on going exactly where we wanted. There were dirt tracks to follow which were even worse than the roads that I had experienced whilst in Uganda (remember?). Then over another mountain and the thick white steam from a geyser was getting closer.

We stopped close to the geyser and I got out to listen to the noise and experience the magnificence of geothermal forces. It was natural and steam erupted from the ground almost all the time. The geyser's power had been harnessed so that the 125 degrees centigrade water could be used as sustainable energy. I walked into the thick cloud of steam and was soon completely invisible to the rest of the world. It was astounding - I was completely on my own and could not even see my hand! The smell was unusual, a kind of strong chemical odour but I was assured that it was completely safe! This had to be one of the most incredible 'earthly' experiences of my whole life!

I became quite giddy and kept going back 'inside'!

We were soon on our way again but driving deeper into snow - and then the inevitable happened! Under the snow was a great deal of ice and as we tried to manoeuvre along the edge of a ridge the vehicle became stuck. The more we attempted to get out of the situation, the more the vehicle became lodged in a deep hole. Basically, the heat from under the Land Rover was melting the ice and we were completely stuck! At first I thought my 'guide' was just having fun and wanting to scare me but when his face became serious - I knew we were unable to move and we were now in an extremely difficult situation! We tried desperately to dig out the snow from under the wheels and threw large stones underneath hoping the tyres would grip onto them and pull us out!

Thank God for mobile phones, we were miles from anywhere and there was no way we could get out of the snow - the vehicle was designed for off-road conditions with four-wheel drive and individual control on the wheels, but we had no option but to call for assistance!

Eventually after nearly an hour, help arrived and we were towed out of the ditch and we were on our way again - back safely to the hotel.

Although it was now getting dark, the city was lit with streetlights in abundance! During the summer Iceland has 24 hours of daylight but in winter there is as little as just three, and since electricity was so cheap, everywhere could be lit up!

This was my last night and so I visited a local restaurant and enjoyed 'lambasteik meo brunni sosu' (highland lamb in a rhubarb sauce!) washed down with a Viking beer - very tasty!

I returned to my hotel to pack and get ready for a very early start in the morning, on my way to Scotland and my last country before home!

Day 222: The journey from Iceland to Scotland

I was up at 4am and on my way to the airport for what I thought would be my journey's final flight to Glasgow in Scotland. Thanks to Icelandic Air who provided me with a discount flight because the ferry service was still not operating due to the winter sea conditions. As we took off, I looked down on this volcanic island, 11% of which is covered by glaciers - I could see very little but thought to myself that this was truly a country where culture meets nature!

The approach into Glasgow was quite something, I could not imagine that so close to home the view of the Grampian Mountains could be so spectacular - I was so excited to be nearly home but still enjoying some wonderful sights! We landed at Glasgow International Airport and my 42nd country!

Glasgow: the last passport stamp and the last leg before Yorkshire. Nearly home!

It had always been suggested that one of my friends would meet me when I arrived in Scotland, but I received a text message on my mobile phone to say he was unable to meet me until Saturday! I was so close to being home and felt so upset - I decided to look at alternative ways to make my final journey back to England.

I made enquiries about hiring a car - although I was tired I did think it would be nice to drive back home apart from the fact that it would take me about five hours. I then visited the British Midland (BMI) desk and spoke with the marketing department. They were very excited about helping me make the final trip to England and offered me a complimentary seat on their afternoon flight to Leeds (England). Well, this was it - thanks to BMI I was finally on my way home!

By late afternoon I was sitting on the very small Embraer aircraft for the one-hour flight to Leeds. No one could imagine how excited I was, but for some reason I also felt very nervous. With a bottle of champagne, courtesy of BMI, I sipped and gazed across the sky and for me, across the world. Yes, I had done it! This was it - my dream to travel completely round the world was nearly accomplished.

From the Alps, the Himalayas, the Andes and the Rockies - across the Indian, the Pacific and the Atlantic Oceans - I was nearly home!

From fires, a car crash, scorching heat, altitude sickness and freezing cold temperatures - I was nearly home!

From the gas chambers in Auschwitz, the children sleeping in street gutters in Addis Ababa, the terrorist bombing in Bali, the extreme bush fires in Australia, the demonstrations in Buenos Aires, War beginning in Iraq and SARS spreading to Canada - I was nearly home!

From the historical buildings in Rome and Athens, the giraffes and elephants in Tanzania, the breath-taking sights of Mount Everest, the Harbour and Opera House in Sydney and the most majestic views on the train across Canada - I was nearly home!

From the impoverished children in Uganda, the head-wobbling people of India, the sulky Immigration Officers of America and the friendliness of so many in Canada - I was nearly home!

Finally, from the fun, laughter and hospitality of the friends I made all over the world - I was nearly home!

At the airport in Leeds I met my sister Sarah and tears took over my emotions as I cried. We drove the final leg of the journey to my home in Wakefield, where I was met by my fiancée Jayne. I was so happy and filled with elation. The hug was the best and I was now home!

Today, I woke up at home and in my own bed!

Day 223: Home!

My life has been changed by the experiences I have had over the last eight months and which have empowered me to make every day a good day.

I had a 'dream' that is defined (among other things) in the dictionary as 'a distant ambition, especially unattainable'. Well, I turned my 'dream', my ambition into a reality and although it was not always easy, pleasurable or in fact simple, I did what I set out to do.

I know that I have inspired people. Many have actually told me that I have been an inspiration, that I have filled people with feelings of confidence, encouragement and exaltation and I am proud and deeply content to know that. I never imagined that I would have the opportunity to share my journey with so many - and I have told everyone I have spoken to, that they had now become part of my journey.

The young people in the schools, colleges, and universities;

The many people I travelled with on buses, trains and aeroplanes;

The family and friends I met on the way;

The readers of many newspapers in so many countries that followed my story;

The listeners of local and national radio stations around the world;

and you! Yes, those of you that have followed my journey every step of the way through the Internet, and now through the pages of this book.

I have enjoyed writing my journal and sharing a part of my journey with so many people and I have also found so much pleasure reading the messages in the guestbook - they had given me support and comfort when I felt lonely and frustrated.

During 222 days and 92,225kms - I visited 42 countries and travelled through 33 time zones. The whole trip included using 31 planes, 25 trains, 24 buses, 9 boats and 7 cars - a total travelling time of 659 hours. I had my passport stamped 68 times, slept in 63 hotels, confused myself with 37 currencies using 116 cash machines - but managed with just one language - English!

With the support of the Salesians of Don Bosco I had the opportunity of visiting lots of projects in underdeveloped countries and gave talks in over 45 community and educational establishments.

So, at last I am home and can now enjoy my creature comforts! One thing is for sure; the memories, experiences and impressions of a global community will remain with me for the rest of my life.

I doubt I will do anything like this again... but who knows?

Home soil: back where it all began; in Wakefield. Will some of these pupils at my old school follow in my footsteps around the world?

2002

DATE	JOURNEY	VIA	TIME	LEG	TOTAL
1/09	Hull (England) to Zeebrugge (Belgium)	Boat	25hrs	400km	400km
3/09	Ghent (Belgium) to Zoetermeer (Netherlands)	Car	3hrs	170km	570km
6/09	Zoetermeer (Netherlands) to Berlin(Germany)	Train	6hrs	620km	1190km
9/09	Berlin (Germany) to Warsaw (Poland)	Train	6.5hrs	580km	1770km
11/09	Warsaw (Poland) to Minsk (Belarus)	Train	11hrs	610km	2380km
14/09	Minsk (Belarus) to Krakow (Poland)	Train	13.5hrs	900km	3280km
16/09	Krakow (Poland) to Oswiecim (Poland)	Train	1hr	70km	3350km
18/09	Oswiecim (Poland) to Kosice (Slovakia)	Bus + Train	8hrs	380km	3730km
20/09	Kosice (Slovakia) to Bratislava (Slovakia)	Train	5hrs	450km	4180km
23/09	Bratislava (Slovakia) to Vienna (Austria)	Bus	1.5hrs	100km	4280km
25/09	Vienna (Austria) to Lausanne (Switzerland)	Train	13hrs	900km	5180km
28/09	Lausanne (Switzerland) to Padova (Italy)	Train	6.5hrs	680km	5860km
1/10	Padova (Italy) to Vatican City	Train	6hrs	540km	6400km
4/10	Rome (Italy) to Naples (Italy)	Train	4.5hrs	250km	6650km
4/10	Naples (Italy) to Palermo (Sicily)	Train Boat	12hrs	700km	7350km
7/10	Palermo (Sicily) to Catania (Sicily)	Train	7hrs	332km	7682km
7/10	Catania (Sicily) to Sliema (Malta)	Air	0.5hr	300km	7982km
12/10	Sliema (Malta) to Catania (Sicily)	Boat + Bus	6hrs	300km	8282km
12/10	Catania (Sicily) to Brindisi (Italy)	Train	12hrs	570km	8852km
13/10	Brindisi (Italy) to Igoumenitsa (Greece)	Boat	9hrs	380km	9232km
14/10	Igoumenitsa (Greece) to Athens (Greece)	Bus Boat	8hrs	400km	9632km
18/10	Athens Greece) to Bethlehem (Palestine)	Air	2hrs	1170km	10802km
22/10	Bethlehem (Palestina) to Nazareth (Israel)	Car	4hrs	200km	11002km
24/10	Nazareth (Israel) to Cairo (Egypt) Via Khartoum (Sudan)	Car + Air	6hrs	850km	11852km
29/10	Cairo (Egypt) to Addis Ababa (Ethiopia)	Air	6hrs	2700km	14552km
3/11	Addis Ababa (Ethiopia) to Kampala (Uganda)	Air	5hrs	2200km	16752km
7/11	Kampala (Uganda) to Nairobi (Kenya)	Bus	14hrs	690km	17442km
14/11	Nairobi (Kenya) to Dar es Salaam (Tanzania)	Bus	13hrs	970km	18412km
15/11	Dar es Salaam (Tanzania) to Kapiri (Zambia)	Train	51hrs	1860km	20272km
17/11	Kapiri (Zambia) to Lusaka (Zambia)	Bus	3hrs	185km	20457km
20/11	Lusaka (Zambia) to Cape Town (S. Africa)	Air	4hrs	2638km	23095km
28/11	Cape Town (S. Africa) to Johannesburg (S.Africa)	Car	16hrs	1460km	24555km
01/12	Johannesburg (S. Africa) to Bombay (India)	Air	9hrs	7020km	31575km
05/12	Bombay (India) to Calcutta (India)	Train	35hrs	1970km	33545km
12/12	Calcutta (India) to Kathmandu (Nepal)	Air	1hr	695km	34240km
17/12	Kathmandu (Nepal) to Bangkok (Thailand)	Air	3hrs	2180km	36420km

2003

DATE	JOURNEY	VIA	TIME	LEG	TOTAL
2/01	Bangkok (Thailand) to Phnom Penh (Cambodia)	Air	2hrs	720km	37140km
6/01	Phnom Penh (Cambodia) to Bangkok (Thailand)	Air	2hrs	720km	37860km
9/01	Bangkok (Thailand) to Satun (Thailand)	Bus	23hrs	1160km	39020km
11/01	Satun (Thailand) to Lankawi (Malaysia)	Boat	2hrs	100km	39120km
14/01	Lankawi (Malaysia) to Kuala Lumpur (Malaysia)	Boat + Bus	9hrs	660km	39780km
15/01	Kuala Lumpur (Malysia) to Singapore	Bus	7hrs	480km	40260km
7/01	Singapore to Jakarta (Indonesia)	Air	2hrs	1050km	41310km
19/01	Jakarta (Indonesia) to Bali (Indonesia)	Bus +Boat	27hrs	1260km	42570km
23/01	Bali (Indonesia) to Darwin (Australia)	Air	3hrs	1860km	44430km
25/01	Darwin (Australia) to Adelaide (Australia)	Air	4hrs	2620km	47050km
30/01	Adelaide (Australia) to Melbourne (Australia)	Car	11hrs	800km	47850km
03/02	Melbourne (Australia) to Sydney (Australia)	Air	1.5hrs	925km	48775km
04/02	Sydney (Australia) to Brisbane (Australia)	Air	1.5hrs	1025km	49800km
09/02	Brisbane (Australia) to Auckland (New Zealand)	Air	3hrs	2300km	52100km
10/02	Auckland (NZ) to Whakatane (NZ)	Air	1hr	300km	52400km
14/02	Whakatane (NZ) to Auckland (NZ)	Air	1hr	300km	52700km
14/02	Auckland (NZ) to Santiago (Chile)	Air	12hrs	9875km	62575km
19/02	Santiago (Chile) to Mendoza (Argentina)	Bus	8hrs	420km	62995km
20/02	Mendoza (Agentina) to Buenos Aires (Argentina)	Bus	14hrs	1200km	64195km
25/02	Buenos Aires (Argentina) to Montevideo (Uruguay)	Air	0.5hrs	300km	64495km
27/02	Montevideo (Ururguay) to Rio de Janeiro (Brazil)	Air	2.5hrs	1850km	66345km
02/03	Rio de Janeiro (Brazil) to La Paz (Bolivia)	Air	6hrs	2900km	69245km
05/03	La Paz (Bolivia) to Puno (Peru)	Bus + Boat	9hrs	300km	69545km
06/03	Puno (Peru) to Cusco (Peru)	Bus	9hrs	370km	69915km
08/03	Cusco (Peru) to Lima (Peru)	Air	1hr	600km	70515km
9/03	Lima (Peru) to Mexico City (Mexico)	Air	6hrs	4320km	74835km
11/03	Mexico City (Mexico) to Torreon (Mexico)	Bus	15hrs	1100km	75935km
12/03	Torreon (Mexico) to Chihuahua (Mexico)	Bus	6hrs	550km	76485km
13/03	Chihuahua (Mexico) to El Paso (USA)	Bus	7hrs	400km	76885km
18/03	Los Angeles (USA) to San Francisco (USA)	Bus	7hrs	660km	78795km
22/03	San Francisco (USA) to Seattle (USA)	Air	2hrs	1400km	80195km
23/03	Seattle (USA) to Vancouver (Canada)	Bus	4hrs	200km	80395km
25/03	Vancouver (Canada) to Toronto (Canada)	Train	75hrs	4600km	84995km
28/03	Toronto (Canada) to Kingston (Canada)	Car	3hrs	250km	85245km
04/04	Kingston (Canada) to Montreal (Canada)	Bus	4hrs	200km	85445km
05/04	Montreal (Canada) to New York (USA)	Bus	10hrs	640km	86085km
07/04	New York (USA) to Reykjavik (Iceland)	Air	6hrs	4260km	90345km
10/04	Reykjavik (Iceland) to Glasgow (Scotland)	Air	2hrs	1450km	91795km
10/04	Glasgow (Scotland) to Leeds (England)	Air	1hr	430km	92225km

With a little help
from my friends

Malcolm, Alan & Greg (from England) - on board P&O ferry
Alex Dockers & family - Waregem, BELGIUM
Fr Henri Alen SDB - Zwijnaarde, BELGIUM
Jeremy Hillman - (BBC) Brussels, BELGIUM
Frederik Bonte - Kortrtijk, BELGIUM
Fien &Trudy Meiresonne - Zoetermeer, NETHERLANDS
Jos Spekman - Zoetermeer, THE NETHERLANDS
Paddy & Olga - Berlin, GERMANY
Rupert (The Emerald Isle) - Berlin, GERMANY
Margaret (Tourist Info Centre) - Warsaw, POLAND
Fr Tadeusz Nieweglowski SDB - Warsaw, POLAND
Darek - Minsk, BELARUS
Janusz Cieplowski - Minsk, BELARUS
Valery & Leonid (on train to Warsaw) - Minsk, BELARUS
Lyuba Pervushina - Minsk, BELARUS
Natascho - Minsk, BELARUS
Joanna Cieplowski - Krakow, POLAND
Joyce Kane & Janice - Ocala, Florida, USA
Monica, Anna & Patricia - Oswiecim, POLAND
Dominika & Onofrejova Family - Presov, SLOVAKIA
Lubica Lachka - Nitra, SLOVAKIA
Stanislav Krivy - Bratislava, SLOVAKIA
Juraj Varchol - Bratislava, SLOVAKIA
Marek, Katarina & Slezak Family - Limbach, SLOVAKIA
Louis Borloz - Verbier, SWITZERLAND
James & Lynne Clark (from England) - Lausanne, SWITZERLAND
Maria Acazi & family - Padova, ITALY
Fili - Padova, ITALY
Fr Paschal Chauvez SDB - Rome, ITALY
Fr Bernard Grogan SDB - Rome, ITALY
Carlo Castiglia - Monte Cassino, ITALY
Mina - Napoli, ITALY
Francesco (Night Porter) Hotel Elena - Palermo, ITALY
Fr Victor Mangion SDB - Sliema, MALTA
Noel & Connie Camilleri - Sliema, MALTA
Gina - Athens, GREECE
Jovana, Ruzica, Milena & Jovana (from Yugoslavia) - Athens, GREECE
Kalil + Family - Nazareth, ISRAEL
Fr Mario Murru SDB - Nazareth, ISRAEL
Marianne - Cairo, EGYPT

Labila Placido - Cairo, EGYPT
Karim, Morad + Ahmed - Shubra, EGYPT
Fr Mario Robustellini SDB - Addis Ababa, ETHIOPIA
Fr Dino Viviani SDB - Addis Ababa, ETHIOPIA
Richard Seifman - Addis Ababa, ETHIOPIA
Fr Jan Marciniak SDB - Bombo-Mamaliga, UGANDA
Kizza Christopher - Kampala, UGANDA
Andrew Laboke - Kampala, UGANDA
Eustace Siame - Nairobi, KENYA
Fr Manuel Pullenkannappallil SDB - Dar es Salaam, TANZANIA
Emily, Marco & Anita (on train to Kapiri Moshi) - Dar es Salaam, TANZANIA
Qussay Mugheiry - Dar es Salaam, TANZANIA
Mayembe - Lusaka, ZAMBIA
Idan Tembo - Lusaka, ZAMBIA
David Dagley (from England) - Lusaka, ZAMBIA
Marc Willmers - Cape Town, SOUTH AFRICA
Sylvia McCallum - Cape Town, SOUTH AFRICA
Theresa Smith - Cape Town, SOUTH AFRICA
Taalib Felton - Cape Town, SOUTH AFRICA
Sheryl Ozinsky - Cape Town, SOUTH AFRICA
Dougie (Altona Lodge) - Cape Town, SOUTH AFRICA
Ogi Mabimba & family - Beaufort West, S. AFRICA
Dr Johann Lochner - Victoria West, SOUTH AFRICA
Elizabeth Araujo - Johannesburg, SOUTH AFRICA
Fr Chris McMahon - Johannesburg, SOUTH AFRICA
Rajesh - Mumbai, INDIA
Fr Xavier Devadas SDB - Mumbai, INDIA
Ashish Chaubeyashish (on train to Calcutta) - Raipur, INDIA
Rakesh - Kathmandu, NEPAL
Sigrid (from Holland) - Kathmandu, NEPAL
Bob & Ann Isaacson (from England) - Kathmandu, NEPAL
Fr John Lissandrin SDB - Bangkok, THAILAND
Dr Wanlop Chiaravanont - Bangkok, THAILAND
Francis Wichai - Bangkok, THAILAND
Boss & Earn, Axe, If, Sit and Ding (the band!) - Bangkok, THAILAND
Leng Sothea - Phnom Penh, CAMBODIA
Fr John Visser - Phnom Penh, CAMBODIA
Alan & Maureen Schofield (from England) - Lankawi, MALAYSIA
Matt & Emma, Steve, Mick, Shaun and Sara (the Reindeer Pub) - Lankawi, MALAYSIA
Fr Andrew Wong SDB - Jakarta, INDONESIA
Kerry & Milton Turner - Bali, INDONESIA
Howard (from England) - Bali, INDONESIA

Heidi, Hannah & Danni (from England) - SINGAPORE
Surin Khan - SINGAPORE
Eileen & Chris - SINGAPORE
Fr Brendan Murphy SDB - Adelaide, AUSTRALIA
Greg Chappell MBE - Adelaide, AUSTRALIA
Greg Sierocinski - Adelaide, AUSTRALIA
Jared Leighton Carr - Adelaide, AUSTRALIA
Peter Smith - Adelaide, AUSTRALIA
Fr John Papworth SDB - Sunbury, Vic, AUSTRALIA
Mark & Angie Allott (from England) - Geelong, Vic, AUSTRALIA
Chloe Cook - Sydney, AUSTRALIA
Di & Cec Pederson - Laidley Heights, Qld, AUSTRALIA
Yvonne Condrick - Ropeley, Qld, AUSTRALIA
Leonard & Barbara Whittaker - Laidley Heights, Qld, AUSTRALIA
Margaret, Colin, Maurice & Brydie Moynihan - Brisbane, AUSTRALIA
Uncle Maurice & Auntie Val - Brisbane, AUSTRALIA
Bob & Debbie Northway - Brisbane, AUSTRALIA
Malcolm Cameron - Kawerau, NEW ZEALAND
Doreen Broadway-Tarawa - Kawerau, NEW ZEALAND
Dave Moran - Auckland, NEW ZEALAND
Fr Andres Morales SDB - Santiago, CHILE
Fr Jorge Rivera Smith SDB - Santiago, CHILE
Maria - Santiago, CHILE
Louis (the taxi driver) - Mendoza, ARGENTINA
Marcelo Castrogiovanni & Family - Buenos Aires, ARGENTINA
Marcelo Nakano - Buenos Aires, ARGENTINA
Fabian Ariel Telezon (Imperial Park Hotel) - Buenos Aires, ARGENTINA
Marcelo Centurion Nakano - Buenos Aires, ARGENTINA
Ivan Rodriguez - La Paz, BOLIVIA
Dr Emilio Hernandez Martinez - La Paz, BOLIVIA
Isabelle - Puno, PERU
Lauren & Alvero - Cuzco, PERU
Gina Alarosa - Lima, PERU
Joseba Maldonado Altuna - Mexico City, MEXICO
Aby, Luis & Families - Mexico City, MEXICO
Alfredo Carrasco - El Paso, TX, USA
BJ Spencer – El Paso, TX, USA
Simon & family - El Paso, TX, USA
Toothless Wolf - Springfield, Hollywood, USA
Fr Nick Reina SDB - San Francisco, USA
Graeme & Sandra Swan - Richmond, BC, CANADA
Matthew & Michelle - Vancouver, CANADA
John & Erin Coughlan - Vancouver, CANADA
Peter Brown (CBC) - Vancouver, CANADA

Carolyn Egerszegi (CBC) - Vancouver, CANADA
June Lenihan (on train to Toronto) - Surrey, BC, CANADA
Derek Kearney (on train to Toronto) - Sudbury, CANADA
Tiffiny Lynn (on train to Toronto) - USA
The Davidson & Fisher Families - Kingston, ONT, CANADA
Dan, Ian & Shi Ting Lu - Kingston, ONT, CANADA
Liliana & John Garieri - Kingston, ONT, CANADA
Teckla Francis - Kingston, ONT, CANADA
Dale Holliday - CFB Kingston, ONT, CANADA
Dale Mundt - CFB Kingston, ONT, CANADA
Lynn Rees Lambert (Kingston This Week) - Kingston, ONT, CANADA
Suzanne Renaud - Kingston, ONT, CANADA
Sam & Neil Anderson - Napanee, ONT, CANADA
Jorge Larrosa - Montreal, CANADA
Shawn Roach (Hotel 41) - New York, USA
Ragnar Lovdal - Reykjavik, ICELAND

Fr Raf Lemmens SDB + pupils from Don Bosco High School -
Zwijnaarde, BELGIUM
Fr Tadeusz Goryczka SDB + pupils from Salezjanie Jagielly -
Oswiecim, POLAND
Fr Sandro Camilleri SDB + pupils from Savio College -
Dingli, MALTA
Fr Gianni Caputa SDB + Theologian students from Int. College -
Cremisan, PALESTINE
Fr Sante Bedon SDB + pupils from Rod el Farag - Cairo, EGYPT
Fr Sandro Giuliani SDB + pupils from Mekanisa -
Addis Ababa, ETHIOPIA
Fr Gianni Uboldi + pupils - Bombo, UGANDA
Fr Gianni Rolandi + Theologian students from Utume -
Nairobi, KENYA
Fr Henri Juszczyk SDB + orphans from Bosco Boys - Nairobi, KENYA
Fr Jose Sequeira SDB + children from Shelter Don Bosco -
Mumbai, INDIA
Pupils at Mission of God School - Calcutta, INDIA
Fr Mathew Parakonath SDB + children from Don Bosco Ashalayam -
Howrah, INDIA
Fr Louis Phonchit SDB + pupils from Savio School -
Bangkok, THAILAND
Pupils at Preataroat School - Phnom Penh, CAMBODIA
Pupils at Don Bosco Technical School - Phnom Penh, CAMBODIA
Ephrem Santos + students from Wisma College - Jakarta, INDONESIA
Pupils at Ropeley State School - Gatton, QLD, AUSTRALIA

Sr Theresa Jones FMA + pupils from St Peter & St Paul School - San Francisco, USA

Fr Joe Boenzi SDB + Theologian Students from Don Bosco Hall - Berkeley, USA

Pupils from Salesian High School - Richmond, CA, USA

Nora McKnight + pupils from Sacred Heart School - Ottawa, CANADA

Jim David + pupils from Regiopolis Notre Dame School - Kingston, ONT, CANADA

Special mentions to:

Idigicon Ltd, Doncaster, UK for running the web-site;

John Allott – The Hollies, Wakefield, UK
and **Vincent Crewe** - Advanced Mortgages, Wakefield, UK for funding the necessary injections;

Mark Pradine - VIA Rail, Vancouver, Canada for treating me as a V.I.P.;

Robert Angwin – BMI, UK for my final ticket home;

Paul Glover – IPWFI Ltd, Huddersfield, UK
and **Kelvin Burke Accountants** – Wakefield, UK for contributions to my travel insurance;

CBC Radio – Vancouver, Canada for making me a radio star;

Wakefield Express – Wakefield, UK for keeping up with me.

Following the Guestbook

Throughout the 'No Onward Ticket' journey, there were the darker moments; but they didn't always come when darkness fell. Many times, alone in a foreign country, and surrounded by people speaking a language I didn't understand, I needed words of support and encouragement. I found them in the guestbook, a collection of encouraging words sent by well-wishers around the globe. This section contains some of those messages...

Foreword

by Di Pederson,
Principal, Ropeley State School,
Lockyer Valley, Queensland, Australia

It has been a long time since I have met someone as passionate about their dreams as what Peter was. Listening to Peter and talking with him energised me. When he spoke about his journey, his dreams and his life he was so animated, energetic and enthusiastic. I couldn't wait for the students, staff and community to meet him and experience the buzz you get from someone like Peter touching your life. The children were mesmerised by his story and asked him lots of questions about his trip. The message that Peter gave to the children was to follow their dreams and that dreams can come true.

We often think of 'Pete the Pom', his amazing journey around the world and how he touched each and every one of us with his enthusiasm and passion for life and learning. Thanks Pete.

255

Name: Ioene & Jim Davidson
City Ontario, Canada
Sent: 10.27 - 25/8
We talked about this adventure years ago. You are the right person for the trip! You can talk your way around the world and will do for the rest of your life!
Looking forward to seeing you on the Kingston part of the trip.
All our love from the Davidsons and Fishers in Canada

Name: justin, allison T,D,J + M
City Dewsbury, UK
Sent: 17.18 - 25/8
Pete....you've talked the talk....now walk the walk. Remember, if you get lost, stay skinny and you probably won't get eaten by some kindly cannibalistic tribesman offering to give you directions to the nearest cooking pot. Don't carry packages for strangers and don't swallow condoms full of drugs.
See you soon. The Hunters ov Doooosbury.

Name: Paul & Vicky
City Wakefield, England
Sent: 11.02 - 2/9
what a start, set the ferry on fire within hours of embarking! Watch out world, this man could be dangerous! Take care, good luck & hurry up home to put Jayne out of her misery!!!!
Love Paul & Vicky

Name: Sarah
City Mirfield, England
Sent: 16.17 - 2/9
when the news hit TV this am, I just closed my eyes, said a few prayers and thought this can only happen to Pete! We're so relieved to hear that you're safe and sound and back on terra firma. Now we've had the dramatic start we would really appreciate less of the adrenaline surges. Take care, love Sarah & co xxx

---

Name: Jayne
City Wakefield, England
Sent: 17.08 - 2/9
I swear you'll do anything for a bit of bloody attention!!!! Good job you had the pyjamas!!!!!
Love always, Jayne xxx

Name: The Holleys
City Wakefield, England
Sent: 22.59 - 2/9
Pete - Cannot believe the extent you will go to have a tale to tell! Have you seen the BBC news web site? We saw a video of the Jon Sopel report - you featured and boy I have never heard you with so little to say!!!!!!
Hope the rest of your travels are not so hairy! LOL Becca, Dave and clan

---

Name: Vincent
City Wakefield, England
Sent: 10.40 - 3/9
Pete, I told you not to smoke in bed! Glad to hear you're safe & well. The adventure begins...
Vincent

Name: Stijn
Homepage: http://users.pandora.be/Fiasco
City Ghent
Sent: 15.07 - 3/9
Hi there Pete you interviewed me today at school here I am
I think that you are doing a fantastic thing here, dedicating urself for such a thing, is very nice of you, but you're a very nice guy too so..
I wish you all the best for your trip, and no more fires and stuff; you don't have to be THAT famous 2 you know. so Pete, bye and good luck!!
Belgium rulez   Stijn OUT

Name: Frederik Bonte
City Kortrtijk/Belgium
Sent: 15.26 - 3/9
Hi Peter
It was very nice sitting with you around the dining table, listening to your travel story. Although you're only just started, you started with a bang. Right away on world wide television.
Hope your journey holds many more adventures, but also hope they end all good.
I know you enjoyed the beer and wine, hope you enjoyed the company too. Have a great trip!
Frederik

Name: Katrijn
City Ghent, BELGIUM
Sent: 16.06 - 3/9
hideliho pete! on our second day at school we already became famous, and that because of you! woe hoe!
I'm very grateful for your (too short) visitation in our class today (I'm in the same class of annelore, from below...) and uihm, tomorrow, you've to buy the "Gentenaar", with our picture in it!! thank you for making me as famous as you already were! and I wish you good luck on your journey; I'll follow it on the internet! please come again, at the end of your journey to tell us all about it!
kiss   katrijn

Name: lien
City gent belgium
Sent: 17.59 - 4/9
Hi Pete! I' am also a student of the school you visited in Belgium. We are very grateful to you that you interrupted our lesson because it was VERY boring. I hope that the rest of your journey will be a great success and that you will meet a lot of other great people. (probably they will be less great then us...) so I wish you all the best! thnx for visiting us and tot ziens! (goodbye in dutch) big kiss, Lien xxx

---

Name: Kenny De Ketele (Belgium)
City Gent, Belgium
Sent: 19.46 - 5/9
Hey Pete, do you remember the cyclist you talked with in Belgium, that's me, so you were about to put my name in your log so all the people around the world would see the name of the future...good luck on your trip, see you!

Name: sophie + katie
City Doncaster, U.K
Sent: 06.55 - 6/9
Hello Uncle Peter!!!
It's lovely to see your pictures. We miss you and hope you are

looking after yourself.

When we saw you on the television we were very proud of you and told all our friends!!

We are back at school now, I'm in year 3 and Katie is in reception. Mummy and daddy seem pleased.....don't know why!!!

We love you. Sophie and Katie xxxxxxxxxxxxxxxxxxxxxxxxx

Name: Paddy
City Berlin, Germany
Sent: 22.28 - 6/9
Well folks no need to PANIC he's here, all bright and bushy tailed as usual. I'll be showing him all the cultural sights of the city and keeping him as far away as possible from boats, ships, ferries, canoes or any other sea fairing vessel that could POSSIBLY catch fire!!! Paddy

---

Name: Rubert
Homepage: http://www.old-emerald-isle.de
City Berlin, Germany
Sent: 15.31 - 7/9
An Irish Blessing for your Journey...
"May the road rise to meet you,
May the wind be always at your back,
May the sun shine warm upon your face,
May the rain fall soft upon your fields
And until we meet again
May God hold you in the palm of his hand."
Hope you have the time of your life....and good luck.

Name: Spiv
City Wakefield
Sent: 08.57 - 9/9
Pete,
How you doing?
Soz didn't get chance to speak to you when I got back from Ukraine. Was very ill with alcohol poisoning.
Bit of advise Pete when your travelling around the former Soviet Bloc -especially on trains (You've probably been told already) -
1) Don't accept any drinks what so ever from strangers (more than likely it'll be drugged and they'll rob you)
2) When going to the bog, don't leave any belonging's what so ever with any one to look after - p.c.,camera, video,etc (they'll rob it all)
3) TRUST NO ONE ESPECIALLY IN EASTERN EUROPE - They'll have the shirt off your back if they could.
Sorry to sound like your mother Pete, but we travelled round Ukraine the other week and heard some horrendous but true stories.
If you do get chance Kiev is a beautiful city and I suggest you have a look at some of the sights (The Ukrainian Woman are gorgeous also!!!!)
Good luck Pete, I'll be following your travels,
Spiv.
P.S. Watch your back and TRUST NO ONE.

Name: margaret
City Warsaw, Poland
Sent: 17.52 - 11/9
Hi Peter! I wish you all the best. I hope that you will manage to get to Moscow. I will be watching your trip and I can not wait to see more pictures from your trip...
Margaret

Name: Lyuba
City Minsk, Belarus
Sent: 06.36 - 15/9
September 14-15. A very unusual and exciting day for me. I met a wonderful person on the train Minsk-Warsaw, Pete. It was very interesting to learn about his intention to travel around the world! He is very enthusiastic about it and I am sure it will be a success! Pete, I wish you good luck, this is a real challenge!
Lyuba Pervushina

Name: tadeusz
City Warsaw
Sent: 14.09 - 15/9
Peter is arrived to Krakow. I spoke with him and he is safe. It was impossible to go to Moscow and to Kiev. There is still another world!

Name: smart alex
City Berlin
Sent: 11.12 - 17/9
hi pete, it's alex from berlin. we met each other in the train from minsk to warsaw. it was very interesting to talk to you. Maybe we meet each other a second time- I'm going to give you some Russian-lessons then. Wish you a great and successful time for the rest of your journey!
alex (sasha)

Name: Joanna
City Krakow
Sent: 21.07 - 17/9
Yesterday I had a wonderful and crazy time with Pete. I showed him old part of city [Krakow]; we ate Birth cake and took a trip to Nowa Huta by tram. He is very funny :) He feels good and he is smiling all time. I'm looking forward to see you again in Krakow, Pete! Greetings from Krakow and Happy Birthday!!!!! [No]

Name: Tadeusz
Homepage: http://www.salezjanie.edu.pl
City Oœwiêcim
Sent: 07.31 - 18/9
we spent very nice time with Pete in Oswiecim at the school. Later some students show him the Muzeum Auschwitz and in the evening he talk to the students who live in the internat.
Dziekuje Ci za twoja wizyte i zyczac szczescia w realizacji zamierzonych planow mam nadzieje Twojej powtornej wizyty.
ks. dyr Tadeusz Goryczka (Director)

Name: Chris
City London, UK
Sent: 21.45 - 18/9
The Hunter is now safely in Presov, Slovakia with my wife, son and her family (On holiday). Spoke with him tonight. He's quite glad to be with people he knows, seems happy and hoping to rest for a day or so. So he thinks anyway my wife will probably drag him around the shops as I'm not there!   Chris

Name: katrijn
City Belgium
Sent: 15.56 - 19/9
go pete go! you're almost 20 days on the road! so far so good!
keep on smilin' one off those crazy belgian girls...   xxx

Name: Stanislav
City Bratislava
Sent: 11.41 - 20/9
I have met Peter in a restaurant here in Bratislava - today 20/9/2002 at 12:00. After lunch I let him to join internet in my office and I help him to find the best tram to his hotel. We will see each other at 19:00 again and I will show him some nice places here in Bratislava. I hope he will like this town.
Stanislav

Name: Monica
City Oswiecim
Sent: 17.28 - 21/9
Hi there!!! I'm from Poland and I showed Peter around Oswiecim. I'm sure you will agree with me that he is a wonderful person. It's so pity that he couldn't stay with us longer but I know there are lots of people wanting to meet him. Peter, I wish you all the best!!!

Name: Juraj (Andy)
City Bratislava
Sent: 20.02 - 23/9
Hey Peter.
It was really nice to meet u. I hope u r going to have great time. Maybe next time when u hear some orchestra u will see some of my friends.

Name: Jayne
City Wakefield
Sent: 12.51 - 24/9
Just to say hi baby!! Hope you have warmed up!

Name: Dr Angela Burton
City West Bretton-/-Cheltenham, UK
Sent: 00.55 - 25/9
Dear Peter, Please forgive me for writing but I really enjoyed reading the journal. I think it would be good to read more from you in future. Re. what I have read today - 1. Happy belated birthday. 2. My Dad, who coincidentally is also called Peter, just returned from Russia on 27/08. My half-brother, Ian, is married to a Russian girl, Natasha, whose mother, Valentina, lives in Novosibirsk. They are very hospitable people, but it sounds as if you have moved on from there now. 3. Great respect to you for going to Auschwitz. 4. Saw you on TV re the Ferry drama & thought you really are the most sassy geezer when it comes down to it, and you just must be destined for one of many kinds of greatness that are much better than drowning at sea.
Safe journey xxx

Name: Katarina
City Limbach, Slovakia
Sent: 09.50 - 26/9
how are You? I would like to send you greetings from my whole family. God bless you, Katarina

Name: Mariachiara
City Padova, Italia
Sent: 21.13 - 29/9
Ciao...a ognuno di voi! Mi sento emozionata di fronte a questo povero computer per poter condividere tanta pienezza e vitalità!
Io Peter già lo conoscevo. Quando ho saputo che sarebbe venuto qui in Italia, subito mi sono precipitata a chiedergli di venire a Padova, così avrei potuto ospitarlo a casa mia. L'ho conosciuto a Torino ad un incontro salesiano europeo e già allora la sua persona mi aveva colpito e la

sua presenza aveva lasciato un segno in me. Ora è vicino a me e ancora non riesco a credere di avere tanta luce accanto. Vi saluto e auguro al nostro caro Peter un buon viaggio.
E un augurio ad ognuno di voi..! Mary

Name: peter gonsalves
Homepage: http://www.sdb.org
City Rome, Italy
Sent: 17.16 - 2/10
Dear Peter,
Glad to have met you here at the Salesian Headquarters, Rome. I was struck by your courage and eagerness to make this journey, to listen and learn from people all over the world. Your desire to visit Salesian youth development projects across the globe is a wonderful sign of solidarity, encouragement and community building.
Wish you good health and may the peace of Jesus be with you wherever you are!
Peter Gonsalves, SDB

Name: carlo
Homepage: http://www.iol.it
City Cassino (Italy)
Sent: 08.27 - 5/10
hi Pete, yesterday it was really nice meeting you at the war graves cemetery here in Cassino. My family enjoyed hearing about your journey it was interesting listening to you, (with your Yorkshire accent!)Take care God bless bye! Carlo.

Name: Mina
City Napoli, Italy
Sent: 09.46 - 7/10
Hi Peter, I hope u remember me... we met last saturday, on the train with "fire"... I'm sorry for my bad english... I'm sure that your journey is great and I'd like to do the same one day... u're really nice, i'll write u soon! a big kiss from Italy, Mina.

Name: Ryan Mifsud
City Mosta, Malta
Sent: 17.05 - 9/10
Hey Pete. I'm from Savio College, Malta. Just want to say thanks for coming to Malta and keep on going until the last point. Don't give up man! Good Luck!

Name: Matthew Bonanno
City Mgarr, Malta
Sent: 18.12 - 9/10
Hey pete, you really are a crazy guy, but i just want to say thank you for coming to savio college and ... It was nice to meet you, but Leeds Utd. are NOT the best team in the world !! Good luck with the rest of your journey.

Name: fr. Sandro Camilleri sdb Headmaster @ Savio College, Malta
City Malta
Sent: 12.44 - 10/10
Thanks a million Pete for allowing Savio College to become a companion on your epic journey. It was a pleasure and a privilege to have met you and listened to your adventurous plan. I wish you all the very best and may the Good Lord bless and protect you! Bon Voyage and keep at it! You've been an inspiration to us! Truly, where there is a will, there definitely is a way! Cheers Pete and all the VERY best!

Name: Mark-Anthony Fenech
City Marsaskala, Malta
Sent: 18.04 - 10/10
Congratulations on your adventurous voyage. I am the one who asked you, "What inspired you to embark on such a journey?" and "China is a communist nation, do you think you are going to make it there?" Thanks for coming to Savio College. No matter the odds you SURELY are going to make it with God's help. And by the way, Leeds Utd are not the best English team, Manchester United are the best team the world has ever seen. Good Luck with the rest of your journey

---

Name: The Simpsons
City Boston Spa, England
Sent: 19.36 - 11/10
In honour of National Poetry day...
There was a young man called Pete
Who went round the World to meet
Lots of new folk
And on the way his train went up in smoke
Or was it just the smell from his feet!!!

Name: giovenni galea
City Sliema, Malta
Sent: 07.29 - 12/10
sexy hair XXXXXXXXXXXXXXXX

Name: Fr. Alfred Sacco sdb
City Sliema - Malta
Sent: 17.46 - 18/10
Great to hear that you are proceeding in your journey according to plans. It seems never a dull moment. Keep it up...never give up. It was wonderful to have you with us here for few days.
Fr. Alfred Sacco and Community of St. Patrick's- Sliema

Name: tadeusz
City warszawa
Sent: 15.50 - 24/10
Saluti per te Peter come pure Fr. Gianni. Sicuramente e' Gianni Caputa da Cremisan!? The situation in Israel is very difficult! Be caryfuly!

Name: Dockers Alex
City Waregem (Belgium)
Sent: 11.08 - 25/10
He Pete, My best greetings to you.
Take care, and let me know when I can help. The Past Pupils of Don Bosco have a great Ambassador with you.
Alex

Name: marianne
City Cairo, Egypt
Sent: 10.34 - 27/10
this's great the website is wonderful... I am really glad that I was a part of this super journey round the world ... you're lucky.. and I am lucky I met you ...take care. I will keep writing to you and follow your journey.... take care... c u sooon   xxx

Name: Claudia
City Herzogenrath
Sent: 19.22 - 27/10
HI peter! How are you doing? One of the girls you meet in roma with my friends at the "fontana di trevi"! i think you are a very lucky person! Good luck! safe and love..... bye Claudia
xxxxxxxxxx

Name: katrijn
City NAZARETH
Sent: 22.47 - 28/10
hi pete, you're in Nazareth????!!! woe hoe!! that's where i live!!! but i live in belgium... very strange... how can you be at two places?! Perhaps, there are TWO Nazareth's..?! but, my Nazareth is the only one!! just come and see!!
keep on smiling! i hope you're having your time of your life!
greetzz, the belgian people (the first foreign people you've met!!) XXX

Name: morad
City Cairo Egypt
Sent: 18.14 - 31/10
h r u im, morad from cairo yu ar wonderful

Name: Borloz Louis
City verbier (switzerland) VS
Sent: 11.50 - 1/11
Hello!! I was with Peter in the train from "Lausanne" to "Martigny". He had a little problem because he did not have any swiss francs just euros, and when he asked for a cheese sandwich, the "train guy" didn't have any change... And that is how I met Peter. Hope you didn't have any other problems in swiss!!
Good luck and take care!!

Name: Stamenkovic Jovana
Homepage: http://bubis@eunet.yu
City Belgrade
Sent: 07.33 - 2/11
Hello Pete,
My name is Jovana.I had opportunity to meet you in Athens two weeks ago. It was great pleasure to talk with you. I have to thank you for giving me (and my friends who were there with me) a chance to present Serbian's spirit, to say something about Serbia. I hope so, that material you made with us will be a part of a whole, because, people today, do not know much about Serbia, Belgrade. If you ever decide to come in Belgrade I will be honoured to see and talk with you again.
with respect Jovana and Milena

Name: musses W.michael
City Addis Ababa, Ethiopia
Sent: 12.34 - 2/11
Dear Peter this are the few opportunities people could have to meet and talk people like you made dreams a reality. i am very much honerd to speak to you on your entire plan and I tell you am inspired to do some thing that has a novel cause like yours. I wish you all the best in your entire trip and hope to hear from you a lote about the rest of the world you will be visiting.
Mussie W.michael
Guest Relations Manager, Sheraton Hotel, Addis Ababa

Name: boni
City Jerusalem, Israel
Sent: 20.22 - 2/11
greetings from us, salesians here in Palestine, we accompany you always in our prayers

---

Name: Marciniak J
City Bombo-Namaliga, Uganda
Sent: 20.22 - 5/11
Dear Peter,
Congratulatins. You made it to our village. It is tough here but you have strength and will keep going! I want the world to know!
FR John Marciniak - Kikomeko / Uganda / Bombo-Namaliga

Name: Andrew Laboke
City Kampala- Uganda
Sent: 15.51 - 6/11
Hello, Andrew Laboke is my name, in Kampala Uganda. I've just met Hunter at 4:30Pm Local time in our Restaurant, "The Canaan Restaurant, Uganda House, Kampala" Found in the middle of the City. He is an interesting man who made us laugh thru' out while with us. Peter says he is heading back to Bombo at 5;00 & catching a bus tomorrow to Nairobi. One thing to note is that he is ahead of his schedule, doing just fine. Peter loves the coffee we make especially to the Muzungu (whites) standard, he had to take it then go. We wish you the best in your Tour round the globe, Hunter and thanks for the time you enjoyed while with us.
Andrew Laboke.

Name: IAIN & LIZ @ NO.27
City Middlestown, England
Sent: 20.52 - 7/11
Hi Pete,
Catching up with you again. Your account of life for the Ethiopian children brought a lump to our throats and the people caring for them are truly unselfish.
I came home today with all the worries of running a busy office dept. but YOU put it all into perspective for me. Tomorrow I will introduce your website to my team. Take care matey!

Name: Joyce Kane
City Ocala, Florida
Sent: 17.18 - 9/11
Hi Pete,
We are the sisters you met on your birthday in the square of Krakow. You look like a busy guy. Hope all is going well on your adventures.
Best wishes, Janice & Joyce

Name: Gianni Rolandi
City Nairobi, KENYA
Sent: 10.11 - 14/11
Dear Peter,
Hi! I hope your journey to Tanzania and beyond is going on well. It was a joy to have you with us; in our community and to know that we contributed, offering you a little rest, which you needed at this particular time. We are happy to have shown to you once more how great it is to be part of the 'Don Bosco Family'! You are always most welcome. 'Karibu tena!' (welcome again), as they say in Swahili!
Have a safe continuation of your journey. Greet very much the Salesians in Tanzania and South Africa.
We keep you in our prayers.
In don Bosco, Fr Gianni, sdb   and the Utume Community

Name: Fr. Manuel pullen
Homepage: http://boscoreachout.8m.com
City Dar Es Salaam
Sent: 19.31 - 14/11
Dear Hunter, it is great your effort to visit us. I hope that your visit to our institutions may bear fruit for your personal enrichment. You are visit to our communities is a testimony that our work is bearing fruits. Keep it up your generosity. Manuel Pullen, Dar Es Salaam, Tanzania

---

Name: jovana, jovana and ruzica
City 11000belgrade
Sent: 00.43 - 17/11
hi Pit! Here we are again! Now everybody can see how kind we are. We hope you are not tired from your journey. Love and kisses from Yugoslavia!!!!   xxxxxxxxxxxxxxxxxxxxxxxxxxxxxxx

---

Name: Theresa Smith
City Cape Town
Sent: 20.34 - 21/11
hi there Peter
let me be the first to note, you're down in sunny Cape Town right now. Don't worry about the cloudy weather tomorrow, it'll change again. We're known for having all four seasons in one weekend.
Enjoy your time here and I hope you get a chance to get up the mountain. T

Name: Altona Lodge
Homepage: http://www.altona.co.za
City Cape Town
Sent: 14.19 - 24/11
It was nice to have Peter and his nephew Ross staying at the Altona Lodge Guest House in Cape Town, South Africa.
It was great to hear of Peter's experience's on his world trip, we look forward to welcoming Peter back!
Dougie

Name: John Ward
Homepage: http://www.donbosco.co.uk/pp
City Uxbridge, Middx, England
Sent: 12.17 - 25/11
Dear Peter
I was so sorry to hear that you have been injured in a car accident. I believe that your friend was not injured and that you have some injury to your arm. I have advised all on National Council. You can depend on their prayers for a speedy return to your amazing adventure.
I trust that you and the car were suitably insured. Do let us know
how you are.
God Bless Peter,
John Ward, Vice President Salesian Past Pupil's Federation (GB)

Name: Helmut De Vos
City Belgium
Sent: 16.15 - 26/11
Ciao Pete,
now that's been quite a shock to hear about your accident. Alex mailed the whole world around to tell what happened ... Hope you're doing well right now and that you're recovering. Don't let this have an effect on your enthusiasm; remember: exploring the

world and talking to people! What you're going trough now might be not what can be expected of 'exploring', but still, you can only learn about it. Try to turn it into something positive! You're a strong person, Pete! You can deal with this; we all stand by your side, we're nearer than ever!

All the best! Helmut

Name: Dr. Johann LOCHNER
City Victoria West, South Africa
Sent: 21.24 - 26/11
I treated the very fortunate (to be alive) Pete and Ross at Victoria West Hospital after their car was written off. Pete sustained bruising of his right arm from mid forearm to the mid upper arm. There is one laceration 5 cm long just above the elbow and multiple lesser lacerations all over his arm. He is in good spirits and will be able to continue his journey soon. He is on preventative antibiotics as well as pain killers. The wounds will be watched carefully. Their new car has arrived. We hope to see them on the road in a couple of days.
Best of luck, Johann.

Name: Steph Wild
City Scarborough. England
Sent: 09.49 - 27/11
can't believe it, don't check the website for a few days and disaster strikes!! Hope you're starting to feel better and doing what the doctors tell you. Keep smiling. Love Steph

---

Name: emily, marco and anita
Homepage: http://www.lens-net.com
City Dar es S, Tanzania
Sent: 10.37 - 28/11
Met Pete on the train from Dar to Kapiri, first time to website. we're really sorry to hear about your accident. Chin up and keep going - you'll only be sorry if you don't. Zambia was fun, hope you enjoyed it too! keep in touch, Emily, Marco and Anita

---

Name: Eustace Siame
City Nairobi - Kenya
Sent: 17.41 - 28/11
it is unfortunate for that accident but don't give up you are an amazing guy and will succeed!

Name: Labila Placido
City Cairo Egypt
Sent: 20.02 - 1/12
Hi Pete, I am very sorry to hear about your accident. I have informed Don Sante and other Salesians in Cairo.
I wish and pray that you will have a speedy recovery both of you. Never give up, but take care!
May God bless you. labila

Name: Jules
City Whitby Ontario Canada
Sent: 05.16 - 2/12
Hello Uncle Pete and Rosco. Sounds like everyone is recovering well which I am glad to hear. Pete I hope that you still have the energy to continue your travels, and inspire us all. I hope that this chain of "adventures" gives you a break soon...although you always seem to have a wild story from anywhere you go. I recently got back from the DR, it was very relaxing...a little different to what you have both been experiencing. Take care guys and enjoy the adventure...it will be over in a flash.

Name: Ross (associate global traveller)
City Mumbai, INDIA
Sent: 17.17 - 2/12
Pete and I just finished what we both have agreed was a top ten all-time meal experience ever!
A proper Indian food feast in Mumbai. It was excellent. Gma, wish you could have been here.
We have seen poverty now 10 times worse than what we saw in South Africa. Mumbai itself is
both fascinating and shocking. We have been lucky to find an internet cafe. Pete realises the
journey log is behind, but I can tell you that computer access was hard to get in Johannesburg,
and phone contact was very expensive.
Pete's arm is really coming along now. It requires fresh dressing and treatment daily to prevent
serious infection.
I took measurements and photos of the accident scene and hope to have a description on this
guestbook by morning. Evidence suggests a blow-out of the rear right tire was the cause of our
serious crash. We have both talked about it a lot and can't believe how lucky we were.
I can tell you all that your guestbook entries and text messages mean a lot to both of us.
Please keep them coming because they help Pete keep focused and positive.
Thanks to you all,
Ross (sat with Pete in Mumbai on Monday 02 Dec 02 @ 2236 hrs)

Name: Qussay Mugheiry
City Dar es Salaam, Tanzania
Sent: 20.48 - 2/12
Please don't forget to contact me as I follow you around the world! You are an inspiration! God
Bless traveller!

Name: Hollie Anne Fisher
City KiOnCanada
Sent: 03.48 - 5/12
Hey Ross and Pete,
I hope you are successful in extending your trip Ross go. Pete, I am glad to read that you are
continuing. I really love checking out all the other entries and love the log book. I can not wait
for the hardcover book. Most of my friends are now reading your site and they agree with me
when I say that your voyage is inspiring. Much better than Lonely Planet because it has Pete as
our voyaging hero. Love you guys and see you soonish.
Ross, Don says hello and wants you to know that the house isn't in too bad shape.
XX Hollie (Jamie and Joey).

Name: Ashish chaubeyashish
City India(raipur) chattisgarh
Sent: 16.46 - 8/12
hi i am ashish met you in a train while coming from Bombay on 6.12.2002, hope both of you
are reached to Calcutta safely, for further journey i am wishing you
all the best.

Name: Yohannes Menghistu
City Addis Ababa
Sent: 07.31 - 9/12
hi, i am yohannes Menghistu from Ethiopia, I felt sorry when I
heard the car accident. I hope you are Ok! now. all the member of
the community of Addisabab Mekanissa are very sad to see and
read this news from your web sight. we are praying for you and I
wish you all the best in all your journeys. may God bless you.
Fr. Yohannes Menghistu

Name: ioene & Jim Davidson
City Kingston Ontario, Canada
Sent: 12.55 - 9/12
Greetings little brother!
Last night we met Ross at Toronto International Airport and had a delightful/shocking drive back to Kingston listening to all the events of the past 17 days. We certainly admire you for your inner strength to continue after so many obstacles. You have certainly left a huge impression on your nephew! (bodyguard!!)Thank you to all the people checking the log/guest book for all your help and encouragement. Peter you will have so much to tell and film to share once arriving back in England. Ioene xox

Name: jovana, jovana & ruzica
City Belgrade
Sent: 23.03 - 11/12
we heard about your accident, and we hope you are ok. When you get tired from your travelling, come to visit us! You are welcome. Good luck! Your friens from yugoslavia.   XXX

Unfortunately the Guestbook was 'lost' for one month!

Name: Idan Tembo
City Lusaka, Zambia
Sent: 17.35 - 11/1
Peter,
How are you doing wherever you are? I hope all is well with you man! Your friend I made for life! Idan

Name: alfonso baños
City Puerto Vallarta, México
Sent: 04.12 - 13/1
Hi Peter...It is so great to read all your stories...! Well done... I am Alfonso, a mexican back-packer that you met in Igoumenitsa coming from Brindisi, some months ago. I am back in México, so you will be more than welcome at home in Puerto Vallarta if you reach this place. Best of wishes and God bless you in your way...
Regards... Alfonso

Name: Alan & Maureen
City Lankawi, Malaysia
Sent: 01.37 - 14/1
Good to be able to accommodate Peter on his trip, thanks for putting Lankawi on the map! Had some great times showing him around and he didn't drink too much! Enjoy the rest of your trip and hope everything goes smoothly for you. See you back in England!
Alan and Maureen (Matthew, Emma, Mick, Steve, Sara & Shaun)

Name: surin khan
City singapore
Sent: 04.52 - 16/1
nice to have meet you in Singapore. trust tat everything will be o.k all the way back to England. Good Luck!!

Name: John & Janet Holmes
City Wakefield, West Yorkshire, England
Sent: 00.09 - 17/1
Hi Peter - sorry for the large gap in contact - we've been really busy with one thing and another, but other people have kept us up to date with your progress (you are still mentioned in

despatches at the garage!). Hope you had a good Christmas and New Year and hope the stitches did the job!

Name: Sebastian
Homepage: http://www.sebastian-baier.de
City Berlin, Germany
Sent: 01.38 - 19/1
Hi Pet, we have met in the changi-airport in singapur at the corner.. you know where... i should not say that.. hei take care and have a nice trip with alot of new experience

---

Name: Jared Leighton Carr
City Adelaide, Australia
Sent: 04.36 - 28/1
Well what can I say, we gave you beer, crabs and directions, it was truly an experience I shall not soon forget, you have met probably thousands of people and if like me, my brother and his friend they will be truly richer for that experience, as was once written if it is what beats your heart you will be drawn to it, I hope that Adelaide will become part of that beat and one day we will see you back on these shores but next time we will show you things you may never dream of good luck and safe travels. Just remember no one is ever far from anyone we all live on this tiny planet and we all are covered by the same roof of stars, well have fun and never forget the true friends you have made and touched this whole journey. Best wishes Jared

---

Name: Tristan
City Mirfield, England
Sent: 13.02 - 26/1
Hey pro pete! You'll be glad to know that all my exams are over now, all that is left to do is coursework, then I'm done with college for good. Not before time i think.
Glad to hear your in safer territory now, although memories of old will never leave you! I'm so proud of you. I bet you didn't think your journey would be as well publicised and as eventful as it has become, i certainly didn't. And I'm sure there will be plenty more goings on before you return home. You will be sorry to know that Leeds Utd are becoming an embarrassment to Yorkshire. Everything is good with me, hope everything is good with you! Take care

---

Name: Greg Sierocinski
City Adelaide, Australia
Sent: 09.51 - 26/1
Go Pete! Havening spent a couple of days with you in Adelaide, nothing except flood, fire or war will stop you in your trek! Good Luck and let me know when you have your book ready!!!
Cheers Greg

Name: Mark Allott
City Geelong (near Melbourne !)
Sent: 13.10 - 31/1
Well folks, I'm sat here with Pete looking at this great website and hearing all his stories. What an experience...I think he needs a couple of days to relax before the next half of this epic journey!
Mark

Name: melody hunter
City Wakefield. England
Sent: 16.28 - 29/1
I love reading the letters the folk send you. You are not forgotten and daily folk ask after you.
It has amazed them. Great and yes I do these letters all by myself.
love you lots and GB Mum & Dad xxx

Name: Malcolm Camerom
Homepage: http://malcolmcamerom0.tripod.com/malcolm
City Kawerau, New Zealand
Sent: 13.05 - 29/1
Pete, know you're busy excited homesick and tired.
Keep going Mate you're a bloody star. Only about 25c in Kawerau today and no rain for 2 wks.
so all the sprinklers are going 24/7. S'pose u will fly into Auckland; the internal 45 min flight to
Whakatane costs about$50 NZ = 15 Quid and I'll meet you in the paddock of an airfield any
time day or night. NZ Customs may be tougher than Aus Watch out. Malcolm

---

Name: Kerry & Milton Turner
City Legian Kuta Bali
Sent: 00.55 - 29/1
Peter it was so interesting to meet and talk with you just a shame it was on your last night in
Bali and you were in the middle of your meal when we found out about your great adventure
have kept up to date with you now that you are in Aus so I hope if you are ever in Bali again
you will drop in for an other great meal at the indo-national bar & restaurant in Legian
Your Hosts Kerry & Milton

Name: Di Pedersen
City Ropeley
Sent: 20.34 - 7/2
Dear 'Pete the Pom',
Well, what can I say. What an absolutely fabulous day we had at Ropeley yesterday. The chil-
dren were so inspired by your visit and loved you so much they didn't want you to leave at the
end of the day. Thank you for allowing our small school to be a part of your journey. You know
that you will always be a part of our Ropeley family. We will keep in touch. Di Pedersen -
Principal

Name: Chloe
City Sydney, Australia
Sent: 03.43 - 7/2
Hey Pete!
Have just logged on to your website and its fantastic! Meeting you in the Royal Botanical
Gardens in Sydney has really inspired me to do something similar in the future...!
For any of you who are a bit confused - I took the pic of Pete with the Opera House and
Harbour Bridge in the background - my little claim to fame! I'm proud to have made a
contribution (however small) to your project and I admire your bravery and passion for what
you're doing.
Take care and keep smiling and don't forget to stay in touch! Chloe x

---

Name: katrijn
City zwijnaarde, belgium
Sent: 21.09 - 6/2
hey pete, just want to tell you, it's snowing here, and i'm jealous of you, being there in the sun!
just know, we're still thinking of you, greetz
katrijn x

Name: Eileen and Chris
City Singapore!
Sent: 17.13 - 8/2
Hi Pete,
It's us from Singapore. Just want to let u know that we have been following ur journey n we r
glad that u are half way round the world....stay safe n brave... u r nearing home!

Name: Yvonne Condrick
City Ropeley, Australia
Sent: 04.48 - 10/2
G'day Peter,
I would like to thank you for a wonderful day we had at Ropeley last Friday(7th). The students were enthralled with your stories and you have inspired us all with your enthusiasm for what you are achieving. The morning tea, bbq lunch, the students singing Waltzing Matilda, staff, parents, past pupils and the media was something we will never forget. I get paid to work here - that's a bonus. I want also to thank Len for being so nosey and accosting you in Darwin. Who knows where your journey would of been if not for him. Not Ropeley that's for sure. I have added my recipe for Choc Caramel slice, I won't tell anyone you had six pieces. It is the next best thing to a mars bar.
Recipe: 1 pkt morning coffee biscuits, 1 tin condensed milk, 2 tablespoons golden syrup (cockys joy), 4 ounces of copha. Line an 8 inch square tin with a layer of biscuits, combine milk and cockys joy in saucepan and cook over a low heat. Boil for 10 minutes stirring continuously. Take off the heat and stir in copha. This takes a long time. Pour over biscuit base and cover with a layer of biscuits.
For chocolate topping. Melt 1 ounce of copha with 1 pkt of Nestle Choc Bits, pour over biscuit layer and refrigerate. Yum! Yum!
Thanks again for a wonderful day and I hope you have a safe and happy journey.
Yvonne Condrick

Name: Maddison
City Ropeley
Sent: 04.31 - 11/2
Hi Peter, How are you going? I enjoyed your visit. Thank you for coming out to Ropeley and visiting the kids and staff. My favourite part of the day was getting to meet you. It was great fun. The thing I liked best about your visit was getting to meet a person who is travelling around the world. I hope you have a safe trip home. Goodluck.
from Maddison, Year 6

Name: Leonard Whittaker
City Laidley
Sent: 20.47 - 12/2
Thought I better clarify something for those in the know. Peter and I drove past 'The Valley' and I pointed it out as an area of interest. I forgot to tell him that in the past it has been known as Brisbane's red-light district. So, no we didn't "visit" The Valley.
Leonard

Name: kizza christopher
City Kampala, Uganda
Sent: 14.13 - 13/2
Hallo Hunter, I hope the journey was interesting and more especially we people you found in uganda. I hope you also had nice time with a lot of experience when visiting different cultures. I also admire such experience though i don't know whether when i grow i will get a good job and i save money for at least in 3 European countries to also experience what you experienced in Africa which was a foreign land to you. Here in uganda , whoever i told about your journey was so surprised to hear about a brave man like you. I chris will never forget a man like you with a great desire for what he always likes. I thought it was me alone in world with such feelings but then i discovered that there those older than me but want and some have already experienced. Anyway we shall

271

always keep in touch with as my true friend. Am now in my vacation of form 4 but not working coz here its so difficult to get even a simple job and most of the people are unemployed but if I had got one, it would have been the start for me to save money for my school fees for higher education. And also for my dream of visiting Europe. Send my greetings to your family and special ones to your beatiful girlfriend you informed us about. May god bless you nice time.
Yours christopher in uganda kampala

Name: Malcolm C
City Kawerau, New Zealand
Sent: 08.51 - 14/2
Gidday Pete
As I type this u r high in the sky en route to Santiago. Great having u stay here over the last week and I compliment u on being one of the tidiest and most considerate house guests I have ever known.
Maybe pick up phrase books for spanish and portugese to help thru the hard parts of Sth America eh?
Yeah Jayne your man is an ace He even shaved twice while here
Pete, steady away does it as u know and good luck, cheers and God speed. You're going up hill now
Malcolm

Name: Robert (Bob) and Debbie Northway
City Brisbane
Sent: 10.06 - 14/2
Peter
I am glad you were able to catch up with things in NZ and get on top of the flu. You are no doubt winging across the Pacific or may even be in Santiago. The Americas are pretty big and exciting, especially the bottom bit so make the most of it. The day before you came our stars said that something good was going to happen. Well, old mate, it looks as if they were referring to you because nothing else has surpassed your visit and you're likely to have had a profound effect on my life. Hope I can live up to it!
Keep up the good work! You'll be home before you know it and wishing you could go back, so make the most of it while you're there!!!
Cheers,
Bob

Name: Bob & Ann Isaacson
City Met in Nepal but from UK
Sent: 10.30 - 14/2
Hi Pete
Glad to hear that your travels are going well and will try to find time to read your log. We like the stories
Just to give you an update on our travels we are still in south India and loving every minute of our time here much nicer than the north. We move on next week dwn to Kerela then make our way up to Calcutta ready to fly to Thailand on the 4th March. Please keep us updated
Kind regards Bob and Ann (Kathmandu)

Name: Jayne
Sent: 15.43 - 14/2
Happy Valentines Day to my gorgeous, sexy fiance! Look forward to speaking soon
xxxxxxxxxxxxxxxxx

Name: sara cremer
City wakefield,uk
Sent: 10.54 - 16/2
Hi Pete how are you? I'm fine really busy with work and back down to earth with a bang since the fantastic holiday when we met you in Malaysia. I'm just saving like mad at the moment to go back again. Yesterday was really sunny here, it was great to see, but today its freezing again! Keep in touch, take care, see you soon, Luv sara xx

---

Name: Ross the Boss
City Kaladar, Ontario, Canada
Sent: 16.37 - 16/2
Pete,
Finally got caught up with your journal after an absence from work due to illness. Cambodia and the rest of Asia were tough by the sounds of it. But Australia, Wow! Why the hell didn't I meet up with you there. I felt warm and relaxed just reading about it. I've been on snowmobile patrol for the past several shifts. Temperatures have been in the -15 to -25 degrees celcius range. There is tons of snow everywhere. After riding around for a bit your face feels like it's going to freeze off. Do you remember renting those ski-doos up in Markdale that time? Well it's a lot damn colder than that! The other day on patrol my partner was driving in front of me when his machine struck a tree stump buried in the snow. The ski-doo shot up in the air and bucked him off, sending him flying into a fence. He broke his wrist and I had to take him to the hospital for X-rays and a cast. It was pretty funny but not for him I guess.
You are getting near us now, we look forward to seeing you and having a good laugh. Stay strong brother, stay strong....and look for buried stumps if you go snowmobiling!
Over-and-out.

Name: Doreen Broadway-Tarawa
City New Zealand (Bay of Plenty Kawerau)
Sent: 20.30 - 16/2
Good luck to u my friend. Well we finished our 'girls' weekend in Auckland with a bang! It was a pleasure to travel from Whakatane to Auckland with u and learning all about yr travels. May god be with u take care x

---

Name: Emily & Balas
City Kingston, Canada
Sent: 23.38 - 17/2
Wow! It is so exciting to read about all your travels... I wish I was somewhere as warm as you!
Emily

Name: Di Pedersen
City Glenore Grove, Australia
Sent: 07.10 - 21/2
Hey Pete
Hang in there. You have undertaken an immense task with your journey and you have achieved a remarkable amount on your trip thus far. Every time you visit somewhere I'm sure you will be changing another person's life. I know that you have an incredibly positive impact on all you meet. Take care and keep safe. Di

Name: Marcelo
City Buenos Aires, Argentina
Sent: 13.47 - 21/2
Hey Peter! Don't forget to watch your back! Enjoy Argentina!!!!
Marcelo

Name: col moynihan
City Brisbane, Australia
Sent: 07.00 - 24/2
Hi Pete. Every thing going OK? Your description of the Andes and border of Chile and Argentina certainly sounded magical. Just a tip re-your trip after Ecuador. Were you aiming to go to Colombia?
If so, I've got some advice from a person I met recently who's just come from there.
1) Flying is the best option from Quito to Bogota.Going overland by bus is risky due to kidnappings etc by guerillas. Especially in border areas around Pasto.
2) Travel inside Colombia is also best done by air. There are no trains, and restrictions travelling by road.
3) The Pacific coast is quite safe but the Caribbean coast is a bit dodgy.
4) They've had a national strike in Venezuala, against the Chavez government. So merchandise, food in shops and restaurants is a little skint. Fuel shortages are also a problem. Otherwise the country is quite safe.
Hope you're feeling stronger and still enjoying the challenge! Kind regards,
Col and Margaret

Name: mossy
Homepage: http://www.totallythomas.co.uk
City The Reindeer Pub, Overton, Wakefield, England
Sent: 02.07 - 28/2
hi pete
just to let you know we are still watching you!! has Graham told you we are going to see Springsteen in Manchester, Elvis The concert in sheffield Again, But he does not know I have tickets to Thomas the Tank Engine the Musical at sheffield arena. Like fools gold dust! keep on keeping on! cheers
alan/adele and all the reindeer crew

Name: lincoln
Sent: 20.04 - 28/2
Peter, Don't get discouraged, you are in a position that we can only dream of. If you loose hope and desire to take in more how will some of us muster up the gumption to get up and go...You said it yourself, you are going into the worlds largest carnival, throw your bag in a locker and PARTY, that's the peter I know, A man who isn't affraid to have a beer!

Name: Ivan Rodriguez
City la paz, bolivia
Sent: 14.27 - 7/3
Hello Peter, it is Ivan from La Paz. I hope all is ok and you are not floating any long. Bye, bye my friend. I pray for you. Ivan

---

Name: joseba Maldonado Altuna
City mexico city
Sent: 00.10 - 10/3
Ive had the luck of being the first mexican meeting peter hunter today. I helped him out to con-tact a friend of his and we drank cappuccino with no foam and had a laugh. best wish. I think this journey it wouldnt b the same without visiting mexico.
Estamos en la oficina de turismo de la ciudad de mexico, Mary mi compañera de trabajo piensa que (pedro) es un pillo. I hope u can come and visit us someother time. mucha suerte!!
joseba y Marie

Name: Gina
City Lima, Peru
Sent: 18.00 - 10/3
Hi Peter
I hope everything is ok with you. Thanks again for the chocolates and have a good time. Bests wishes for you; was very exciting to meet you . XXX

Name: Ted Carless
City Liverpool, UK
Sent: 23.18 - 11/3
Hi Peter, I have spent over an hour on your fascinating website and although I shall never be able to achieve the mammoth challenge you are engaged in, you have inspired me to really have a go at doing the 3 peaks walk in Yorkshire this year while I'm still young enough (68). Take care!

Name: Ivan
City Mexico D.F.
Sent: 21.59 - 13/3
Hi Peter:
Remember the trees whit flowers purple? ehel there are: "Jacarandas". So where are you? My parents ask me abaut you. This house is thiferent now because you not are here, be caerful and don forguet us because we never can forguet you.. sorrry for the wramar bay and keep in touch

---

Name: Bj,Spencer
City EL Paso,Tx
Sent: 05.38 - 14/3
Hello Sir, thanks for the few words and post card, we shared in the lobby at the Travelodge Center downtown. May the Angels, ride, walk, speak and guide you home. Be safe.
Spencer.

Name: Lauren & Alvaro
City Lima, Peru
Sent: 15.57 - 15/3
Peter,
It was great meeting you in Cuzco, and lord knows I am still trying to think up some American idiomatic expressions that could possibly stump you. Meanwhile we hope you are having a good journey into the US, and just remember that the beautiful land of California sunshine is soon to come.
Buen viaje y Dios te bendiga (and Bob's your uncle),
Lauren and Alvaro

Name: Mike and Karen
City Hollywood California
Sent: 07.43 - 17/3
Greetings, Peter!
Hopefully we're not the first to welcome you to the United States! Well, I should say thanks for taking our picture down there at Hollywood Blvd and Highland. Sure is strange how we just so happened to bump into you! Often makes you wonder at the people you see everyday - Where they've been, or where they are going. Our hopes and prayers go along with you. You've gone this far without too much incident- get North America over with! You're well on your way home.
PFC. Michael J. Adamczyk, United States Marine Corps
Karen M. Bates, University of Dayton, Ohio

No Onward Ticket

Name: malcolm cameron
City Kawerau New Zealand
Sent: 12.42 - 18/3
Now then Pete don't flag on the 3rd 2 last leg but I can sure understand the physical and psychological traumata u have experienced over the last 2 weeks!!! Seriously u av done out of this world mate an there r a lot of people feel the same
Keep R hand on backpack and L in the most important pocket huh
They have still got your card pinned up at the Corner Bar in Kawerau Kool
Malcolm in NZ the safest place 2 b as the world moves into War Huh

---

Name: Isabelle
Homepage: http://www.msnusers.com/IsaandJustinsTravelPics2003
City La Paz, Bolivia
Sent: 23.57 - 19/3
Just a Hi from Isabelle (who you met on the bus from Puno to Cuzco in Peru)
Did you like Cusco? Hope you enjoy your travels. The inka trail to machu Picchu is absolutely fantastic. You should do it if you come back one day. I am back at home in Bolivia now and back at work. We do have new website (and I will post the inka trail pictures soon). Enjoy the US, safe travels and happy marriage after you come home.
Oh and I heard about a Don Bosco school here in Cochabamba today (had never heard about them before I met you) Isabelle

---

Name: John Muir
City Albany, California
Sent: 05.02 - 20/3
Hello Peter,
We met at Fortune Hotel in Bangkok. Looks as if you are having a great trip. If you are still in San Francisco when you read this call me at 510-559-****. I'm about 5 minutees from Berkeley.

Name: Dale Holliday
City Kingston, ON CANADA
Sent: 17.32 - 20/3
Hi Peter: My boss and I are both on your website now reading your journal. We're jealous. I'm sure the west coast is beautiful and the people are friendly. I hope that when you arrive in Kingston, we get to meet you. Be safe.
Dale

Name: eric panganiban
City El Sobronte, USA
Sent: 03.29 - 21/3
Hey. Im one of the students from san francisco at Sts.Peter and Paul. Its very cool what u did. I hope u come again.cya

---

Name: Sr. Theresa
City San Francisco, California
Sent: 22.52 - 23/3
Dear fellow Salesian family member Peter Paul Hunter,
What a delight you are! Love for life dances in your eyes, oozes from your pores, communicates itself in every fiber of your being. What a vibrant, positive contrast you are to the "culture of death"; what a powerful message you communicate to our young people by your very being! How honored we here at Sts. Peter and Paul School feel to have been graced with your immediate connecting presence and enriched by your captivating presentations. Thank you so much for spending time and sharing with us and with me. I so enjoyed chatting with you over lunch.

Thank you for making your admirable world journey not only a personal quest, but also a documented resource of wealth to tap, sharing your innumerable adventures and experiences with our Salesian family members and beyond. Your impact is tremendous. God's continued blessings upon you! Continue to let all the good in you shine through.

With prayer-filled gratitude,

Sr. Theresa Jones, FMA

Name: Tristan Abhay Brennan-Torell

City San Francisco

Sent: 02.02 - 25/3

Thank You for putting me on the Photo page with my pin that read, "No to War, No to Racism".

Name: Grace Murphy

Homepage: http://www.yahoo.com

City San Francisco

Sent: 02.30 - 25/3

Hey Peter, I hope you are having fun. Thanks for visiting Saints Peter and Paul Salesian school! It was so great to see someone who accomplished such an amazing dream. It really inspired me. Sincerely

Grace Murphy

Name: Sigrid

City Gouda/Holland

Sent: 11.38 - 25/3

Hi Peter, Maybe you don't remember me, but we met in Kathmandu. I'm also over 200 days traveling now. But I didnn't travel as much kilometers as you. After Nepal I went to Myanmar, Thailand and I'm in Laos now. Tomorrow I leave Laos to go to Vietnam. After Vietnam I will visit Cambodja, back to Thailand and at the the end of may I fly back home. I wish you a great time in Canada!

Name: Tim & Pat

City Horbury, Wakefield, England

Sent: 12.55 - 25/3

Hi Pete

We have kept up with your travels & travails, as best we could. best of luck for trip through Canada & then back to blighty, you are right the world has changed a great deal since you left home.

Hope to see you over a beer in Boons in the not too distant future.

Love from Tim & Pat

Name: Pete Hollis

City Flockton, England

Sent: 18.39 - 25/3

Hi Pete just a quick line from all at the George & Dragon everyone sends there Love and best wishes David says the cards are still arriving ok we are all looking forward to your safe return and to hear about your adventure first hand Take care Pete PETE

Name: Carolyn

Homepage: http://www.vancouver.cbc.ca

City Vancouver, BC

Sent: 23.58 - 25/3

Hey Peter! It was great meeting you here in Vancouver. I'm so glad you were able to come down to CBC Radio for another inter-

view with Peter Brown on That Saturday Show. Enjoy your Via Rail journey across Canada. You'll be travelling through some of the most beautiful scenery in the world so I know it will be great. Good luck and stay safe. You have my card, drop me an email when you get home!!
Cheers, Carolyn

Name: The Coughlan's
City Vancouver
Sent: 02.06 - 26/3
Hi everyone,
I have just returned home after seeing Peter off at the train station here in Vancouver where he will be travelling First Class no less across Canada to Toronto. The people at Via Rail have given him a first class ticket free of charge so he is very excited. He will not be able to communicate with any of you until he reaches Toronto on Friday.
It was fantastic meeting him again and chatting, it was great. We will be keeping track of his progress, it is fantastic what he is doing!!!!!
Cheers, Erin, John, Melissa & Shane Coughlan

Name: Greg
City Adelaide
Sent: 04.10 - 26/3
Peter, The world hasn't been the same since you left home, for the sake of World Peace-Go . home! LOL All the best and enjoy the last leg-I'm sure you will be out of harm's way in Canada and where else Iceland-too cold for terrorists there!!! Brrr!

Name: melody hunter
City Wakefield
Sent: 16.32 - 26/3
Feel so excited that you will be home soon. Just been reading your letters and longing to hear all about your adventures .We loved the train across Canada and we were well looked after and the sights were lovely. The snow and the frozen lakes! Wow! See you soon God bless and lots of love - Mum & Dad.

Name: June Lenihan
City Surrey, British Columbia, Canada.
Sent: 20.07 - 27/3
Just wanted to let everyone know that Pete is on the train to Toronto and doing well (actually he is wonderful). I left him when I got off at Portage La Prairie, Manitoba. He has one more day on the train. Being on the train with him was like an Agatha Christie novel. All the best for the future, Pete.

Name: John Coughlan
Homepage: http://www.transcold.ca
City Vancouver
Sent: 14.32 - 28/3
Peter. Had a great evening with you in Vancouver, loved the chat about all the Ups and Downs on your journey. You are one of a kind Peter. Well done, you are nearly home.
One question? What's next ? Do we expect to see Peter's journey around Mars?!
Cheers! Your Friend John

Name: Robyn Hume
Homepage: http://www.user.dccnet.com/rhume/
City Vancouver
Sent: 23.21 - 28/3
Hi Peter. I just heard your interview with Peter Brown and I must tell you, the most exciting

thing for me was listening to how beautifully articulate you are! It is a joy for radiophiles like me to hear such an eloquent and thoughtful and intelligent speaker, with that great accent and enthusiastic manner. Thank you for that. PS. The trip sounds pretty good too.

Name: Michelle
City Vancouver, B.C.
Sent: 23.34 - 28/3
Guess I'm not the only one listening to the CBC huh?
Just a quick note to welcome you to Canada! I hope you have a safe, but exciting 'last leg' of your journey, and come back again when you can spend more time with us!
Safe journey

Name: wendy Tippett
City Black Creek
Sent: 23.55 - 28/3
Hi Peter--just heard the interview on Roundup this afternoon & zoomed right to the computer-- have read the first 60 pages of your journey--what an adventure its been. Great interview too. Good luck for the rest & I'm SO happy you got to follow your dream!!!

Name: Richard Quintal
Homepage: http://loosenuts.cjb.net
City Montreal, Quebec
Sent: 23.58 - 28/3
Mr. Hunter
I heard you whilst driving home from work today and thought that you must be the last true adventurer. The thought of doing your trip is mind-boggling. Best of luck on the balance of your epic journey, and I'd gladly stake you to a pint when you pass through Montreal

---

Name: Garth Kennedy
City Calgary, Canada
Sent: 01.23 - 29/3
Hey Peter. Heard your interview on the CBC in my car today - ended up sitting there in the driveway so I could hear the end of it. Nice work! I went around the world in '97-'99 and I think despite the current situation (or maybe because of it), it is important for people to hit the road and make connections with our neighbours elsewhere in the world. Hope you enjoyed Western Canada and have a safe trip home.

Name: lois
City creston, bc
Sent: 04.40 - 29/3
Like the others, heard your interview on CBC today and previously, wow, what a trip, reminds me of one I took 33 years ago, but not as extensive! Good for You!
Great pics. Have fun in Canada, Enjoy your trip home. Are you writing a book? Are you going to be a motivational speaker?
Cheers.....and Take care!

Name: nancy
City montreal quebec
Sent: 05.48 - 29/3
Like others elsewhere in Canada, I had to sit in the driveway this afternoon, to catch today's update on your dream voyage.
Bravo - what an incredible and unforgettable experience.
Bon voyage.

Name: Poppy
City Darwin, NT, Australia
Sent: 13.16 - 29/3
Not to sure if you remember, but I was one of the Darwinites who you spoke to whilst you were in Darwin. I worked with the regional airline. I have been following your journey ever since then, but unfortunately have not been able to write in the Guestbook until now. I just wanted to say good luck, take care and stay sane.

Name: Alfredo Carrasco
City El Paso, TX
Sent: 18.55 - 29/3
Qué tal Peter!
I read your journal, it's good to know your bus ride from El Paso to LA was successful. I was your translator on the bus. If you ever need Mexican curios/souvenirs or if you find yourself in El Paso let me know... you missed the highlights of the Southwest!! Good luck on your Canadian tour, you should be "aboot" there by now.

Name: sara
City Ottawa Ontario Canada
Sent: 19.49 - 1/4
This is a message thanking you on both the behalf of myself and Mrs Mcknigt's english class from sacred heart in stitsville ottawa. we greatly enjoyed your stories and your message that was presented. I think that you are doing a great job and have done a great thing that prove our abilities. thanks for showing us your life and your world. it's been a wonderful experience and don't thank us but we are thanking you for what you gave us in return for listening
sincerly
sarah and gang

Name: Jeff
City Richmond, Ontario Canada
Sent: 20.24 - 1/4
Ha just wanted to thank you for that great class where I didn't have to do any work. And I'd like to thank you on behalf of myself and the non French-Canadian students in the class for the great presentation so well. I never heard that word before that you kept using, the one that stared with 's' and ended in 't' I think!!!!!
anyways have a great rest of trip eh
Jeff

Name: Petra Leffler
City Stittsville
Sent: 14.26 - 2/4
Hey Peter....your "can do" spirit came through, loud and clear. Your verbal sharing with us about your adventures, some of the heartaches, and huge joys, was truly inspiring. You are truly dynamic, in that your words embrace your story, and capture the moment of vision, and adventure. Be safe, and eat, eat, eat, now that your in North America,......especially Fruit Loops...Petra xxx

Name: Kayla
City Kingston, Canada
Sent: 20.02 - 2/4
Today (april 2) you came in and talked to my english class. What you said was very inspirational and thought provoking. THank you for coming in and talking to us.
Have a safe trip home!

Name: Elisa
City Kingston, ON, Canada
Sent: 17.06 - 2/4
Today (april 2nd) you came to my class and spoke, it was very interesting!!! I have a suggestion, since you love Tim hortins so much you should buy one of those tim hortins coffee makers with tim hortins coffee, it may not be tim hortins itself, but its close enough. I thought that your speech was very insightful and it was an inspriation to me.

Name: Chris (the 'fro kid)
Sent: 20.48 - 2/4
Good luck in the future, and be more careful when driving!
You're a great speaker, and I can safely say that you've had an impression on every single person in our class.
Thanks for coming in, and have fun on the way home.

Name: Dave Owens
City Kingston, CANADA
Sent: 21.53 - 2/4
hey, you came into Regi today and talked with us, It was Awesome! your journey is really inspiring, I've always wanted to travel, and always knew I was going to. Your stories were really interesting, and I liked how you were laid back and treated us as as full adults and didn't try to sugar coat anything because we were younger. Have a great time on the rest of your trip, and thankyou again.

Name: Marsha
City Kingston, Canada
Sent: 22.01 - 2/4
Hey!
Thnx for coming in today! You were awesome, I don't think I have laughed so much in my entire life! I will always remember now what time english class ends now! I just wanted to say that your trip is very inspiring and I hope you get back home safely. Thank you again so much for comming in to talk to us! I think Mr.David is lucky, he got to listen to your stories twice. I will always remember your Tim Hortons story! Anyway, I hope you get back safely, thanx again

---

Name: nora
City Ottawa
Sent: 03.03 - 3/4
Hi Peter
Thanks for keeping the students enthralled with tales of your adventures from around the world. You have a powerful message about perseverance and fulfilling dreams. I hope that you meet with warmer weather as you continue on your journey until you reach that country in the middle (well at least it is on some maps).

Name: Kristina
City Kingston, Ontario
Sent: 03.18 - 3/4
Hello Peter!
I am so happy that you got to talk to my class and me about your travels around the world! I am from Regi and you talked to Mr.David's first period class, which I was in. Anyways. I just wanted you to know that you have inspired me to travel the world! I always wanted to, but now I know I definitely am going to. I think it's something every one should be able to experience, because it's good to know what other parts of the world are all about. Thank you very much and good luck on your journey!

Name: Ash
City Hollywood
Sent: 03.36 - 3/4
Hey Peter!
Guess you've roamed the world and seen God's portraits both in People and Nature. The world is so small, aint it? Guess thats why they say its a small world. The beauty is in all the cultures that through centuries has passed down from a generation to the next, all the way to individual that are here now. Imagine if you could trace yourself through your own history. We all have come a long way, so why can't we just Love each other and understand there is good in all of us. We were all a child once. Hope you had fun. Be safe.

Name: Derek
City Sudbury, Canada
Sent: 16.37 - 3/4
Hey Peter!
Glad to hear you made it to Kingston. You helped make my trip from Edmonton to Parry Sound the best ever. Hope you enjoyed your first two moose (chocolate that is). As I told you, the next day I was running freight trains down the same section of track and we saw 5 of the other variety (real). This was very unusual but some trips are like that. Fortunately we didn't hit any as they were either off to the side or got out of the way (there's not enough time to slow down). The car made it through a blinding rain-storm with lightning back to Sudbury although I got stuck on the side of the road when I pulled over to let traffic by. Some good people stopped and with their help I soon got out. I think you've met similar people all over the world from some of the stories you told. Best of luck.

Name: Jason Woudsma
City Kingston ont
Sent: 23.36 - 3/4
This is to Peter of course, a big thanx from myself and all of us at regiopolis notre dame, i cant express how lucky we felt when you came to talk to us. the talk in it self was simply amazing, i was inspired intrigued and astounded at the level at which you talked to us. its amazing the determination you must have had to go through the whole journey without quiting, i must say again i feel very privledged that you took the time out of your veryvery busy schedule to tell us of all the things you've seen, i felt that your msg was really well put across, thanx of giving us the oppurtunity to be part of journey, now just in case you don't remember who everyone is especially me, i was one guy with spiky hair, i was one of the guys you toook an interview with and my word for canada was "home" its all good if you can't put a face to that anyways i would love it if you wrote back however don't let it be a pressure Jason

---

Name: Veronica Garland
City Wakefield, England
Sent: 23.45 - 3/4
Hi Peter, Just wanted to say well done and thank you for a fascinating journey. Hope the remainder of your journey home goes according to plan. Enjoy Canada and the family. Safe journey home,
Love Veronica Garland & family

Name: Dale Mundt
City Kingston, Ontario K7K 2X2
Sent: 04.07 - 4/4
Peter,
You have enlightened many people throughout your world journey, as their messages to you can testify. I have enjoyed reading about your adventures with Ross, Jane and citizens of the countries you visited. I am envious of you for all of the sights, sounds and challenges you have

encountered. I can't wait to purchase the movie and/or book of your world trip in the near future. I was glad to see you at Jim and Ioene Davidson's house on Sunday March 30th and at CFB Kingston today (April 3rd) and hear about your adventures. Your journey is nearly over, with a stop in New York, Iceland, Scotland and then home to England. Wishing you a great trip home. Cheers!

Name: Dale Holliday
City Kingston, ON CANADA
Sent: 16.21 - 4/4
Hi Peter: You are a breath of fresh air and a sweet young man. Meeting you yesterday was like meeting a friend. Following your journal I got to know you. Everything that popped out of your mouth was interesting and I enjoyed listening to you. I'm already following up on the Tim Horton's coffee. It will be my gift to you for entertaining us with your adventures and I know, know, know how much you love Tim Horton's coffee. I though I'd E-mail you now, as I have to go to Ottawa for a week of training and I wanted to thank you before I left. I'm glad you enjoyed yourself in Canada as we enjoyed having you.
Be safe, one of your faithful followers
Dale

Name: Nuwa B. Kim
City Kampala
Sent: 08.47 - 5/4
Good adventure Hunter, We meet in Kampala at Post Office. well I will get to you soon with that fascinating journey. Talking to you in Kampala was not enough to disclose the details. I need to be your pal. You are inspirational. Keep it up. All my love from Kim x

---

Name: David Delcloo
City Kingston, ON, Canada
Sent: 20.04 - 6/4
VIA Rail employee from Kingston, Ontario wishing you well on your journey. Cheers!

Name: Jayne
City England
Sent: 14.08 - 9/4
I cannot put into words how excited I am! It has been a long hard slog sometimes over the past 7&1/2 months for both of us but I know how important it has been for you and we've made it (nearly!!) I am so proud of you for what you have achieved and it is so great to know that so many people around the world know how special you are too!!
Love you so much babe! Won't be long now!
Jayne xxxxxx

Name: Jorge Larrosa
City Montreal
Sent: 18.10 - 9/4
Hi, Pete. I am glad to see you are almost in Britain home again!
I am back in Montreal, after 4 days NY. The unexpected snow storm was hard, how do you managed to go to ground zero with this weather?
Jorge

Name: Andrew from Avis
City Glasgow, Scotland
Sent: 14.43 - 10/4
Hope the photo outside Glasgow Airport makes it onto your

Webpage (it's not often Glasgow has better weather than New York or Canada). More importantly, hope you got back to Leeds safely. Good luck with the book.
Andrew, Glasgow Airport.

Name: Joe
Homepage: http://www.boscohall.org
City Berkeley in California
Sent: 17.12 - 10/4
Hello Pete: good to see that you have crossed the continent and are on the way to Iceland. Have a great trip across the Atlantic and back toward home turf.

Name: Jon
Homepage: http://www.hotelleifur.is
City Reykjavik
Sent: 20.29 - 10/4
Hi! Just wanted to know if you got home safe from Iceland. Hope you enjoyed your stay with us and the jeep tour! Best regards from Iceland,
The staff at hotel Leifur Eiriksson (www.hotelleifur.is)

Name: Ioene & Jim Davidson
City Kingston, Ontario, Canada
Sent: 00.06 - 11/4
Wonderful, Fabulous, Congratulations, Fantastic, Wow, Brilliant, Awesome, Amazing, Terrific endurance, Great stick-at-it ability, You did it!!!!!!!!!!!
Love always Ioene and family in your home from home in Kingston Ontario Canada.
P.S. Who says good news doesn't travel fast!?

Name: Shannon
City Kingston, Ontario, Canada
Sent: 23.44 - 12/4
Hi Peter,
Wow, congratulations on getting around the world! I finished reading your journal the other day. Now I really understand what it was like for you to be away from home for so long but also what it was like experiencing the world through your own eyes. I can't wait to read the rest of your journal and your book! Thanks again from everyone at Regiopolis Notre Dame.
P.S. I hope you got to see the elk roaming the streets in Jasper! Shannon

---

Name: Sarah
City Mirfield
Sent: 20.56 - 14/4
Well you did it Pete and you can be so very proud of yourself
- I know we are. It was so good to see you in person at Leeds Bradford airport last Thursday evening and for all you sentimental folk out there - it was pure emotion and by the time I got him home to Jayne well need I say anymore!!! I soon made myself scarce and besides I needed time out to take in all that Pete had told me - how do you fit 8 months escapades into a 90 min car journey (actually Pete didn't do too badly considering I never got chance to say much). I guess we'll be kept entertained for a good long while to which I am looking forward to.
Love you loads, Sarah

Name: Fr Patrick Sherlock SDB
Homepage: http://www.salesians.org.uk
City Stockport, UK
Sent: 10.50 - 15/4
Peter, I'm so glad you have now completed your amazing adventure. The scale of what you've achieved, the way you've accomplished it, and the effect you've had on the thousands of

Salesian contacts around the world is overwhelming. You've been a worthy ambassador for the Salesian Family!
Best wishes for the future from Fr Pat, Bro Donald and all your Salesian friends in Stockport.

Name: Joanna
City Krakow, Poland
Sent: 22.47 - 28/4
I'm very happy that you're ok. So, you finish the journey, now you can relax at home and talking with family and friends. Do you know that you'r journey take the same time as Tomas Cook's journey? In the early 1870s he organized the first round-the-world tour, lasting 222 days. [he was the first person to develop mass tourism- i learnt at school].
Here in Krakow nothing has changed [i think] My animals are in good condition. My english isn't good enouh to write you everything what i will :-P I'm learning from special book for tourism classes so theres not much new words and gramatic.
Greetings from Krakow
Joanna x

Name: Julian Bailey
City wakefield, england
Sent: 15.19 - 29/4
Congratulations Peter i saw you on BBC news and couldn't believe it ,you have achieved a journey i have only been able to dream about, i love to travel myself but unfortunately due to ill health i have to stay in the UK but who knows i might just make it myself one day, anyway congratulations again and the best of luck for the future

---

Name: Victor Mangion
City Malta
Sent: 17.14 - 29/4
Hi Peter,
Home at last but proud to have done it. I am sure it has been an enriching experience. It is said that after such trips one's life will never be the same again. all the very best and CONGRATULATIONS.
Fr Victor from Malta

Name: Malcolm and Christine
City Ossett, England
Sent: 00.52 - 2/5
Hi Pete
Welcome home Pete! We've followed your journey all the way, and I have to say your achievement has been nothing short of fantastic. Just finished the last page of your journal. It has been an amazing story, and like all good stories I'm sad to see it end.
However, knowing what you have put into this most remarkable feat, it makes it all the more amazing to have seen it through so successfully.
I sincerely hope that you carry on to turn your story into a book which deserves to be a best seller and can be read by a much wider audience thereby giving enjoyment and inspiration to many, and due recognition to yourself for having achieved something to which few people are likely even to come close.
Best Wishes
Christine and Malcolm

Foreign phrases

Quite apart from dealing with strange cultures and currencies, I also had to deal with different languages too. You'll have seen some of the phrases elsewhere in the book; this section explains what they mean...

Auf wiedersehen Berlin und bis bald!
Good bye Berlin, see you soon!

Germany

'szla dzieweczka do laseczka do zielonego....'
'one day a lady went to the forest and she meets a young man and she was in love with him...' (from an old Polish song)
Te wesole slowa pozostawiam dla wszystkich Polaków.
These happy words I send to all Polish people.
Zycze wszystkiego najlepszego i dziekuje za goscine
I wish you all the best and thank you for help

Poland

Cnacisa za npizuauiemie nocetiyu ienapycb za nasazemme
Thank you for inviting me to visit Belarus, see you

Belarus

In Wien find'st nur die kultur, im reslichen osterreich herrscht nature pur!
In Vienna you find only culture; the rest of Austria is full of great nature!

Austria

Alles hat eine ende, nur die wurst hat zwei!
Everything has its end, except sausages which have two!

Switzerland

Ix-xemx shuna ta' Malta tirrifletti fil-qlub generuzi tal-Maltin
The warmth of the sun in Malta is reflected in the generous hearts of the Maltese

Malta

No Onward Ticket

Italy	*Il popolo Siciliano ha un cuore grande!* The Sicilian people are big hearted!
Greece	*una fazza una razza* one face one race
Palestine	*Marhaba* Hello friend
Egypt	*Bel hanawel shefa!* Eat and be happy with good health! *Maael Salama!* Go in Peace!
Ethiopia	*Tenaistilign* Greetings *Egziabiher Yistilign* Farewell and go with God
Tanzania	*Kwaheri Tanzania nakutakia mema!* Goodbye Tanzania, I wish you all the best!
Zambia	*Mulishani mwena Zambia, natemwa bana ukwisa muzambia!* Hello from Zambia, you will be looked after in Zambia!
India	*Namaste India!* Greetings from India! *Main jab India aaya to bada khush hua. India ek loktantrik desh hai. Yahan ke logion main anekta main ekta hai! Main jab Mumbai aaya to aur khush hua. Dhanyavad!* When I got to India I was very happy. India is a populous country. The people live in unity, I was very happy to visit Mumbai. Thank you!
Nepal	*Namaste Nepal* Greetings from Nepal
Thailand	*Sawadee pated Thai!* Good day Thailand! *Sawadee Pee Mai* Good day to you *koobkun Samrab wanwelatidee-dee naimaungthai* Thank you for the good days spent together in Thailand

Chob m roaom? Hi, how are you?	**Cambodia**
Selamat Jalan Bahasa! May the language (of Malaysia) continue to have a happy journey of use!	**Malaysia**
Wo hen gao xing lai clao xing jia po, zhe li de ren hen qin qie. *Huan jing hen zhen jie, duo duo bao zhong!* I am very happy to visit Singapore. The people here are very warm-hearted and their welcome is heartfelt, take care!	**Singapore (Mandarin)**
tiang polih pengalamon becik ring bali! persons who do good will receive good in return!	**Indonesia**
Buenos Noches Good Night	**South America**

Hunter's detours - 5

Greenland would have been good, but I'd have waited weeks for the ice to melt, so I pressed on to Iceland...

Home: Wakefield, England

Hunter's detours - 4

The flight deal was too good to miss, with the chance to get into Mexico at a bargain price - Sorry, Caribbean!